D0081748

GOTTLOB FREGE, 1848–1925

CONCEPTUAL NOTATION

To "Doc",
with fond memories
of Chester High
and you.
                TB

GOTTLOB FREGE

CONCEPTUAL NOTATION

AND RELATED ARTICLES

———

Translated and edited
with a Biography and Introduction by
TERRELL WARD BYNUM

OXFORD
AT THE CLARENDON PRESS
1972

Oxford University Press, Ely House, London W. 1

GLASGOW NEW YORK TORONTO MELBOURNE WELLINGTON
CAPE TOWN IBADAN NAIROBI DAR ES SALAAM LUSAKA ADDIS ABABA
DELHI BOMBAY CALCUTTA MADRAS KARACHI LAHORE DACCA
KUALA LUMPUR SINGAPORE HONG KONG TOKYO

© OXFORD UNIVERSITY PRESS 1972

DISCARDED
WIDENER UNIVERSITY

WIDENER UNIVERSITY
WOLFGRAM
LIBRARY
CHESTER, PA.

B
3245
.F22
B94
1972

PRINTED IN GREAT BRITAIN
AT THE UNIVERSITY PRESS, OXFORD
BY VIVIAN RIDLER
PRINTER TO THE UNIVERSITY

TO

GOTTLOB FREGE

PREFACE

THE present volume is the culmination of a project begun in 1962 at the University of Delaware where I first became acquainted with Frege's philosophy. After reading several of Frege's works, I attempted to learn more about the man himself, only to discover that very little was known about him and only a few of his forty or more publications had been translated into English. I was surprised to discover that the book in which Frege was said to have revolutionized logic, the *Begriffsschrift*, was (except for Geach's translation of most of Chapter I) untranslated and unavailable at major universities even in the original German. My curiosity had been aroused, however, and I managed to acquire a microfilm of the *Begriffsschrift*, so I began translating parts of it. The more I learned about Frege, the more interested I became in his life and work.

During the year 1963–4 a Fulbright Fellowship in England provided the time and wherewithal to seek out information on Frege and find some of his lesser-known works in European libraries.

The summer of 1965 proved to be the most fruitful and exciting time for the project. A grant from the Danforth Foundation and one from the Robert Wetherill Trainer Memorial Fund of Chester, Pennsylvania, made it possible to go to Europe. My wife and I visited the Frege Archives in Münster, Germany, and received permission from Professor Hans Hermes to read some of Frege's unpublished works and letters. At Fribourg, Switzerland, we met Ignacio Angelelli, who generously provided information and biographical data which he had gathered over several years. In London I talked with Rudolf Carnap about his experiences as a student in Frege's courses at Jena University. At Bertrand Russell's home in Wales I discussed with him his discovery of Russell's Paradox and his subsequent correspondence with Frege. Conversing with Russell over tea and reading Frege's original letters at Russell's desk are among the most memorable events of the project for me.

By the end of the summer of 1965 I realized that a 'Frege renaissance' was under way in America and Europe. Frege's philosophy was being studied avidly, and some of his works, including the *Begriffsschrift*, were to appear in English. I was disappointed to learn that my translation would not be the first into print; but my project was well advanced, and I resolved to finish it. A Frege biography now would be even more timely, and a second translation could be beneficial in bringing out differences of interpretation.

The first draft of the present volume was written at Princeton University during 1965 and 1966 on a grant from the Danforth Foundation. In completing the translations, I benefited especially from Dr. Dietrich Schulz and from my wife, Aline, who also shared with me the fascinating, but seemingly endless, job of compiling the bibliography.

The volume was prepared with two major objectives in mind: (1) to serve as an introduction to Frege's early philosophy, and (2) to serve as a tool for further Frege research. The student using the book as an introduction may want to skip some of the more technical passages, while the initiated scholar could forgo the more elementary remarks. Frege's works themselves, rather than appearing chronologically, occur in an order that makes them easier to understand— two later works, which discuss respectively the justification and the aim of the *Begriffsschrift*, occur before the *Begriffsschrift* itself. The reader will find some overlap here and there between the biographical essay and the Editor's Introduction, since each was written to stand on its own without reference to the other.

Throughout this project I have benefited greatly from the help of many people. I am especially indebted to my friend Ignacio Angelelli who generously allowed me to profit from his wide knowledge and wise counsel. I owe much to my friend James A. Thomas who has helped in ways too numerous and too subtle to describe. I am indebted to Bertrand Russell and Rudolf Carnap, and I regret that they passed away before I could express my gratitude in print. I am grateful to Peter Geach, Carl G. Hempel, and Leah E. Jordan for reading the manuscript and making many valuable criticisms and suggestions. I have benefited also from suggestions by Alonzo Church, Dagfinn Føllesdal, Hans Freudenthal, Montgomery Furth, William Kneale, Günther Patzig, and Richard Rorty. Bernard Baumrin, who first introduced me to Frege, has often been a source of encouragement and wise counsel. I am grateful to the late John R. Parsons and sorry that he did not live to see his portrait of Frege on the Frontispiece. The Clarendon Press has provided valuable advice and assistance in preparing the book for publication; and Sandy Savage Shufelt was of great service in helping to prepare the Index of Names. Acknowledgements are also due to Georg Olms Verlagsbuchhandlung and Harvard University Press for permission to publish my translation of the *Begriffsschrift*.

It is impossible to express fully my gratitude to my wife, Aline, whose encouragement, translating skills, and critical and secretarial efforts were indispensable to the success of this project.

Albany, New York
20 March 1972

CONTENTS

* 'Conceptual notation' is the English translation of Frege's term '*Begriffs-schrift*'. In the present volume, when 'conceptual notation' appears in italics, it refers to Frege's book; when it is enclosed in double quotation marks, it denotes Frege's symbolic language; when neither occurs, it means simply a language like Frege's.

† Items in the bibliography are referred to in the text by their serial numbers.

ON THE LIFE AND WORK OF GOTTLOB FREGE

§1. INTRODUCTION

DURING the past twenty years, Gottlob Frege has become one of the most studied modern philosophers. Because of the present strong emphasis in philosophy upon logic and linguistic analysis, the works of Frege are of primary interest, since he (1) revolutionized logic and semantics, (2) initiated the "linguistic turn" in philosophy, (3) made a major contribution to the philosophy of mathematics, and (4) significantly influenced leading scholars like Peano, Husserl, Russell, Wittgenstein, Carnap, and Church.

Given these facts, it is astonishing that no major biography of Frege was ever published; and it is tragic that the present biographical sketch was made only after the Second World War, in which valuable records and documents were destroyed (including a biography of Frege by his adopted son Alfred).[1] Even before the war, the amount of material available would have been small. Now, relevant information is scarce indeed; and the following account had to be pieced together from biographical fragments gathered from many places.

Very little is known about Frege's personality and private life; so the present effort must deal, for the most part, with his works and the main events in his career. A sketchy account, at least, can be given of his person and character. A description from Wittgenstein[2] and an extant photograph[3] reveal that "Frege was a small, neat man" with a short beard, "who bounced around the room when he talked". It is clear from existing records and Frege's writings that he was a

---

[1] Listed (1935) in the article S253 (items in the Bibliography of the present volume are referred to by their serial numbers) as among the documents in the Frege Archives at the University in Münster, Germany. However, Professor Hans Hermes at Münster has informed me that the biography is unknown to him and must have been lost during the Second World War.

[2] Included in S22.

[3] The portrait which appears as the frontispiece of the present volume is based upon that photograph, which was generously provided from the Archives of Jena University by Professor Dr. G. Uschmann. I am indebted to Professor Ignazio Angelelli for informing me of the photograph's existence and enabling me to obtain it.

subtle and creative thinker with remarkable energy and persistence. He was an effective and conscientious teacher, with a gift for clearly explaining very complex material.[4] He had keen logical insight which could cut to the heart of a problem; and he was always a formidable polemicist. When aroused, he often had a spicy tongue.[5] Apparently, his only major interests were his work and his family.

Throughout his life Frege was plagued by tragedy. When he was just a boy, his father died. Later, after he was married, his children died young, and then his wife. After twenty-five years developing a formal system in which to derive arithmetic from logic, Frege learned that one of his assumptions can generate a lethal paradox. In spite of his monumental achievements, Frege received little recognition while he was alive; and his death in 1925 was virtually unnoticed by the scholarly world. It is only recently that a general interest in his life has arisen, and his works are being widely read and discussed.

§2. FAMILY BACKGROUND

Friedrich Ludwig *Gottlob* Frege was born in Wismar, Germany (in Mecklenburg on the Baltic Sea) on 8 November 1848. Apparently, he was named after his grandfather, Christian *Gottlob* Emanuel Frege (1779–1811), who was a businessman and Consul of Saxony in Hamburg. Frege's father, *Karl* Alexander (1809–66), was the founder and director of a private girls' school. His mother Auguste Bialloblotzky (?–1878)—to whom Frege was devoted[1]—was a teacher and later principal of the girls' school. Her maiden name may indicate Polish extraction; though it is also possible that, like many people in the area, the Bialloblotzky's were related to Slavonic peoples who had inhabited the Mecklenburg region since the sixth century A.D.

Arnold Frege, a writer born in Wismar in 1852, may have been Frege's brother.[2]

§3. BOYHOOD

Almost nothing is known about Frege from the time he was born until he entered university at the age of 21. He apparently spent this

---

[4] See S1.
[5] The best example of Frege's wit and sarcasm is F29.

[1] Indicated in a *Lebenslauf* which Frege wrote in Göttingen on 2 August 1873.
[2] Suggested in a letter to Professor Ignazio Angelelli from the Frankfurt Goethe Museum, 15 November 1960.

whole period in Wismar (a flourishing commercial town, with a population of about 12,000, and one of the best harbours on the Baltic). Frege's family, like most families in the region, was Lutheran. His father died in 1866 while Frege was still at the *Gymnasium* in Wismar, which he attended for five years (1864–9) under the headmasters Krain (father and son). He passed his graduation examination (*Abitur*) in the spring of 1869 and immediately entered Jena University.

This is all that is known at present about Frege's early life. There may have been many more details about this period in the biography of Frege that his adopted son Alfred gave to Professor Heinrich Scholz for the Frege Archives in Münster in the 1930s.[1]

§4. UNIVERSITY STUDIES

Again, unfortunately, almost nothing is known about Frege's life as a university student, except the courses and professors he had. It is clear, however, that he impressed his teachers as a bright, assiduous young man;[1] but it is unknown, for example, where or how he lived, or what induced him to move to Göttingen University after two years at Jena.[2]

Frege spent four semesters at Jena, from the spring of 1869 to the winter of 1870. His professors were Geuther in chemistry; Fischer in philosophy; and Abbe, Schaeffer, and Snell in mathematics.[3] During his five semesters at Göttingen (Easter 1871–December 1873) he studied philosophy of religion under Lotze; physics under Weber and Riecke; and mathematics under Clebsch, Schering, and Voss.[4]

[1] See S253 and footnote 1 to §1 above.

[1] This was the description of Frege as a student included in an official memorandum from Professor Carl Snell to Professor Ernst Haeckel at Jena University, Spring 1874.

[2] Perhaps Ernst Abbe, who had gone to both Jena and Göttingen himself, and who donated millions of dollars (through the Carl Zeiss *Stiftung*) to Jena in an effort to make it as good as Göttingen, persuaded Frege to go to Göttingen in order to get the best education possible, and then return to Jena to teach. Abbe was always impressed with Frege's great ability in logic and mathematics.

[3] From a *Lebenslauf* submitted by Frege to Göttingen University on 12 August 1873.

[4] The courses which Frege took at Göttingen were the following:

Summer 1871: Analytic Geometry with Professor Clebsch, Images of Surfaces with Professor Clebsch, Functions of Complex Variables with Professor Schering, Philosophy of Religion with Professor Lotze.
Winter 1871–2: Experimental Physics with Professor Weber.

[cont. on p. 4

One of his major interests as a student was the theory of complex mathematical functions, which he studied with Abbe in Jena[5] and with Schering in Göttingen. His *Habilitationsschrift*,[6] which develops a functional calculus containing the seeds of his great contributions to logic,[7] was apparently composed at Göttingen before his graduation.

In late 1873 Frege presented his doctoral dissertation, *On a Geometrical Representation of Imaginary Figures in a Plane*,[8] and was granted the degree of Doctor of Philosophy in Göttingen on 12 December of that year.

§5. HABILITATION

As soon as he received his Ph.D., Frege (probably sponsored by Ernst Abbe) applied for a teaching position at Jena. Among the several documents he submitted was a statement from his mother that she would support him,[1] since the position he sought was unsalaried.[2] At that time she was already a widow; but apparently the income from the girls' school, which her husband had founded

Summer 1872: Experimental Physics with Professor Weber.

Winter 1872–3: A four-hour physics lab. with Professor Riecke, Mathematical Theory of Elasticity with Professor Riecke.

Summer 1873: Calculus of Variations with Professor Schering, Selected Topics from Electrodynamics with Professor Riecke, Selected Topics from Higher Geometry with Dr. Voss.

(This information was supplied from the Frege Archives at Münster, Germany, by Professor Hans Hermes.)

[5] From Snell's memorandum mentioned in footnote 1 of the present section.

[6] *Rechnungsmethoden, die auf eine Erweiterung des Grössenbegriffes gründen.* This is F2. It contains much material of interest and importance; but, thus far, it is virtually unstudied. Fortunately, this circumstance may soon change, since Professor Angelelli's reprint of Frege's *Kleine Schriften* (F′52) includes the *Habilitationsschrift*.

[7] Although there seems to be no hint at this time of Frege's logicism, there is in this work an expanded notion of function related to the one he would later use so extensively in his logistic programme.

[8] *Über eine geometrische Darstellung der imaginären Gebilde in der Ebene.* See Bibliography, F1. This is also virtually unstudied and may contain interesting and important material. It is also included in F′52.

[1] From a report by Professor Ernst Haeckel to the University officials recommending Frege for the position of *Privatdozent*, 19 April 1874.

[2] At this time a university lecturer (*Privatdozent*) received no salary. His only income from his university position was a meagre standard fee that each student paid him to attend his course; but this was generally insufficient to live on.

and which she was then directing, was sufficient to support herself and her son.

Another document which Frege submitted was the article "Methods of Calculation Based upon an Amplification of the Concept of Magnitude", which was his *Habilitationsschrift*.[3] In March 1874 Professor Ernst Abbe submitted to the University officials a report on this paper.[4] The report shows that the Jena mathematics faculty were most impressed by Frege's *Schrift*. Abbe found it to be erudite, clear, and to the point; bearing the mark of true originality and extraordinary creative powers; and containing novel points of view, sagacious explanations, and surprising relations among widely separated regions of analysis. He speculated that it might contain the seeds of a comprehensive new point of view which, when fully developed, would attain a durable significance for mathematical analysis. Thus, Abbe's report was a truly impressive recommendation and, as it turned out, a remarkable piece of foresight.

Since Frege's documents were acceptable, he was admitted to an oral examination on 18 April 1874.[5] The questions asked were very general ones related to topics in Frege's *Habilitationsschrift*. At the end the committee was satisfied that Frege had mastered his subject matter and achieved defensible views; but they were less impressed than they had been by the *Habilitationsschrift* itself, since Frege's answers were "neither quickwitted nor fluent".[6]

Having sustained his oral examination, Frege was recommended by the committee for acceptance into the University. They requested speed in accepting him, because Professor Snell was not well, and Frege was willing to take over part of Snell's duties. On 6 May he was admitted as a lecturer (*Privatdozent*), provided that he would sustain a public disputation and present a satisfactory trial lecture. By 18 May these requirements had been fulfilled;[7] and Frege had become a member in good standing of Jena's mathematics faculty.[8]

[3] See footnote 6 of §4, and also F2 of the Bibliography below.
[4] Apparently sent to Professor Ernst Haeckel on 30 March 1874.
[5] Given by Professors Abbe, Fortlage, Geuther, Haeckel, E. Schmid, M. Schmidt, and Strasburger.
[6] From a report on Frege's examination to the University officials submitted by Professor Haeckel on the afternoon of 18 April 1874.
[7] The public disputation was held on Saturday, 16 May 1874 at 10 a.m.; and the trial lecture was given at noon on the following Monday.
[8] Frege worked most of his life on problems in mathematics and philosophy; and it is likely that he discussed his work with fellow faculty members in those two disciplines. Mathematics and philosophy faculty members who were at Jena

§6. BETWEEN HABILITATION AND *CONCEPTUAL NOTATION*

Thus, in the summer semester of 1874 Frege began his teaching career. His life during forty-four years at Jena was not so secluded and hermit-like as is commonly thought today. He was a member of the *Deutsche Akademie der Naturforscher* (Leopoldina), the *Circolo matematico di Palermo* (from 1906 to 1925), the *Jenaische Gesellschaft für Medicin und Naturwissenschaft* (from 1874 to 1917), and the *Deutsche Mathematiker Vereinigung* (from 1897 to 1925). He read several papers at meetings of some of these organizations.[1] For three years—1899–1901—he was Assistant Treasurer (along with Johannes Thomae) of the last-mentioned organization. He corre-

at some time during Frege's forty-four years there include (dates indicate time at Jena):

Mathematics:
Carl Snell (1844–86)
Karl Julius Traugott *Hermann* Schaeffer (1850–1900)
Ernst Karl Abbe (1863–1905)
Paul Victor Langer (1875–8)
Carl *Johannes* Thomae (1879–1921)
Adolf Piltz (1884–97)
Carl Friedrich *August* Gutzmer (1899–1905)
Rudolf Julius Rau (1902 to at least 1908)
Robert Karl Hermann Haussner (1905–31)

Philosophy:
Karl *Volkmar* Stoh (1843–66; 74–85)
Arnold Rudolf *Carl* Fortlage (1846–81)
Karl August Julius *Fritz* Schultze (1871–6)
Julius Hermann Guido Wilhelm Walter (1873–5)
Eberhard Schrader (1873–5)
Rudolf Christoph Eucken (1874–1920)
Johann *Heinrich* Stoh (1876–1905)
Friedrich Otto *Richard* Falckenberg (1880–9)
Friedrich Ernst *Otto* Liebmann (1882 to at least 1908)
Wilhelm Rein (1886 to at least 1908)
Franz Bruno Erhardt (1891–8)
Hugo Moritz John Dingler (1896 to at least 1935)
Max Scheler (1900–6)
Paul Linke (1907 to at least 1950)
Hermann Julius Nohl (1908–?)

Perhaps the writings and correspondence (should any be found) of some of these scholars could shed light on some areas of Frege's career.

[1] The articles F6, F8, F10, F12, F13, and F16 were read before the *Jenaische Gesellschaft für Medicin und Naturwissenschaft*; while the paper F27 (in an earlier draft than the published version) was read before an annual meeting of the *Deutsche Mathematiker Vereinigung* (16 September 1895 in Lübeck).

sponded with many European scholars, including such important people as Husserl, Peano, Russell, Hilbert, Löwenheim, and Wittgenstein.[2] He met Łukasiewicz, Wittgenstein, and Vailati (and, no doubt, many others). He published 40 works during his lifetime, including 4 books, 24 articles, 8 reviews and 4 comments and remarks.[3] He also wrote a score of other works which did not appear before his death, but have recently been published in one volume.[4]

The happiest period of Frege's professional career appears to have been the beginning, while he was a lecturer (*Privatdozent*). He was

[2] The following is a list of those who are known to have had correspondence with Frege. Wherever possible, the date of the correspondence and the number of extant pages (if any) are included. Many of these letters contain interesting and important technical discussions which ought to be published.

Avenarius	1882	1 page
Ballue	1895–7	6
Couturat	1899–1906	12
Darmstaedter	1913 and 1919	2
Dingler	1917	6
Falchenberg	1890	1
Hilbert	1895–1903	22
Hönigswald	1925	5
Huntington	?	3
Husserl	1891–1906	10
Jourdain	1902–14	29
Klein	1881	1
Knoch	1893	2
Koebner	1891	2
Korselt	1903	5
Löwenheim	?	none
Mayer	1896–8	4
Pasch	1894–1903	10
Peano	1894–1903	20
Russell	1902–12	51
Scheibe	1919	1
Schlömilch	1881	1
Ulrici	1881	1
Vailati	1904–6	3
Wittgenstein	1910 or 1911	none

An unknown number of Frege letters were lost during the Second World War. These include the large correspondence with Löwenheim mentioned in S253. Wittgenstein mentions his correspondence with Frege in the quotation included in S22; but so far there is no trace of them. Perhaps the Second World War claimed them as well.

(Most of the extant letters, and perhaps all of them, are collected at the Frege Archives in Münster, Germany.)

[3] See the Bibliography below.

[4] These are edited by H. Hermes, *et al.*, and published (1969) by Felix Meiner in Hamburg, Germany. See F45.

highly regarded by the faculty and the best mathematical students at Jena. He was young and vigorous, with great hopes for the future. During this busy five years Frege taught an extra-heavy load of courses and published three reviews, an article on geometry, and a little book (*Conceptual Notation*) on logic and mathematics that later scholars would come to recognize as monumental.

From the beginning, his teaching load was unusually large, particularly in 1878, when Professor Carl Snell was very ill. Frege volunteered to take over most of Snell's work in mathematics and carry his own load besides.[5] In so doing, he prevented an intolerable gap in the mathematical teaching programme until Johannes Thomae could be acquired a year later. His extra teaching certainly forced him to sacrifice much of his research time—and just when he was making great strides in logic.

Frege was a very conscientious teacher, who designed his lectures for the sake of the student, making them clear and thoughtful and avoiding unnecessary complexity.[6] As a result, his courses were much appreciated by the conscientious students who attended them. This seems to have been true from the start of Frege's career right to the end. Rudolph Carnap, who attended Frege's courses in 1910–13, and who is perhaps Frege's greatest student, reports: "the most fruitful inspiration I received from university lectures did not come from those in the fields of philosophy proper or mathematics proper, but rather from the lectures of Frege on the borderlands between those fields".[7]

Frege was not only an effective teacher, but also very demanding upon those who attended his lectures. In evaluating his work for the University officials in January 1879, Abbe reported that Frege's courses were little suited to please the mediocre student "for whom a lecture is just an exercise for the ears". He continues: "Dr. Frege, by virtue of the great clarity and precision of his expression and by virtue of the thoughtfulness of his lecture, is particularly fit to introduce aspiring listeners to the difficult material of mathematical studies.—I myself have repeatedly had the opportunity to hear lectures by him which appeared to me to be absolutely perfect on every fundamental point."[8]

---

[5] From S1, which was written by Abbe on 10 January 1879. (I am indebted to Professor Dr. Uschmann of Jena, Professor Ignazio Angelelli, and the Jena University Archives for a copy of this document.)

[6] Also from S1.   [7] From A34, p. 4.   [8] S1.

For Frege it was especially important to get the fundamental points absolutely perfect—to make completely clear the root concepts and basic assumptions upon which a discipline is built. Indeed, this was the chief aim of all his major works and the root of most of his criticism of other scholars.

This desire for clarity and correctness at the fundamental level, together with a seemingly insignificant review which Frege published during his first year of teaching,[9] may have been the origin of his idea for a project that shaped his career and consumed most of his working life—namely, proving that arithmetic is a branch of logic. The book that Frege reviewed was H. Seeger's *The Elements of Arithmetic*,[10] which was meant to explain to students the fundamentals of arithmetic. Frege's main criticisms are that the basic laws of arithmetic are left unproved and the fundamental concepts are poorly defined:

After some partially unfortunate explanations of the calculating operations and their symbols, some propositions are presented in the second and third chapters under the title of "the fundamental theorems and the most essential transformation formulas". These propositions, which actually form the foundation of the whole of arithmetic, are lumped together without proof; while, later, theorems of a much more limited importance are distinguished with particular names and proved in detail. . . . The amplification of concepts which is so highly important for arithmetic, and is often the source of great confusion for the student, leaves much to be desired. . . . The result of all these deficiencies will be that the student will merely memorize the laws of arithmetic and become accustomed to being satisfied with words he does not understand.[11]

Perhaps it was his disappointment with Seeger's book that gave Frege the idea of writing a clear, exact presentation of the fundamental notions of arithmetic. The very things that he finds lacking in Seeger's book—clear definitions of fundamental arithmetical concepts and proofs of the basic laws of arithmetic—become the major aims of his whole logistic programme. *Conceptual Notation*,[12] the first of four volumes devoted to the project, was completed four years after the appearance of the review in question—enough time to conceive a plan and publish a little book about it.

We shall probably never learn whether or not this actually was the path that led Frege to his logistic programme. From this point on,

[9] F3.
[10] H. Seeger, *Die Elemente der Arithmetik* (Schwerin i. M.: A. Hildebrand, 1874).   [11] From F3.   [12] F7.

however, we know how the project developed, since we have Frege's own account in his books. Confronted with the task of proving the basic laws of arithmetic, he had to decide what would constitute a proof. He tells us that "we divide all truths which require a proof into two kinds: the proof of the first can proceed purely logically, while that of the second must be supported by empirical facts".[13] For reasons which he later detailed in his book *The Foundations of Arithmetic*,[14] Frege believed that the laws of arithmetic are independent of experience. Therefore, according to his own principles, proofs of the laws of arithmetic must proceed *purely logically*. To give such proofs, however, he believed he had to define the fundamental concepts and operations of arithmetic, using only concepts and operations of logic. To achieve this end, he devised the plan to (1) "reduce the concept of ordering-in-a-sequence to the notion of logical ordering";[15] (2) advance from here to the definitions of 'number', 'magnitude', and so on; and finally, (3) prove the basic laws of arithmetic using only these definitions and logic.[16] His first book, *Conceptual Notation*, is concerned with the first part of this plan—"reducing the concept of ordering-in-a-sequence to that of logical ordering". His second book, *The Foundations of Arithmetic*, deals with the definitions of 'number', 'zero', 'one', and so on. Finally, his two-volume *magnum opus*, *The Basic Laws of Arithmetic*,[17] contains his proofs of the fundamental principles of arithmetic.

§7. *CONCEPTUAL NOTATION*

In the beginning, Frege attempted to use ordinary language (German) in reducing the concept of ordering-in-a-sequence to that of logical ordering; but he was very quickly discouraged by ambiguities and inaccuracy that made rigorous, dependable arguments impossible:

So that something intuitive could not force itself in unnoticed here, it was most important to keep the chain of reasoning free of gaps. As I

---

[13] From the Preface of F7. [14] F14.

[15] Frege's way of putting it, in the Preface of F7 is, "den Begriff der Anordnung in einer Reihe auf die *logische* Folge zurückzuführen". It is clear from §26 of that work (see p. 173 below) that what Frege called "the concept of ordering-in-a-sequence" is today called the "proper-ancestral of a relation"; thus, in today's terminology, Frege wished to give a purely logical formulation of the proper-ancestral.

[16] See the Preface of F7. [17] F23 and F30.

endeavoured to fulfil this requirement to the strongest degree, I found an obstacle in the inadequacy of the language; despite all the unwieldiness of the expressions, the more complex the relations became, the less precision—which my purpose required—could be obtained. From this deficiency arose the idea of the "conceptual notation".[1]

Thus confronted with the inadequacy of ordinary language, Frege was forced to use a more exacting one. Basing himself upon Leibniz's programme for a universal language,[2] and drawing upon his training and interest in functional analysis, he developed a language custom-made for his purposes. In order to achieve the most accuracy and avoid all error, he laid down very strict requirements:

(1) Ambiguity must be banned. Each symbol or combination of symbols must keep in the same context the meaning it is originally given in that context.[3]

(2) *All* assumptions must be clearly stated. There must be no implicit presuppositions.[4]

(3) The modes of inference must be as simple as possible and restricted to as few as possible. They must be syntactically defined, so that strict adherence to grammar will ensure correctness of reasoning.[5]

(4) The two-dimensionality of the writing surface must be exploited for the sake of perspicuity. The various logical interrelations among the parts of a proposition or a proof must be clearly illustrated in a two-dimensional display, thus making the notation as easy to read as possible.[6]

Because of these rigorous requirements, Frege could not have used ordinary language, or even the various systems of logical notation that were then available. Ordinary language obviously would not suffice: its words and phrases are often, indeed nearly always, ambiguous, having many different meanings which are

[1] From the Preface of F7.
[2] See, for example, Leibniz's "A Specimen of the Universal Calculus".
[3] See F11.   [4] See F11 and the Preface of F7.
[5] See F7 and F11.
[6] See F11 and F12. Frege attached no logical or ontological significance to the two-dimensionality of his notation. The two-dimensionality was purely pragmatic: merely a means of achieving maximum perspicuity.

frequently only shades apart. Also, it is written in a one-dimensional notation (words and sentences follow one after the other); but Frege wanted a two-dimensional display, to achieve maximum perspicuity. Finally, in ordinary discourse, assumptions are frequently implicit, and modes of inference are numerous and loose; to state them clearly and carefully would lead to insufferable prolixity. Frege was apparently unaware, at the time of this project, of existing symbolic notations such as those of Boole and Schröder; but those notations would not have fulfilled his requirements anyway. They too contained ambiguities and were one-dimensional. Furthermore, Frege needed some logic different from the Aristotelian kind, even in the modernized and further developed form in which Boole, Schröder, and others had presented it.

Thus, Frege devised his own notation. He had not planned to develop a symbolic logic; he was forced to do so, becoming a logician almost by accident, and achieving quite unintentionally the first major advance in logic since Aristotle.

With his symbolic language, Frege wished to express and analyse *assertions* (or "judgements", as they were called then) of mathematics and *assertions* of logic (Frege called them "laws of pure thought").[7] He believed that the formal relations which concerned him related the *meaning contents*—"conceptual contents" is Frege's term for these[8]—of such assertions. Thus, he sought a symbolic language of *conceptual contents* of assertions, which he appropriately called a "conceptual notation".[9] A more modern name for conceptual contents of assertions would be 'propositions';[10] so, in more familiar terms, one would say that Frege sought *a symbolic logic of propositions*.

Five of the basic things one wants to do with propositions are (1) assert them, (2) deny them, (3) conditionalize them, (4) conjoin them, and (5) disjoin them. Frege chose symbols for the first three of these, and then used negation and conditionality to define conjunction and disjunction.[11] Since he also wished to be able to state the fact that two formulas express the same conceptual content, he added a sign for identity of content.

[7] *die Gesetze des reinen Denkens.* See the Preface of F7.
[8] *begriffliche Inhalte.* See F7.
[9] *eine Begriffsschrift.*
[10] For a discussion of 'proposition' and Frege's term *'beurtheilbare Inhalt'* see the Editor's Introduction, 6 below.
[11] See F7, §7.

He then had tools for expressing logical relations *among assertible contents (beurtheilbare Inhalte)*;[12] but he still had to express relations *within* such contents. It is at this point that he made, perhaps, his greatest contribution to logic. Drawing upon a rich background in the mathematical theory of complex functions, and the ground-breaking research which he had done on functions as a student,[13] Frege ingeniously regarded sentences as functions of the names occurring within them, treating property-expressions as functions of one argument, and relation-expressions as functions of two or more arguments, and adding what would later be called "variable-binding quantifiers".

Frege was at last equipped to begin the first phase of his logistic programme—reducing the concept of ordering-in-a-sequence to that of logical ordering; and he published the results in his book *Conceptual Notation*, a work which is now recognized as a landmark in the history of logic, making 1879 "the most important date in the history of the subject".[14] It attained a standard of rigour and correctness that went unrivalled for more than forty years;[15] and the list of inventions and "firsts" that appear in its brief eighty-eight pages is truly impressive:[16]

(1) The invention of logical functions;
(2) The invention of quantification theory;
(3) The first appearance of the functional calculus of first order;
(4) The first application of the logistic method;
(5) The first formulation of the propositional calculus as a logistic system;
(6) The first definition of an ancestral of a relation;
(7) The first logical analysis of proof by mathematical induction or recursion;

[12] *Beurtheilen* means "to judge"; so *'beurtheilbare Inhalt'*, taken literally, means "judicable content", and indeed this is how Jourdain (see F38) translates it. Russell (in S241) uses "propositional content", Geach (in F'47) employs "possible content of judgement", and Bauer–Mengelberg (see F7) suggests "content that can become a judgement". Bauer–Mengelberg's rendering seems to be, strictly speaking, closest to the mark, though unwieldy and inconvenient.

Because a judgement for Frege is an asserted content, I render *'beurtheilbare Inhalt'* by "assertible content". A content for Frege becomes a judgement by being asserted, and only assertible contents can become judgements; so "assertible content" seems to be the best convenient translation.

[13] See F2 and the discussion of it in the present volume, p. 5.
[14] From S167, p. 511.   [15] See S54, p. 268 and A70, p. 126.
[16] See S66, A40, A124, and A125.

(8) The first use of the "truth table method" to define propositional connectives and justify axioms;[17]
(9) The first use of the material conditional in a logistic system;
(10) The first clear, consistent account of the notion of a variable;[18]
(11) The first clear distinction between axioms and rules of
inference.

Besides all these achievements, the *Conceptual Notation* also
ushered in the so-called "linguistic turn" in philosophy.[19] In the
Preface, Frege suggests that some philosophical problems are really
only illusions arising from imperfections in our language; and he
asserts that philosophers could use his newly invented logic to expose
and resolve such illusions. The logical language developed in Chapter
I is the first so-called "ideal language" designed to tackle philosophical problems. (Specifically: What is the nature of mathematical
propositions? Do their proofs require empirical evidence? Are they
purely logical?) The second chapter contains the first application
of an "ideal language" to a philosophical problem—namely, "What
are the laws of thought and the interconnections that hold among
them?"

After the publication of the *Conceptual Notation* the "linguistic
turn" had been made; but "analytic philosophy" grew very slowly at
first, and it was Frege's later writings (*The Foundations of Arithmetic*,
"On Sense and Denotation", *The Basic Laws of Arithmetic*)[20] that
influenced philosophers like Russell, Carnap, Wittgenstein, and

[17] Strictly speaking, Frege did not use tables that could be mechanically used
regardless of interpretation. The nearest analogues in his work are interpreted
meta-sentences.
[18] Frege himself disapproved of using the term 'variable'. See footnote 33, p. 61
below.
[19] There are many reasons for considering Frege the seminal figure in the
"linguistic revolution" in philosophy. Some of these are:
    (*a*) Many influential scholars in the linguistic movement (e.g. Russell,
    Wittgenstein, Carnap, Church) openly and consciously take Frege's work as
    a model.
    (*b*) An important tool of linguistic philosophy is modern logic, which
    Frege himself invented and first used in attacking philosophical problems.
    (*c*) Frege frequently espoused views which are generally associated with
    linguistic philosophy. For example, he claims that the grammatical structure
    of a sentence in ordinary language frequently does not correspond to its
    logical structure (see §3 of F7); this creates illusions and pseudo-problems
    for the philosopher which can best be resolved by careful logical analysis
    (see F11 and the Preface of F7).
[20] F14, F20, and F23 respectively.

Waismann. It was more than two decades after the *Conceptual Notation* first appeared that these latter scholars began to do philosophy with logical analysis.

With the publication of Frege's book, a logical renaissance occurred;[21] but no one seemed to see it at the time. More than twenty years passed before the greatness of Frege's achievement was sensed by Bertrand Russell;[22] and fifty more years elapsed before it could be generally appreciated.[23]

Frege himself seemed to be unaware that he had made monumental strides in logic. For him, his "conceptual notation" was not a logical calculus, but a *language* to serve as a tool for his logistic programme; and early in 1879 he lectured to his colleagues in the *Jenaische Gesellschaft für Medicin und Naturwissenschaft*, demonstrating how his notation could be used to express propositions of geometry and arithmetic.[24] At that time he did not mention any new advances in logic.

Though he apparently did not realize what a milestone he had established in logic, he was aware that he had improved it to *some* degree, for in the Preface of his book, he claimed to have done so, and he correctly judged that one of his most important contributions would prove to be the introduction of logical functions.

Some other advancements which he noted in the Preface were that his notation would allow us to (1) fill in the logical gaps in existing symbolic languages like those in arithmetic, geometry, and chemistry; (2) combine these separate languages into a single one; and (3) construct other symbolic languages for fields such as kinematics and mechanics. Thus, he believed that his *Conceptual Notation* was a step towards Leibniz's dream of a universal language, rather than an attempt to develop an abstract logic or *calculus ratiocinator*.[25]

§8. RECEPTION OF *CONCEPTUAL NOTATION*

Because of the publication of the *Conceptual Notation*, 1879 was an important year in Frege's life. It was important also because he was

[21] See A127.

[22] See S241 and A139.

[23] In the 1950s, interest in Frege began to grow; translations appeared and wider distribution of his works resulted.

[24] This was the paper F8.

[25] When he discusses these Leibnizian terms, Frege refers to Trendelenburg, "Über Leibnizes Entwurf einer allgemeinen Charakteristik", *Historische Beiträge zur Philosophie*, vol. 3, pp. 1–47. See S122.

promoted to the position of *ausserordentlicher Professor*.[1] With this promotion he received a salary for the first time and could support himself and even a family.

The promotion was granted on the strength of a recommendation by Ernst Abbe,[2] who apparently was Frege's best friend and strongest supporter at Jena. Abbe cited the fact that Frege had given the University five years of excellent teaching, had carried an overload, and had taken on the work of the ailing Professor Snell. Then, in discussing the publication of the *Conceptual Notation*, Abbe made some perceptive comments. The book contains, he said, very original ideas that reveal unusual mental powers. He speculated that mathematics "will be affected, perhaps very considerably, but immediately only very little, by the inclination of the author and the content of the book". He noted that some mathematicians "find little that is appealing in so subtle investigations into the formal interrelationships of knowledge", and "scarcely anyone will be able, off hand, to take a position on the very original cluster of ideas in this book"; thus, "it will probably be understood and appreciated by only a few".

Abbe's speculations were remarkably prophetic. The ideas that Frege presented in the *Conceptual Notation*, and the logistic position he adopted, helped to revolutionize mathematics—but not immediately, only three decades later, and only indirectly, through the *Principia Mathematica*[3] of Russell and Whitehead, whose chief debt "in all questions of logical analysis" was to Frege.[4] Abbe's pessimistic prediction that the *Conceptual Notation* "will probably be understood and appreciated by only a few" proved to be an understatement. For years, virtually no one but Frege understood the *Conceptional Notation*, and no one important appreciated it.

Part of the responsibility for this unfortunate state of affairs was Frege's. He presented in his book many new and profound ideas; but they were abstract and difficult, at best, for the unprepared reader to grasp; and Frege did not prepare his readers well. He did not thoroughly explain the purposes of his symbolic language; he did not make it clear that his notation was a device to ensure correct reasoning in proofs of mathematical propositions. Also, he did not explain why the notation had an unusual two-dimensional form, or why existing notations (he probably did not know about them) such as those of Boole and Schröder would not suffice for his purposes.

---

[1] Approximately equivalent to assistant professor.
[2] S1.   [3] S242.   [4] See the Preface of S242.

For these reasons it was a very difficult book to read; and because of all the symbols it was a bit frightening at first sight.

As a result, many readers misconstrued the aim of the book, and it was misjudged and rejected by those who should have welcomed it. This was tragic, for Frege, an exceptionally lucid lecturer, was adept at introducing complicated mathematical notions to beginning students;[5] and it is a mystery that he failed to exercise his rare talent in his book.

At least six scholars, some of them very able logicians, reviewed Frege's book in the journals;[6] but none of them saw the great logical advances. Lasswitz,[7] the most sympathetic of the reviewers, considered the *Conceptual Notation* "a valuable contribution to the theory of thinking", thus more of an epistemological or even psychological study than an effort to devise tools for rigorous demonstrations of mathematical propositions. He correctly judged, however, that Frege's notion of functions is interesting and perhaps important; although he made no further claims for it.

Hoppe[8] was also sympathetic, but he missed the point completely. Frege, in a few passages,[9] mentions certain features of classical logic that he excludes from his own logic because they are not needed for his purposes. Hoppe interpreted these remarks as criticisms of classical logic and the main thrust of the book. He expressed doubt that anything new had been gained from Frege's notation itself, but saw much of value in the criticism of existing logic. He concluded that the book was worth while.

Michaëlis[10] had a less favourable reaction. He considered the *Conceptual Notation* an effort to advance logic, and concluded that it was not an improvement, but, indeed, a step backwards! Frege excludes from his logic certain things from classical logic, such as the subject-predicate distinction and the distinction between apodictic and assertoric statements. Michaëlis saw this as removing part of the already meagre content of logic; and he criticized Frege for not adding more things: "One must not only criticize, he must contribute constructively."

One of the most negative reviews was that of Paul Tannery[11] in France. Apparently, he merely skimmed the book and really did not

---

[5] See S1 and the discussion of it in this volume, p. 8.
[6] These reviews are S135, S176, S205, S256, S283, and S292.
[7] See S176.   [8] See S135.   [9] See F7, §§3–4.
[10] See S205.   [11] See S283.

know what was in it. He asserted that it contains little more than an explanation of the symbolism, though this constitutes only the first of three chapters. He claimed that the applications remain only promises; while, in reality, the second chapter provides proofs of fifty-nine "laws of thought", and the third chapter contains derivations of fifty-nine propositions from "a general theory of sequences". He considered fruitless Frege's replacement of the notions of subject and predicate with those of function and argument, though actually it was a major advance in logic.

Perhaps the most disappointing reviews were those of Venn[12] in England and Schröder[13] in Germany. Both men were formidable logicians, who should have welcomed the *Conceptual Notation* as a great advance in logic. Instead, they rejected Frege's notation as clumsy and hardly the equal of Boole's logic. They missed Frege's great achievements, because they constantly compared the *Conceptual Notation* to Boole's *The Laws of Thought*[14] and considered the aims of both books to be the same.[15] Given this assumption, one could easily come to think, upon first sight, that Boole's logic is better than Frege's. Since Boole's notation employs familiar symbols from mathematics, it looks much less forbidding than Frege's inventions. Fregean notation is two-dimensional and, thus, uses more space than Boole's, and appears to be more complicated. For these reasons Venn considered Frege's notation "cumbrous and inconvenient", and Schröder dubbed it "a monstrous waste of space" which "indulges in the Japanese custom of writing vertically".

Since Frege did not mention Boole in his book, Venn assumed (perhaps correctly) that Frege had never heard of Boole. He concludes that Frege's work "is one of those instances of an ingenious man working out a scheme—in this case a very cumbrous one—in entire ignorance that anything of the kind had ever been achieved before".[16]

---

[12] See S292.

[13] See S256.

[14] G. Boole, *An Investigation of the Laws of Thought, on which are founded the mathematical theories of logic and probabilities* (London, 1854). Reprinted in America by Dover Publications (New York, 1951).

[15] The only comments that appear in the margins of Venn's personal copy of the *Conceptual Notation* are translations of some of Frege's formulas (on p. 5 of the original German text) into Boolean notation. (I am indebted for this information to the Cambridge University Library, which has a collection of Venn's personal copies of books on logic.) See A162.

[16] From S291.

There seem to be several reasons why Venn and Schröder so completely misconstrued the aim and nature of Frege's logic. First, when Lasswitz reviewed the *Conceptual Notation*, he attacked the Boole–Schröder notations as "onesided" and considered Frege's symbolic language preferable in some respects. Schröder had read this review before he wrote his own,[17] and he was thus led to consider Frege's "conceptual notation" as a threatening alternative to his own modified Boolean notation.[18]

The misconstrual of Frege's aim might have been avoided, perhaps, if he had chosen a different title for his book. He seems to have made a singularly unfortunate choice. The whole title reads *Conceptual Notation, a Formula Language of Pure Thought Modelled upon the Formula Language of Arithmetic*. Now, formulas in Boolean notation actually look like equations of arithmetic, so Boole's symbolic language is certainly "modelled upon arithmetic". Furthermore, since the symbol for a *concept* (*Begriff* in German) could be called a *term*, a *concept-notation* (*Begriffsschrift* in German) could easily be taken to be a *symbolic logic of terms*, which would be a good description of Boole's logic.

In the Preface of the *Conceptual Notation* one finds still another unfortunate choice of phrase that could lead the reader to think that Frege's aims are the same as Boole's: in describing the project that led to his book, Frege says that it was "to test how far one could get in arithmetic by means of logical deductions alone, supported only by the laws of thought".[19] This sounds remarkably like a project that could be described by the whole title of Boole's book, *An Investigation of the Laws of Thought on which are Founded the Mathematical Theories of Logic and Probabilities*.

For all these reasons, it is easy to see how Venn and Schröder could have thought that the aim of Frege's book was the same as Boole's and, being on the wrong track from the beginning, fail to see Frege's achievements. If only they had studied Frege's book more carefully or, as Frege himself said later,[20] had tried to translate into Boolean notation some of the formulas in Chapter III of the *Conceptual Notation*, they would have seen at least some of the advances that Frege had made.

---

[17] He mentions Lasswitz's review in his own review.

[18] See, for example, his book *Der Operationskreis des Logikkalküls* (Leipzig, 1877).

[19] See the Preface of F7.   [20] In the article F12.

Before the reception that greeted his *Conceptual Notation*, Frege had every reason to be optimistic. He had established a good reputation at Jena, received a handsome promotion, and published his first book; but the joy and success that seemed assured were not to be. The happy years had ended, for the reception of Frege's book marked a turning point in his life. Henceforth frustration and tragedy were to haunt him. From 1879 to 1891 his works were ignored or misunderstood. From 1891 to 1901 they were slowly acknowledged; but this period was dramatically and ironically capped by Russell's recognition of Frege's greatness and almost simultaneous discovery of an antinomy in Frege's carefully laid foundations for mathematics.[21] Even in his personal life sorrow and frustration plagued him; for after he was married to Margaret Lieseburg (1856–1905) of Grevesmühlen, the couple started a family only to see all the children die young.[22] About 1900[23] they adopted a son Alfred; but Frege's wife died in 1905 and left him to raise the boy alone.

§9. BETWEEN *CONCEPTUAL NOTATION* AND *FOUNDATIONS OF ARITHMETIC*

The poor reception of the *Conceptual Notation* altered Frege's plans. In the Preface of his book it is clear that he had hoped to proceed immediately from the *Conceptual Notation* to the definition of number and other basic mathematical concepts:

Arithmetic, as I said at the beginning, was the starting point of the train of thought which led me to my "conceptual notation". I intend, therefore, to apply it to this science first, trying to analyze its concepts further and provide a deeper foundation for its theorems. For the present, I have presented in the third chapter some things which move in that direction. Further pursuit of the suggested course—the elucidation of the concepts of number, magnitude, and so forth—is to be the subject of further investigations which I shall produce immediately after this book.

Instead of proceeding as planned, Frege rallied to the defence of his symbolic language and spent most of the next three years answering

---

[21] See §16 of the present biographical sketch.   [22] See S22.

[23] It is not known when the Freges adopted Alfred; but it must have been before 1905 when Mrs. Frege died. It could not have been much before 1905, however, since Alfred was still a schoolboy when Wittgenstein visited Frege in 1911. See S22.

his critics. He did maintain an active interest in geometry and physics, publishing a review[1] of Hoppe's *Textbook of Analytical Geometry*[2] and lecturing to the *Jenaische Gesellschaft für Medicin und Naturwissenschaft* once on geometry[3] and once on physics;[4] but most of his efforts went into the defence of the *Conceptual Notation*.

To answer his critics, Frege wrote a long, brilliant paper, "Boole's Calculating Logic and the *Conceptual Notation*",[5] in which he carefully examined the aims and properties of his own notation and compared them to Boolean logic. In this paper Frege uses the great explanatory talent he failed to use in the *Conceptual Notation*. He clearly shows that he could not have used Boole's logic in his book; and he carefully explains the advantages of his own notation over Boole's. He submitted this paper to three journals, hoping that one of them would publish it and thus correct the misconceptions of his work. However, it was a very long paper, full of complex symbols, and all three journals rejected it.[6] He also wrote a much shorter version, "Boole's Logical Formula Language and my *Conceptual Notation*", which he submitted to a journal that had published several technical discussions of Boolean logic; but even this short paper was rejected.[7]

These further difficulties could only have added to Frege's frustration and disappointment; however, he wrote another paper, "On the Scientific Justification of a Conceptual Notation",[8] which was much shorter and contained no special symbols. Unlike any of Frege's other works, it was very general and contained a liberal dose of psychological and epistemological speculation. Perhaps this was included to make the paper more attractive to the editor of the *Zeitschrift für Philosophie und philosophische Kritik*, who accepted and published it in 1882.

---

[1] F9.

[2] R. Hoppe, *Lehrbuch der analytischen Geometrie I* (Leipzig, 1880).

[3] Published as the article F13; delivered on 2 November 1883.

[4] Published as the article F10; delivered on 15 July 1881.

[5] This is one of the papers in the Frege *Nachlass* recently published in F45.

[6] Rejected by F. Klein of the *Mathematische Annalen*; O. Schlömilch of the *Zeitschrift für Mathematik und Physik*; and H. Ulrici of the *Zeitschrift für Philosophie und philosophische Kritik*. Their letters of rejection can be found in the Frege Archives in Münster, Germany. See F45, p. 9.

[7] Rejected by R. Avenarius of the *Vierteljahrsschrift für wissenschaftliche Philosophie*. His letter of rejection can be found in the Frege Archives in Münster, Germany. See F45, p. 53.

[8] F11, included below, pp. 83–9.

Frege's major claim in this paper is that in complex scientific contexts, in order to avoid errors in reasoning, one needs a much more exact tool for reasoning than ordinary language, either spoken or written. Spoken language, he asserts, is fleeting: once a statement is spoken and unrecorded, it is gone and cannot be recaptured for careful scrutiny. The written word has the advantage of permanence and immutability; a written argument can be checked and rechecked for correctness. But in *ordinary* written language, there are subtle differences in the meanings of words; and modes of inference are numerous, loose, and fluctuating. Thus, mistakes and presuppositions can be easily overlooked. For exact scientific reasoning one needs an unambiguous, rigorously constructed language, with only a few carefully specified modes of inference. Frege's "conceptual notation" is such a language.

Frege surely felt better once this paper was accepted for publication, for at least he was able to publish a very general justification of his new symbolic language. He still had not answered the specific objections of his critics, however, and no doubt welcomed the opportunity to do so in a lecture at a meeting of the *Jenaische Gesellschaft für Medicin und Naturwissenschaft* in January 1882. The lecture was published later under the title "On the Aim of the *Conceptual Notation*".[9] In it Frege presents a brief account of Boole's notation, criticizing it on some fundamental points, and citing several reasons why he could not have used Boolean logic in his own book. These reasons are, first, that Boole borrows symbols of arithmetic for logical purposes; but Frege needed these symbols for ordinary formulas of arithmetic, and could not use them for logical operations. Because he wished to avoid ambiguity, Frege could not use the same symbol (such as the sign '+', which Boole used as a logical symbol) part of the time in a mathematical sense and part of the time in a logical sense. Second, Frege's aim was not merely to produce a *calculus ratiocinator* like Boole's, but to help develop a *lingua characteristica* (including propositional functions).[10] As a result, many of the statements from Chapter III of the *Conceptual Notation* cannot be expressed at all in Boolean notation.

Frege also offered a defence against Schröder's claim that the two-dimensional "conceptual notation" is clumsy and a waste of space:

[9] F12, included below, pp. 90–100.
[10] For a discussion of the difference between a *calculus ratiocinator* and a *lingua characteristica* see S122.

Frege's notation for "a or b" (using the exclusive sense of 'or') is

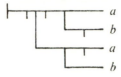

while Schröder's is $ab_1 + a_1 b = 1$

and Boole's is even shorter,

$$a + b = 1.$$

Schröder used this example to show that Frege's notation is "a monstrous waste of space"; but Frege answered:

This criticism is based upon the view that my "conceptual notation" is supposed to be a presentation of abstract logic. These formulas [of my "conceptual notation"] are actually only empty schemata; and in their application, one must think of whole formulas in the places of a and b—perhaps extended equations, congruences, projections. Then the matter appears completely different. The disadvantage of the waste of space of the "conceptual notation" is converted into the advantage of perspicuity; the advantage of terseness for Boole is transformed into the disadvantage of unintelligibility. The "conceptual notation" makes the most of the two-dimensionality of the writing surface by allowing the assertible contents to follow one below the other while each of these extends [separately] from left to right. Thus, the separate contents are clearly separated from each other, and yet their logical relations are easily visible at a glance.[11]

Having published this second defensive paper, Frege was apparently satisfied that he had sufficiently answered his critics and

[11] For example, let a be $(a+b)(c+d) = (7+6)(4)$ and b be the equation $ac+bd+bc+ad = (7+6)(4+3)$. Then to form the exclusive disjunction of and b, Frege could write the very perspicuous

$$
\begin{array}{l}
(a+b)(c+d)=(7+6)(4) \\
ac+bd+bc+ad=(7+6)(4+3) \\
(a+b)(c+d)=(7+6)(4) \\
ac+bd+bc+ad=(7+6)(4+3)
\end{array}
$$

while Schröder's version would be the unintelligible

$((a+b)(c+d) = (7+6)(4))(ac+bd+bc+ad = (7+6)(4+3))_1 + ((a+b)(c+d) = (7+6)(4))_1(ac+bd+bc+ad = (7+6)(4+3)) = 1$

and Boole's result would be

$\quad ((a+b)(c+d) = (7+6)(4)) + (ac+bd+bc+ad = (7+6)(4+3)) = 1.$

The matter becomes worse and worse for Boole and Schröder as the assertible contents that replace a and b get more and more complex.

justified his new symbolic language. He was now ready to move on to the next step in his logistic programme, the preparation of his book *The Foundations of Arithmetic*.

§10. *FOUNDATIONS OF ARITHMETIC*

The poor reception given the *Conceptual Notation* taught Frege a hard lesson. In writing *The Foundations of Arithmetic* he was much more careful to prepare the reader for the new ideas that he would present and to make the book as easy to read as possible. This time, the text was written in bright, vigorous German; there were no special symbols to discourage the less tenacious reader. The scope and purpose of the book were clearly stated; and more than half of the text was devoted to a lively critique of relevant views of other scholars, including famous Continental philosophers like Descartes, Leibniz, and Kant; important British philosophers such as Locke, Hume, and Mill;[1] and current mathematicians and logicians like Jevons, Schröder, Cantor, and Grassmann.

In preparing the manuscript of the book and developing his own definitions of the basic concepts of arithmetic, Frege was naturally led to a careful study of the relevant views of these other scholars; and he was dismayed with what he found. Ambiguity and disagreement were everywhere, even in discussions of one of the most basic arithmetical concepts of all: the notion of a natural number. Frege considered this a scandal,[2] for mathematics had just undergone two hundred years of rapid development, and most of the growth had been based upon more and more extensions of the concept of number —negative, fractional, irrational, imaginary numbers, and so on.[3] Instead of a solid, logical foundation for this vast new edifice, Frege found a quagmire of disagreement and confusion. He believed that arithmetic was tottering and would not be secure until this shaky ground was forsaken and replaced by a solid foundation rooted in "the laws of thought". He took upon himself the enormous task of righting the situation by (1) reforming or discrediting whole schools of thought in number theory, and then (2) rebuilding the foundations of arithmetic almost from scratch. Thus, starting with the book *The*

---

[1] Frege's knowledge of the relevant views of Hobbes, Locke, Berkeley, and Hume appears to have been only indirect, through Baumann's *Die Lehren von Zeit, Raum und Mathematik* (Berlin, 1868). Whenever he cites these scholars, he cites Baumann's book.

[2] See the Preface of F14.

[3] See S165, pp. 27–30.

Foundations of Arithmetic, Frege's original logistic programme became only a part of a more comprehensive and ambitious project.

A major part of that project was to be a critique of prevailing schools of thought in number theory, and more than half of *The Foundations of Arithmetic* is devoted to this task. In that work, Frege argues in particular against what he calls "psychologism", "formalism", and "pebble and gingerbread arithmetic". Psychologism is the view that numbers are mental constructs, and that certain descriptions of psychological processes are proofs of basic arithmetical propositions; but in his book Frege insists that descriptions of mental events are *not* proofs and definitions of mathematics:

> It may, of course, serve some purpose to investigate the ideas and changes of ideas which occur during the course of mathematical thinking; but psychology should not imagine that it can contribute anything whatever to the foundation of arithmetic. To the mathematician as such these mental pictures, with their origins and their transformations, are immaterial. . . . Never let us take a description of the origin of an idea for a definition, or an account of the mental and physical conditions on which we become conscious of a proposition for a proof of it. A proposition may be thought, and again it may be true; let us never confuse these two things.[4]

The second important school of thought which Frege attacks is "formalism",[5] according to which numbers are just the numerals (like '1', '2', and so on) which one writes on paper or on the blackboard: they are just empty symbols, and the so-called "laws of arithmetic" are mere rules (like the rules of a game) for the manipulation of these symbols. The "formalist", Frege asserts, believes that he can create new numbers just by creating new symbols; but, Frege insists,

> the mathematician cannot create things at will, any more than the geographer can; he too can only discover what is there and give it a name.

This is the error that infects the formalist theory of fractions and of negative and complex numbers. It is made a postulate that the familiar rules of calculation shall still hold, where possible, for the newly-introduced numbers, and from this their general properties and relations are deduced.

---

[4] From the Preface of F14, Austin's translation. See the Bibliography below under F14.

[5] This movement should not be confused with the later project of David Hilbert, which is also often called *formalism*. In this present essay the double quotation marks will always be used with the term 'formalism' in reference to the earlier movement, to remind the reader that the term being used does not refer to Hilbert's programme.

If no contradiction is anywhere encountered, the introduction of the new numbers is held to be justified, as though it were impossible for a contradiction still to be lurking somewhere nevertheless, and as though freedom from contradiction amounted straight away to existence.[6]

The third major school of thought which Frege attacks is that of the extreme empiricist, such as John Stuart Mill,[7] who claims that the laws of arithmetic are only empirical generalizations based upon induction, and that fundamental arithmetical concepts are mere empirical concepts gained through the observation of aggregates of physical objects. Frege considered this point of view a major setback to centuries of efforts by mathematicians to clarify the basic concepts of their science:

Often it is only after immense intellectual effort, which may have continued over centuries, that humanity at last succeeds in achieving knowledge of a concept in its pure form, in stripping off the irrelevant accretions which veil it from the eyes of the mind. What, then, are we to say of those who, instead of advancing this work where it is not yet completed, despise it, and betake themselves to the nursery, or bury themselves in the remotest conceivable periods of human evolution, there to discover, like John Stuart Mill, some gingerbread or pebble arithmetic! It remains only to ascribe to the flavour of the bread some special meaning for the concept of number. A procedure like this is surely the very reverse of rational, and as unmathematical, at any rate, as it could well be.[8]

Frege's critique of these three influential schools of thought is vigorous, often perceptive and convincing; and the conclusions he draws are that numbers are *not* subjective mental constructs, nor mere empty symbols, nor properties or agglomerations of physical objects. He believes he has provided firm grounds for these criticisms, and has thus cleared the way for his own account of the matter. This account, of course, is the logistic position that (1) the fundamental concepts of arithmetic (such as 'number') can be defined using only concepts of formal logic; and (2), given these definitions, the basic laws of arithmetic can be proved using only logical modes of inference and laws from formal logic.

Now it is clear from Frege's definition of cardinal number[9] that, for him, formal logic included a set theory very much like Cantor's.[10]

---

[6] From p. 108 of Austin's translation of F14.
[7] See J. S. Mill, *A System of Logic* (London, 1843).
[8] From the Preface of Austin's translation of F14.   [9] In §72 of F14.
[10] See G. Cantor, *Grundlagen einer allgemeinen Mannichfaltigkeitslehre* (Leipzig, 1883).

Indeed, it could have been the study of Cantor which led Frege to his famous definition of cardinal number. In *The Foundations of Arithmetic* (§§85–6) Frege discusses Cantor's work, so it is clear that he was familiar with it. He may have noticed that certain special sets (which Cantor called "powers") have all the mathematical properties of cardinal numbers. Frege apparently considered these sets to be the cardinal numbers; and his logistic programme required that he should define them purely logically.

The three essential concepts in Cantor's notion of "power" are "class (or set)",[11] "class-membership", and "one-to-one correspondence" (of the members of one class to the members of another class). Now, according to Frege, logic had long concerned itself with the notions of "concept", "falling under a concept" (that is, "being an entity to which the concept applies"), and "the extension of a concept" (that is, "the class of all and only those things to which the concept applies"). He considered these to be notions from pure logic; and thus he could use them to define 'class-membership' and the relevant classes: the classes that concerned him he defined as extensions of certain given concepts; and membership in a class which is the extension of, say, concept F he considered to be simply "falling under the concept F".

Having given purely logical definitions of 'class' and 'class-membership', Frege had only the third concept—"one-to-one correspondence"—to define purely logically; and he cleverly saw how to do this by using the functional logic he had developed in the *Conceptual Notation*. He was thus able to give in *The Foundations of Arithmetic* a definition of cardinal number which he believed to be purely logical; and using the notion of the ancestral of a relation which he had presented in the *Conceptual Notation*, plus some aspects of his version of set theory, he was able to provide, as well, a sketch of a proof that the series of natural numbers has no last member.

Frege claimed that these promising achievements were strong evidence for his logistic thesis that arithmetic is a branch of logic:

I hope I may claim in the present work to have made it probable that the laws of arithmetic are analytic judgments and consequently a priori. Arithmetic thus becomes simply a development of logic, and every proposition of arithmetic a law of logic, albeit a derivative one. . . .

[11] At the time he wrote *The Foundations of Arithmetic*, Frege believed that Cantor's notion of class was the same as his own. He later discovered that Cantor was unclear and perhaps even inconsistent about the notion of class, and he notes this in a review of Cantor's theory of transfinites. See F21.

I do not claim to have made the analytic character of arithmetic propositions more than probable, because it can still always be doubted whether they are deducible solely from purely logical laws, or whether some other type of premiss is not involved at some point in their proof without our noticing it. This misgiving will not be completely allayed even by the indications I have given of the proof of some of the propositions; it can only be removed by producing a chain of deductions with no link missing, such that no step in it is taken which does not conform to some one of a small number of principles of inference recognized as purely logical. To this day, scarcely one single proof has ever been conducted on these lines. . . .[12]

Frege was not satisfied, however, with this state of affairs. He wanted to prove his logistic thesis beyond all doubt; and he believed that arithmetic would not be secure from error and contradiction until such a proof were given. Thus, his next big project was to provide, from formal logic alone, detailed, "gapless" proofs of the basic laws of arithmetic.

§11. RECEPTION OF *FOUNDATIONS OF ARITHMETIC*

As he began preparations and research for the next phase of his project, Frege waited for the reaction to his *Foundations of Arithmetic*. He had written the book in a style intended to attract a wide range of scholars; and he hoped it would clear the ground for the most technical and complex part of his logistic programme. His hopes were soon dashed, however, by a reception that was worse than that given the *Conceptual Notation*. Most mathematicians and logicians —even famous scholars—seemed to disregard the book completely. Apparently, it was reviewed only three times—by Hoppe,[1] Lasswitz,[2] and Cantor.[3] The reviews were unfavourable; and for nearly twenty years after it appeared Frege's book was practically ignored. The only person, besides the reviewers, who discussed it seriously in print was Edmund Husserl, who criticized it in 1891 in *The Philosophy of Arithmetic*.[4]

---

[12] From pp. 99 and 102 of Austin's translation of F14.

[1] S138.   [2] S177.   [3] S60.
[4] S139. Frege's book is also mentioned twice in passing: once by Dedekind in 1893 in A52, and once by Peano in 1895 in S220. These, apparently, are the only times Frege's book was mentioned in print (except by Frege himself) from 1885 to 1903, when Russell's *Principles of Mathematics* appeared. See S241.

Cantor's review was an unfortunate mistake, for his own effort to develop a theory of transfinite cardinals was strongly supported in *The Foundations of Arithmetic*. Cantor was apparently so much harassed by criticism from others that he failed to recognize Frege's friendly encouragement.[5] He did realize that Frege's critique of prevailing schools of thought is an asset of the book; but he apparently did not study Frege's own view very carefully, for he wrongly construed Frege to be defining the cardinal numbers as sets of physical objects, rather than sets of concepts. The criticism that he offered in his review is thus misdirected. Frege pointed this out in a brief reply published in 1885;[6] but this was also ignored or unnoticed, even by Cantor himself.

Another reviewer of *The Foundations of Arithmetic* was Reinhold Hoppe, who, as editor of the *Archiv der Mathematik und Physik* for many years (1873–1900), was influential and respected. Hoppe was a staunch advocate of psychologism in logic and mathematics; and he apparently took Frege's critique of psychologism very personally. His review was emotional, highly critical, and satirical. He referred to Frege as "the doctrinaire logician" and used the very same kinds of psychologistic arguments that Frege's book had undermined. He predicted that other scholars would consider Frege's theories fruitless and unworthy of serious consideration.

Much to Frege's sorrow, Hoppe's prediction held true for more than fifteen years: practically everyone, including researchers in the same field, ignored Frege's book—at least in print. This is surprising, for Frege was a respected scholar in an established university. He lived in a country and in a period in which basic research in his field was of serious concern to many others. In this second book he employed none of the special symbols which frightened the timid reader from his *Conceptual Notation*; and he included vigorous, convincing arguments, dealing with a wide spectrum of views and scholars. Today *The Foundations of Arithmetic* is one of Frege's best-known works; and it is still read and valued as a lively and interesting contribution to the philosophy of mathematics.

Given these facts, it is remarkable that Frege's work was ignored for so long. No single factor explains the silence. The only explanation seems to be that several factors, which could not account for the matter when considered individually, worked together at the same time. First, Frege was a much more subtle and careful reasoner than

[5] An explanation suggested by Kneale in S165.   [6] F17.

his peers, and the new ideas he presented were difficult for most of them to master. Second, his first book was fraught with unusual symbols, whose appearance may have discouraged even the most tenacious readers[7] and turned them away from Frege from the start. Third, psychologism, "formalism", and extreme empiricism were all formidable movements in nineteenth-century philosophy of mathematics; and Frege was opposing a strong tide in attacking them. Finally, at least five influential scholars in three different countries— Venn, Schröder, Hoppe, Cantor, and Tannery—had given Frege poor reviews; and this could hardly have encouraged others to make the effort to master Frege's work.

These factors contributed to the disappointing silence that greeted *The Foundations of Arithmetic*; but despite the bad reception, Frege stubbornly continued to work on his grand project, hoping that someone somewhere would understand and appreciate his work.

§12. BETWEEN *FOUNDATIONS OF ARITHMETIC* AND *BASIC LAWS OF ARITHMETIC I*

The nine years which elapsed between the publication of *The Foundations of Arithmetic* and the appearance of Volume I of *The Basic Laws of Arithmetic*[1] (1884–93) were among the busiest and most fruitful in Frege's career. He published five articles, two reviews, and an answer to Cantor's critique of his *Foundations of Arithmetic*.[2] He prepared a large preliminary manuscript for *The Basic Laws of Arithmetic*, only to scrap it when he discovered that his logic had to be modified and supplemented.[3] He encountered semantical problems

---

[7] In a discussion in the summer of 1965 Bertrand Russell told me that he and others had ignored Frege for so long because they had been too lazy to learn Frege's symbolism. Frege's symbolism has long been unjustly considered clumsy and difficult to learn and read. On the contrary, it is the most perspicuous notation yet developed for logical analysis. Because its statements are two-dimensional displays, it can make a very complex proposition quite clear and easy to grasp at a glance. This gives it a great advantage over one-dimensional notations, which must in most cases resort to many parentheses, brackets, braces, dots, and other devices to indicate the grouping in a complex statement. Such devices make very complex statements difficult indeed to read. (See footnote 11 on p. 23 of the present volume.)

The only important disadvantage of Frege's symbolism is the difficulty and cost of printing it; but modern methods of photo-reproduction have greatly reduced this problem.

[1] F23.   [2] F15, F16, F17, F18, F19, F20, F21, F22.
[3] See the Introduction of F23.

which he answered with a major contribution to the philosophy of language.[4] He wrote, but never published, two polemical articles[5] on Benno Kerry's critique of logicism.[6] About 1891 Frege's work began at last to influence others when the Italian logician Peano read his works and cited them in print, and the German philosopher Husserl started to correspond with Frege[7] and study his works intensively.

During this time Frege's interest and attention were almost entirely on his grand project of reform and logical reconstruction in the foundations of mathematics. In his critique[8] of Cohen's *The Principle of Infinitesimal Method and its History*[9] his emphasis is on the correct definition of mathematical concepts and the meaning and basis of mathematical propositions. Even in his article "On the Law of Inertia" (1891),[10] in which he considers Ludwig Lange's account [11] of this law, Frege includes a discussion of logic and concepts:

The expression ['concept'] should be dealt with in logic, for logic has dealt with it since olden times and needs such an expression to formulate its laws. For this purpose, logic requires that a concept be exactly determined. . . . If a concept is not sharply defined, it cannot be a concept of logic. . . . A logical concept has no development, no history. . . . I do not agree with Lange that it is very necessary to talk of the development of a concept. . . . Instead, it could be said that "there is a history of defining that and that concept", or "there is a history of attempts to understand that concept"; and that would be more pertinent. A concept is something objective which we do not construct and which also has not developed in us; but something which we try to understand, and in the end we do understand, provided we have not sought erroneously after something where there is nothing.[12]

[4] Contained especially in F20 and the first part of F23.

[5] These have recently been published in F45. They contain interesting comments on the nature of concepts and objects, and also on Dedekind's work on the foundations of arithmetic. See S253. With regard to Dedekind see A52.

[6] S160.

[7] These letters are among those collected in the Frege Archives in Münster, Germany.

[8] F15.

[9] H. Cohen, *Das Prinzip der Infinitesimal-Methode und seine Geschichte* (Berlin, 1883).

[10] F18. An English translation was recently published by R. Rand. See the Bibliography below.

[11] In L. Lange, *Die geschichtliche Entwicklung des Bewegungsbegriffs und ihr voraussichtliches Endergebnis* (Leipzig, 1886). Lange published an answer to Frege in 1902 in S173.

[12] The present translation of this passage owes much to Rand's translation.

In the summer of 1885 Frege delivered to his colleagues in the *Jenaische Gesellschaft für Medicin und Naturwissenschaft* a lecture[13] concerning two different "formal" theories of arithmetic. One theory was the "formalism" which he had attacked so effectively in *The Foundations of Arithmetic*, and he continued the assault here with further damaging arguments. The other "formal" theory was his own logistic thesis that arithmetic is a part of logic; and his description of that view is perhaps the clearest he ever published (and well worth quoting at length):

Of all the arguments which speak for this point of view, I want to cite here only one which is based upon the comprehensive applicability of arithmetical theories. One can indeed count everything which can be a subject of thought: ideals as well as reals, concepts as well as objects, temporal entities as well as spatial entities, events as well as bodies, methods as well as theorems; one can even count the numbers themselves. Strictly speaking, the only thing that is required is a certain sharpness of definition, a certain logical perfection. As a result, at least this much can be inferred: the basic propositions upon which arithmetic is constructed cannot be based upon a narrow domain whose particular characteristics they express—as [for example] the axioms of geometry express [the peculiar characteristics] of space. These basic propositions of arithmetic must cover everything thinkable, and one is certainly correct to include such a general proposition within logic. Now, from this logical or formal nature of arithmetic I draw several conclusions:

First, there is no sharp boundary between logic and arithmetic; from the scientific point of view, both constitute a single science. . . . If this formal theory is correct, then logic cannot be so unfruitful as it may appear when considered superficially. . . .

My second conclusion is that there is no peculiarly arithmetical mode of inference which cannot be reduced to the general modes of inference in logic.

[Finally], it is clear that the boundaries of a science are fixed by the nature of its fundamental concepts. Thus, if arithmetic is to be divorced from all particular properties of things, then the same must hold for its fundamental concepts—they must have a purely logical nature. Thus, for example, I have displaced [in my *Foundations of Arithmetic*] the expression 'class' {'*Menge*'}, which is often used by mathematicians, by the expression 'concept' {'*Begriff*'}, which is customary in logic; and this is not merely an indifferent change of nomenclature, but is important for knowledge of the true state of affairs.

[13] F16.

Frege's most important efforts during this period were additions that he made to his logic, and the great strides he achieved in semantics and philosophy of language. After he had recognized the inadequacy of the preliminary manuscript of *The Basic Laws of Arithmetic*, he responded with a major creative effort: he extended even further the expanded notion of "function" presented in the *Conceptual Notation*. This new extension included (1) elaborating upon the distinction between function and object; (2) permitting any object to be the argument of a function; and (3) distinguishing levels of functions,[14] so that objects would be arguments of *first-level* functions, while first-level functions would be arguments of *second-level* functions. Since a single function can have more than one argument, there could also be *equal-level* and *unequal-level* functions. Finally, with respect to functions, he introduced "courses-of-values" and "value-ranges" of functions, and defined a "concept" as a "function of one argument whose value is always a truth value".

To give a clear, consistent account of the meaning of an identity statement, Frege replaced the old "identity of content" sign with the customary identity sign from mathematics, and replaced the studiedly vague notion of "content" with the distinction between the sense (*Sinn*) and the denotation (*Bedeutung*) of an expression. An identity statement, he decided, asserts that *two expressions have the same denotation*. For the special and very important case of the sense and denotation of *sentences*, Frege held that they express a thought—which is their sense—and denote one or the other of the two logical objects *the True* and *the False*.

Besides these things, Frege added a notation for the definite article; gave rules for correct definition; provided a formal analysis of descriptions; and distinguished *use* from *mention*,[15] *ordinary* from *oblique* contexts.

The result of all these additions and modifications to the "conceptual notation" was a magnificent achievement—a formal philosophy of language with great power, scope, and subtlety—which is widely studied and imitated today, and which has exerted—through the works of Russell, Wittgenstein, Carnap, Church, and others (and

[14] As early as F14 Frege had distinguished levels of concepts (see §53); but it was only after that that he elaborated upon this distinction and carried it through his whole account of functions.

[15] Among other things, Frege's "use-mention" distinction and his account of correct definition were meant to avoid the mistakes of the "formalists" who mistook numerals for numbers and believed they could define numbers into existence.

finally, since 1950, through Frege's works themselves)—a profound influence on logic and philosophy.

To prepare the prospective readers of his forthcoming book for all these subtle and technical innovations (and, he hoped, to avoid the frustrating fate of his earlier books), Frege explained many of them in a lecture, "On Function and Concept",[16] to his colleagues in the *Jenaische Gesellschaft für Medicin und Naturwissenschaft*, and also published two articles—"On Sense and Denotation"[17] (now a classic in semantics) and "On Concept and Object"[18] (answering Kerry's objections to Frege's account of concepts). The stage was set, at last, for the appearance of *The Basic Laws of Arithmetic*.

§13. *BASIC LAWS OF ARITHMETIC I*

After working more than fifteen years on his project, revolutionizing logic, and making a major contribution to the philosophy of language, Frege was ready at last to publish the final, step-by-step proof of his logistic thesis. His works had been rejected or ignored for many years, but vindication and triumph appeared to be in sight.

This hope was soon shattered by a new frustrating problem: no publisher would risk printing Frege's book. The manuscript was very long and filled with two-dimensional displays of Frege's special notation. This made printing more difficult and more expensive than for a book in ordinary language or customary logic. Furthermore, Frege's earlier works had been coldly received, and there was no guarantee that the new volume would not receive similar treatment. It seemed a great financial risk to print Frege's book; and apparently no publishing house was willing to take that risk.[1]

The problem was finally resolved, however, by a compromise: the publisher Hermann Pohle in Jena, who had printed Frege's lecture "On Function and Concept",[2] agreed to print the book in two instalments, the publication of the second part to be dependent upon a good reception of the first.[3] So, in late 1893, the first volume of *The Basic Laws of Arithmetic* appeared.

---

[16] F19. Reviewed by Hoppe in S136 and Schotten in S255.
[17] F20   [18] F22.

[1] There is a note by Heinrich Scholz in the Frege Archives in Münster, Germany, stating that Frege had to pay for the publication of Volume II out of his own pocket. See also A34.
[2] F19.   [3] See the Preface of F23, p. v.

Frege had no great expectations, however; for it is evident in the Preface that he feared the worst. Here, obviously pessimistic, he seems to try hard to prod or persuade prospective readers to study his book. He tells of disappointment over the reception—or lack of it—of his earlier works; and he informs the reader that the appearance of Volume II will depend upon a good reception of Volume I. He describes unfavourable attitudes and trends of the day, working against the acceptance, or even the reading, of his book; and he challenges other scholars to do better or find something essentially wrong with *his* work. He criticizes "formalism" and viciously attacks psychologism, as if to provoke an answer. Finally, he asks for support from other mathematicians against the corrupting influence of the "psychological logicians".

Of all the threats to his work, and to the well-being of mathematics itself, Frege considered psychologism to be the worst. He believed that, by reducing everything to idea—to the subjective—the proponents of psychologism blot out subtle distinctions which are necessary for truth in logic and mathematics; thus they destroy objective truth itself and end up in a mire of contradiction and confusion.[4]

As a concrete example of psychologism Frege selected the view of Benno Erdmann[5] and subjected it to a *reductio ad absurdum*. His arguments are lethal and crushing, but also merciless and satirical; reflecting, perhaps, Frege's frustration and loss of patience after years of arguing to deaf ears. The bitterness of the attack may also have been an intentional effort to irritate the "psychological logicians" and provoke them into a reply; for Frege expresses in his Preface the belief that "as soon as [the psychological logicians] so much as condescend to occupy themselves seriously with my book, if only to refute it, then I have won".[6]

Many others besides the "psychological logicians" were sure to be repelled by the content—even the appearance—of Frege's book; and Frege sadly admits that this is so:

An expression cropping up here or there, as one leafs through these pages, may easily appear strange and create prejudice. . . . Even the first

---

[4] See F23, pp. xvii–xxv.   [5] In Erdmann's *Logik*, Band I (Halle, 1892).

[6] This and all other quotations from Volume I of *The Basic Laws of Arithmetic* are from Furth's translation (originally published by the University of California Press, reprinted by permission of The Regents of the University of California). See the Bibliography under F23.

impression must frighten people off: unfamiliar signs, pages of nothing but alien-looking formulas. . . . I must relinquish as readers all those mathematicians who, if they bump into logical expressions such as 'concept', 'relation', 'judgment', think: *metaphysica sunt, non leguntur*, and likewise those philosophers who at the sight of a formula cry: *mathematica sunt, non leguntur*; and the number of such persons is surely not small. Perhaps the number of mathematicians who trouble themselves over the foundation of their science is not great, and even these frequently seem to be in a great hurry until they have got the fundamental principles behind them. And I scarcely dare hope that my reasons for painstaking rigor and its inevitable lengthiness will persuade many of them.[7]

Under the circumstances, Frege could hardly be optimistic for his book. To offset some of the difficulties, he provided in the Preface hints on how to read the book to achieve the quickest and easiest general understanding of its contents; and in the text itself, before he began a rigorous proof, he included a rough introductory outline of it, to make its course and general significance easier to see. In addition, Frege voiced the hope that someone would have "enough confidence in the matter beforehand to expect in the intellectual profit a sufficient reward" for the labour that a deep study would require. He expressed the belief that a determined reader would soon discover that he had overrated the toil involved, and that the rigour of the book actually facilitates understanding, once the novelty of the notation is overcome.

According to Frege, his rigorous method is basically Euclidean:

The ideal of a strictly scientific method in mathematics, which I have here attempted to realize, and which might indeed be named after Euclid, I should like to describe as follows. It cannot be demanded that everything be proved, because that is impossible; but we can require that all propositions used without proof be expressly declared as such, so that we can see distinctly what the whole structure rests upon. After that we must try to diminish the number of these primitive laws as far as possible, by proving everything that can be proved. Furthermore, I demand—and in this I go beyond Euclid—that all methods of inference employed be specified in advance; otherwise we cannot be certain of satisfying the first requirement. This ideal I believe I have now attained.[8]

Frege did, indeed, essentially achieve a methodological ideal: the standard of rigour and formal correctness of *The Basic Laws of*

[7] pp. xi–xii   [8] p. vi.

Arithmetic had never been achieved before (even in the *Conceptual Notation*), and would remain unrivalled for nearly three decades.[9]

Although Frege was satisfied with this rigorous, scientific form of Volume I, he was disappointed by its meagre content. He was forced to publish, at first, only part of his work; and much of the initial instalment had to be devoted to an explanation of his improved "conceptual notation". Because of this, the only other things he managed to include were an account of cardinal numbers (finite and infinite), plus "ordering-in-a-sequence", relative products, mapping by relations, and the like. This by itself was a monumental work in logic, mathematics, and philosophy; but it still lacked an account of negative, fractional, irrational, and complex numbers, as well as addition, multiplication, and other arithmetical operations. Frege was forced to reserve these for Volume II. Even so, he believed that Volume I contained enough material to give the reader a good idea of his method and position; and he was firmly convinced that an honest reader would accede to all his arguments.

The only thing about which he expressed some reservation was his Basic Law V. This assumption of his logical system stated essentially that, "the set of *F*s is identical with the set of *G*s if and only if all *F*s are *G*s and all *G*s are *F*s".[10] Frege conceded that this is a principle "which logicians perhaps have not yet expressly enunciated"; but he nevertheless asserted, "I hold that this is a law of pure logic". He evidently believed that any objections to this could be met; for the final paragraph of the Preface rings with confidence:

It is *prima facie* improbable that such a structure could be erected on a base that was uncertain or defective. . . . As a refutation in this I can only recognize someone's actually demonstrating either that a better, more durable edifice can be erected upon other fundamental convictions, or else that my principles lead to manifestly false conclusions. But no one will be able to do that.[11]

§14. RECEPTION OF *BASIC LAWS OF ARITHMETIC I:* FREGE AND PEANO

The reception accorded *The Basic Laws of Arithmetic I* was another frustrating blow to Frege's hopes and plans. There were only

[9] See p. 268 of S54 and p. 126 of A70.
[10] This is the fateful assumption that can be used to generate Russell's Paradox in Frege's logical system.   [11] p. xxvi.

two reviews, both unfavourable; and except for these there was neither approval nor rejection from the scholarly world—just silence. As a result, the publisher refused to print Volume II; and Frege's grand project—one of the monumental works in the history of thought—was unfinished. As it turned out, Frege did not give up—he was just delayed. (He was determined to see his project through; so, finally, ten years after the appearance of Volume I, he paid for the publication of Volume II out of his own pocket.[1])

The first review of Volume I was by Reinhold Hoppe.[2] It is so brief that it hardly merits being called a "review". It consists of only three sentences, giving a very inaccurate summary of the contents of the book and accusing Frege of being secretive about his purposes. Apparently Hoppe had merely glanced over the Preface and Appendix, without reading the book itself. As a discussion of Frege's work his review is insignificant; but it may have discouraged some would-be readers.

The second review was by the Italian logician Peano.[3] It also was unfavourable, but much more important. It initiated a fruitful exchange of letters between Frege and Peano, and in 1900 or 1901 led Bertrand Russell to read Frege's works,[4] starting the chain of events which eventually led to a general recognition of Frege's achievements.

Peano's review was much more detailed than Hoppe's. As Frege had already done, Peano and his associates[5] were developing a symbolic logic to analyse mathematical statements; and in his review Peano compared some of the basic ideas and notations of Frege's logic with those of his own. He also included a brief discussion of Frege's account of the notion of a cardinal number.

Peano's intention, however, was not, it seems, to present a careful or exhaustive account of Frege's logic; but rather to prove the superiority of his own logic over Frege's. He saw Frege as a rival, but he never really learned Frege's system; he knew only some similarities and differences between the two notations. He misunderstood some things (such as Frege's use of German, Greek, and italic letters) and completely overlooked others, such as the detailed analysis of logical functions and the carefully worked-out philosophy of language that insures maximum rigour and welds Frege's system into a coherent whole. For these reasons Peano missed some of the greatest achieve-

---

[1] See footnote 1 of §13 of the present biographical sketch.
[2] S137.   [3] S220.   [4] See S212.
[5] Vailati, Castellano, Burali, Giudice, Vivanti, Bettazzi, Fano, and others.

ments in Frege's work, and failed to see that Frege's logic was much better than his own.

Indeed, Peano proudly asserted in his review that his own logic is more practical and more profound that Frege's. It is more practical, he said, because the two-dimensionality of Frege's notation hides associative and commutative properties from the eye, while his own notation does not. (Peano was naturally more at home in his own symbolism, and thus the logical properties expressed and reflected were easier for him to see in his own notation than in Frege's. Anyone accustomed to reading Frege's notation knows that Peano's claim here is false.)

Peano's argument for the assertion that his logic is more profound was this: mathematical logic is an analysis of the ideas and propositions of logic and mathematics into primitive and derivative; "and this analysis is unique". According to Peano, his logic and Frege's are alternative attempts to perform the same analysis. He claimed to use only three primitive notions and define all the others in terms of these, while Frege used five primitives. Thus, Peano concluded, his logic gives a more profound analysis than Frege's.

Frege was most disturbed by Peano's claim to have a more profound logic. He believed this claim to be false, and he wrote a letter to prove it to Peano,[6] asking him to publish the letter in the *Rivista di matematica*. Peano learned the hard way what an able polemicist he had challenged. Frege's reply was crushing; and it pointed out weaknesses and mistakes in Peano's work, forcing Peano to print a recantation[7] and thank Frege for making improvements in his logic.

The major points in Frege's reply are these:

First, merely counting the number of primitive signs does not give sufficient grounds for judging which notation yields the deeper analysis. Other things must be considered, such as "the strictness of the rules of definition" (which Frege found lacking in Peano) and how much can be accomplished with the primitives. Frege points out that it is easy enough to reduce the number of primitive signs by merely failing to take account of known distinctions. He notes that Peano himself recognizes the difference between (1) the case in which a thought is merely expressed, but not asserted; and (2) the case in which it is also asserted. Frege has a primitive symbol to capture this distinction, while Peano does not. Gaining fewer primitive symbols in this way makes Peano's notation, if anything, a *less* profound rather

---

[6] F28.   [7] S219.

than a *more* profound analysis, "since the actual difference remains" whether Peano is able to express it or not.

Second, even if the number of primitive signs *were* good grounds for judging the depth of analysis, Peano's position would be untenable, because his claim to use only three primitive symbols is easily disproved. Frege notes that Peano never defines at all one of the signs he claims to define with his three primitives. Also, Peano's definition of the identity sign is circular; and there are at least four other symbols that Peano does not define with his three primitives.

Third, perhaps the most important reason which Frege cites to show that Peano's logic is not more profound is that Peano's definitions are faulty. They are, in the first place, merely *partial definitions* that give the meaning of the symbol in question *only for certain specified cases*. Thus, Peano's concepts are *not completely determinate*. But "logic can only recognize sharply delimited concepts; only under this precondition can it establish exact laws". The law of excluded middle is just another expression of this requirement; and Peano's logic thus violates that law. Besides this general problem with Peano's definitions, Frege points out flaws in specific definitions given in Peano's *Formulaire de mathématiques* I;[8] and he notes that Peano often gives more than one definition for the same sign, but fails to supply a proof that these definitions do not contradict each other.

Peano was obviously impressed by Frege's reply; for in his published recantation he says that it "will contribute to the clarification of a number of controversial and difficult points in mathematical logic"; and he gratefully acknowledges that his own logic is not the work of an individual, but one of collaboration; and he will always receive with gratitude remarks which contribute to its growth and perfection.

Because of Frege's reply, Peano was forced to admit that his logic does use more than three primitive symbols—indeed, uses at least nine. Also, Frege's polemic against his definitional procedures forced him to add the sign '= Df' ("identical by definition") to his primitives, and to change some faulty definitions. Hence, because of Frege, there was an essential improvement in the rigour and precision of Peano's logic between Volume I and Volume II of the *Formulaire de mathématiques*.[9]

---

[8] Turin, 1895.

[9] Although Peano received Frege's letter in 1896, he did not publish it until 1899, after he had already incorporated Frege's improvements into Volume II of *Formulaire de mathématiques* (1897).

This contribution by Frege to Peano's logic is definitely known. In addition, Peano may also have adopted other things from Frege. From its inception, Peano's logic was a gathering of ideas and techniques from many different scholars, rather than his own individual creation. For example, he apparently acquired his famous postulates for arithmetic from Dedekind.[10] Many logicians are mentioned in Peano's published works,[11] and Frege is among them. Also, Frege and Peano corresponded between 1894 and 1906. For these reasons, there may be other things that Peano owes to Frege. A careful study of the matter has never been made.[12]

One of the things that Peano may have acquired from Frege is quantification theory, which originated in 1879 in Frege's *Conceptual Notation*. It first appeared in Peano's works in 1894 in *Notations de logique mathématique*;[13] but Peano had seen Frege's *Conceptual Notation* at least three years before that, since he cited it in *Principii di logica matematica* published in 1891.[14] Peano uses the same abbreviation technique as Frege; namely, completely leaving out quantifying notation when the scope of the quantification is the whole proposition. Also, in *Formulaire de mathématiques* II, Peano explicitly credits Frege's *Conceptual Notation* with pointing out the need for some notation to show which variables in a formula are to be quantified.[15] All these things are evidence that Peano acquired quantification theory from Frege.

§15. BETWEEN *BASIC LAWS OF ARITHMETIC I* AND *RUSSELL'S PARADOX*

Sorrow and frustration continued to plague Frege after the publication of Volume I of *The Basic Laws of Arithmetic*. The cold reception the book received was another exasperating blow. Although his new book was a monumental contribution to logic and mathematics, no one realized the fact. However, instead of marking a premature end to Frege's grand project, the poor reception of Volume I

[10] See A166.
[11] For example, Boole, Cayley, Clifford, Delboeuf, Dedekind, DeMorgan, Ellis, Frege, Grassmann, Günther, Halsted, Jevons, Liard, MacFarlane, MacColl, Nagy, Peirce, Poretzky, Schröder, Venn.
[12] Perhaps the Frege–Peano letters will shed some light on the matter. They can be found in the Frege Archives in Münster, Germany.
[13] Turin, 1894.
[14] In the *Rivista di matematica*, 1 (1891), p. 10.
[15] Turin, 1897. See the discussion of proposition 361.

initiated a special effort on his part to tie up the loose ends and bring the project to a successful conclusion. Between 1894 and 1902 Frege wrote a torrent of papers—published and unpublished, working out details of his own position and attacking opposing views. Near the end of this period he completed the manuscript of Volume II of *The Basic Laws of Arithmetic* and arranged to publish it at his expense.

Fortunately, Frege's persistence was rewarded with some success, and happy events made his troubles more bearable and renewed his hope. In 1896 he was promoted to the rank of Honorary Ordinary Professor. About 1900 he and his wife adopted a son. Also, he scored a success in 1894 in his fight against psychologism by converting the German philosopher Husserl to anti-psychologism; and his influence in logic began to grow when he made additions and corrections to the logic of Peano.[1]

Frege was probably offered not just an Honorary Ordinary Professorship, but a full Ordinary Professorship. He had given Jena twenty-two years of excellent, conscientious teaching and had published twenty-six works, including three books. (Later, in 1907, he was even granted the prestigious title of *"Hofrat"*, so at Jena his work was certainly appreciated.) It is most likely that he was offered a full professorship;[2] but—as Ernst Abbe, his teacher and friend, had done before him—Frege refused it, because he wished to devote full time to teaching and research; he did not want the added administrative duties of a full professorship.

The position of Honorary Ordinary Professor was unsalaried and slightly less prestigious than the position of Ordinary Professor, but it gave Frege more free time for research. He was able to accept this unsalaried position because he was offered the generous stipend of 3,000 marks per year from the Carl Zeiss *Stiftung*,[3] a foundation that gave hundreds of thousands of marks to Jena University every year. It is most likely that Frege's friend Ernst Abbe was responsible for the generous grant to Frege. From the time that Frege was his

[1] See §14 of the present biographical sketch for a discussion of Frege's contributions to Peano's logic.
[2] This assumption is plausible because: (1) it was not unusual for a teacher who wanted more research time to prefer the Honorary Ordinary Professorship to the full Ordinary Professorship; (2) Frege was very busy completing his project at the time he was offered the promotion; (3) the fact that he was granted the title of *Hofrat* is strong evidence that his work and achievements were appreciated at Jena University; and this is further confirmed by the fact that Frege was made a co-director of the Mathematical Seminar at Jena in 1899.
[3] See A146.

student, Abbe was impressed with the originality and revolutionary character of Frege's work. It was Abbe who recommended that Frege be admitted to the Jena faculty in 1874, and Abbe again who suggested that Frege be promoted to Professor Extraordinarius in 1879.[4]

Abbe had helped the Zeiss family establish their lens and camera factory; and for this he received 45 per cent of all the profits. He used this money anonymously to establish and sustain the Carl Zeiss *Stiftung*. Later he bought out Rhoderich Zeiss's share of the factory and donated his profits to the *Stiftung* as well.

Frege took full advantage of his extra research time. In terms of pages of manuscript, this period was the most productive part of Frege's career. He corresponded with Ballue, Couturat, Hilbert, Husserl, Knoch, Mayer, Pasch, and Peano. He published (1) a crushing review of Husserl's *Philosophy of Arithmetic* I;[5] (2) a damaging critique of Schröder's *Lectures on the Algebra of Logic*;[6] (3) a lethal reply to Peano's review of *The Basic Laws of Arithmetic* I;[7] (4) a thoughtful comparison of his own logic and Peano's;[8] (5) a convincing refutation of Ballue's "formalist" definition of 'whole number';[9] and (6) a witty, satirical attack upon Schubert's philosophy of arithmetic.[10]

He prepared, but did not publish, (1) three large manuscripts in "conceptual notation"—two (301 and 210 pages respectively) on the theory of magnitude, and one (258 pages entirely in symbols) on irrational numbers; (2) an essay on logical mistakes in mathematics; (3) a paper on the establishment of his strict principles of definition; and (4) two articles which argue *ad absurdum* the "peppercorn standpoint" of Weierstrass, Kossak, and Biermann that numbers are aggregates of objects.[11] Besides all this, Frege completed the manuscript of Volume II of *The Basic Laws of Arithmetic*.

Of the six papers which Frege published during this time, the most important and influential was his review of Husserl's book *The Philosophy of Arithmetic* I. It delivers a devastating attack upon the

---

[4] See S1 and §6 of the present biographical sketch.

[5] Husserl's book is *Philosophie der Arithmetik*, Erster Band (Leipzig, 1891). Frege's review is F24.

[6] Schröder's book is *Vorlesungen über die Algebra der Logik* (Leipzig, 1890, 1891, 1895). Frege's article is F25.

[7] Peano's review is S220; Frege's reply is F28.   [8] F27.

[9] That definition occurs in Ballue's article "Le nombre entier considéré comme fondement de l'analyse mathématique", *Revue de métaphysique et de morale*, 3 (1895). Frege's article is F26.

[10] F29.   [11] See S253.

psychologistic foundations of Husserl's position. Frege's crushing arguments marked a turning point in Husserl's career.[12]

While he was a student of mathematics at Vienna, Husserl attended out of curiosity the lectures of Franz Brentano, and was so impressed by Brentano's personality and philosophical lectures that he gave up his plan to become a mathematician. He devoted himself instead to philosophy; and under Brentano's influence became a staunch advocate of psychologism in philosophy, logic, and mathematics.

In 1891 Husserl published the first volume of his *Philosophy of Arithmetic*, in which he expounded a view firmly rooted in psychologism. He included an attack upon Frege's philosophy of arithmetic, which prodded Frege into a reply; so in 1894 Frege reviewed the book and subjected it to his exceptional polemic powers. Analysing each of Husserl's major arguments, Frege exposed the contradiction and confusion that lurked in their psychologistic underpinnings. So completely did he undermine the foundations of Husserl's position, that there was little left to stand upon. As Husserl's biographer explains:

Frege had struck at the very basis of [Husserl's] views so that, unless he desired to stand dogmatically and obstinately by the doctrines to which Brentano had accustomed him, it was now quite impossible for him to carry on further without first assuring himself of fundamental questions. . . . He set himself the prodigious task of making a thorough analysis of the root principles of logic in particular and philosophy in general, and practically the whole of his later work was given over to clarifying basic positions without attempting to build up a system on them.[13]

Frege's review thus marked a turning point in Husserl's career. Before its appearance, Husserl had been a staunch *advocate* of psychologism; after it, he became an *opponent* of psychologism. However, he did not become a disciple of Frege, but went on to develop his own special philosophical position.

Although Husserl was not a Fregean disciple, he apparently did adopt some important ideas from Frege. His personal copies of Frege's works (some of them given to Husserl by Frege himself) are filled with marginal comments, indicating that he studied them thoroughly.[14] Also, the two philosophers corresponded between 1891 and 1906; and one of the most important of Frege's letters to Husserl (24 May 1891)[15] contains a careful explanation of Frege's distinction

---

[12] See S213.   [13] From S213, p. 51.   [14] See S140, S141, S142.
[15] These letters can be found in the Frege Archives in Münster, Germany.

between the sense and the denotation of an expression, which apparently led Husserl to his own distinction between the object and the *noema* of an act of thought.

Frege replaced the classical distinction between an expression and its meaning with the trichotomy of (1) the expression, (2) the sense of the expression, and (3) the denotation (or reference) of the expression. Similarly, Husserl replaced Brentano's distinction between an act of thought and the object of that act with the trichotomy of (1) the act of thought, (2) the *noema* of the act, and (3) the object of the act. Now, for Frege, the *sense* of an expression is that *in virtue of which it has a denotation*; while, for Husserl, the *noema* of an act of thought is that *in virtue of which it has an object*. Thus, Husserl's *noema* corresponds to Frege's *sense*; and, indeed, Husserl considered his notion of *noema* as sense generalized in some special way.[16]

Here, then, is a strong link between Frege and the school of phenomenology. The notion of "*noema*" is crucial in phenomenology; and indeed this philosophical movement, initiated by Husserl, could be reasonably described as an effort to study *noemata*.

Unlike his review of Husserl's work, Frege's critique of Schröder's *Lectures on the Algebra of Logic* had no impact upon philosophy; but from Frege's point of view it was important, because it disproved Schröder's claim to have a better logic. When, back in 1880, Schröder reviewed[17] Frege's *Conceptual Notation*, he proudly asserted that his own logic (and Boole's) was superior to Frege's in every respect; and he produced a most critical and misguided review. Frege had countered this attack in his lecture "On the Aim of the *Conceptual Notation*"[18] (and in the unpublished paper "Boole's Calculating Logic and the *Conceptual Notation*;"[19]) but the convincing last word on the matter appeared sixteen years later in Frege's critique of Schröder's logic. In that work Frege specifies many difficulties and inconsistencies, tracing them to five major sources. Schröder had

(1) Failed to distinguish between a class as a physical collection (pile, cluster, agglomeration) of individuals and a class as an abstract (non-physical) object;

(2) Failed to distinguish between sign and thing signified;

---

[16] For a thorough discussion of this matter see S97.
[17] The review is S256. For a discussion of its contents see the present biographical sketch, §8.
[18] F12.   [19] See S253.

(3) Failed to distinguish between (i) an individual's falling under a concept, and (ii) one concept's being subordinated to another concept;

(4) Failed to distinguish between a name which does not refer and a concept under which nothing falls; and

(5) Attempted to create something by fiat or definition.

Thus, like Peano and Husserl, Schröder also learned the hard way what a formidable polemicist he had challenged.

The unlucky author who was the target of Frege's most caustic criticism was H. Schubert, who was chosen to write an article on the foundations of mathematics for the first edition of the *Enzyklopädie der mathematischen Wissenschaften*. The result was a singularly incompetent essay, and after all the years of careful work which he and others had invested in the foundations of mathematics, Frege thought it was a scandal that the *Enzyklopädie* should print such an article. He wrote a scathing satire on Schubert's views, publishing it privately under the title *On the Numbers of Mr. H. Schubert*.[20] This paper, more than any other, reveals what a spicy tongue Frege could have when aroused. The humour, irony, even ridicule, which it contains are the best examples of Frege's efforts as a satirist.

§16. RUSSELL'S PARADOX: FREGE AND RUSSELL

Beginning with his advancement to Honorary Ordinary Professor in 1896, Frege's luck seemed to improve; and by early 1902 he was enjoying some success. The second volume of his *Basic Laws of Arithmetic* was in press; and he was sure he had proved beyond all doubt that arithmetic is a branch of logic. He believed he had rescued mathematics from a quagmire and re-established it upon a solid foundation rooted in "the laws of thought".

Besides providing this apparently decisive proof of his own view, Frege had dealt a damaging blow to current alternative theories which he believed were detrimental to mathematics. Extreme empiricism (Mill, Weierstrass, Kossak, and Biermann), psychologism (Erdmann and Husserl), and "formalism" (Hankel, Ballue, and Thomae) had all been effectively attacked. Also, Frege had disclosed contradictions and shortcomings in the logical studies of Peano and Schröder, both of whom had claimed that their own logic was superior to Frege's.

[20] F29.

At the height of this happiness and success the "impossible" happened! Someone—a young British logician named Bertrand Russell—discovered an antinomy in the "solid" logical foundation for mathematics which Frege had laid with such pain. In June 1902 Russell wrote to Frege to disclose his discovery.[1] Frege was shocked.

The antinomy was the now famous Russell's Paradox concerning the set of all sets which are not members of themselves: if it is *not* a member of itself, then it *is*; and if it *is* a member of itself, then it is *not*.[2]

The trouble lay in the set theory which Frege employed in defining the numbers and establishing their mathematical properties. The Paradox affected not only Frege's work, but also the work of all scholars (such as Cantor and Dedekind) who had used set theory for the foundations of mathematics.[3] In Frege's system the difficulty could be traced to his Basic Law V[4]—the only fundamental principle about which he had expressed some reservations.[5]

Frege believed that without a solution to the Paradox three decades of work would be in jeopardy, and mathematics would again be tottering on weak foundations.[6] During the summer of 1902 he corresponded with Russell and attempted to work out a solution to the Paradox; but the bad news had depressed him and he felt ill. In late July he reported to Russell that he lacked the strength to reply to Russell's letters as quickly as he wished.[7]

Finally, as the end of the summer drew near, the appearance of the second volume of the *Basic Laws of Arithmetic* was rapidly approaching, and Frege hoped to include an appendix to honour Russell's discovery. He devised an amendment to his Basic Law V which would prevent the generation of Russell's Paradox in his logical system; and he included the amendment in an appendix in which he expressed confidence that he had successfully coped with

---

[1] See S240.

[2] For a discussion of this paradox see Russell's *Principles of Mathematics*, Chapter X. See S241.

[3] See the Appendix to F30.

[4] See the same; also §13 of the present biographical sketch, p. 37.

[5] In the Preface of F23.

[6] In the Appendix of F30, he says: "I do not see how arithmetic can be scientifically founded . . . unless we are allowed—at least conditionally—the transition from a concept to its extension" (from Furth's translation); i.e. unless something like Frege's Basic Law V holds.

[7] In a letter dated 28 July 1902. A copy of this letter can be found in the Frege Archives in Münster, Germany.

the Paradox and secured his logistic foundations of arithmetic. Russell, in an appendix to *The Principles of Mathematics*,[8] agreed.

We know today that Frege's "way out" was unsuccessful, for by adding very simple axioms—e.g. $(Ex)(Ey)$ $(x \neq y)$—to his repaired system new contradictions may be derived.[9] We do not know whether Frege ever became aware of such shortcomings; but it *is* clear that for many years he believed any difficulties could be overcome. As late as 1913–14 he was presenting and defending his logistic programme in courses at Jena University.[10]

After the appearance of *Basic Laws of Arithmetic* II, Frege published no more major ground-breaking efforts in logic or the foundations of arithmetic. However, the impact upon logic, mathematics, and philosophy of his earlier achievements had just begun. Through the work of other scholars (chiefly Russell, Wittgenstein, and Carnap) his influence increased and spread. Bertrand Russell gave the first great impetus to Frege's influence.

For decades inaccurate views have circulated about Russell's relation to Frege and his work. For example, it has often been said that Frege's work was virtually unknown till Russell discovered it and drew attention to it in his *Principles of Mathematics*. Russell himself fostered such a view with statements like these:

In spite of the epoch-making nature of his discoveries, he [Frege] remained wholly without recognition until I drew attention to him in 1903.[11]

In spite of the great value of this work [*Conceptual Notation*], I was, I believe, the first person who ever read it—more than twenty years after its publication.[12]

Other scholars have echoed Russell's claims down through the years. Lewis and Langford say, for example,

Frege's work passed unnoticed until 1901, when attention was called to it by Mr. Bertrand Russell.[13]

---

[8] S241. [9] See S102, S229, S234, S270.

[10] See A34. There are more details in a letter to the present writer from Carnap, dated 4 April 1967.

[11] B. Russell, *A History of Western Philosophy* (London: Allen and Unwin, 1946), p. 858.

[12] From Russell's *Introduction to Mathematical Philosophy* (London: Allen and Unwin, 1919, 1920), p. 25 n.

[13] From their *Symbolic Logic* (New York: Century, 1932; Dover, 1951, 1959), p. 16.

It is clear from information already presented in this biographical sketch that these claims are overstatements. This fact was not clearly pointed out, however, until 1963, when Nidditch did so in his article "Peano and the Recognition of Frege";[14] and many people are still unaware of the facts.

Frege's work hardly "passed unnoticed" before Russell discovered it; for it had been reviewed or criticized by many others, including notable scholars like Venn, Schröder, Cantor, Husserl, and Peano.[15]

Russell was certainly not the first person to read the *Conceptual Notation*. It had been reviewed six times[16] and cited in Peano's works[17] and in Venn's *Symbolic Logic*,[18] both of which Russell himself had read.

Finally, Frege did not remain "wholly without recognition" until 1903; for, as we have seen,[19] both Husserl and Peano had already recognized Frege as an important scholar, and indeed had been essentially influenced by him.

Though Russell was not the first to "discover" Frege, he *was* the first to see that Frege had made revolutionary advances in logic and the philosophy of mathematics. The correct account seems to be, then, that Husserl and Peano "discovered" Frege, while Russell discovered Frege's greatness.

Starting with the *Principles of Mathematics*, Russell taught—as Frege had done before him—that applying the "new logic" to old philosophical problems could yield impressive results. Through Russell, contemporary analytic philosophy, which had originated with Frege, began to grow. Ironically, as Russell's fame increased, Frege was relegated to the background; so he never lived to enjoy the recognition he deserved. Russell and Whitehead's *Principia Mathematica* was acclaimed a monumental work, while Frege's *Basic Laws of Arithmetic* was neglected and ignored; even though much of what the *Principia* had achieved (with the notable exception of a solution to Russell's Paradox) had been done first and more rigorously[20] in Frege's book. Russell lived to see himself called the

[14] S212.
[15] See S60, S139, S220, S256, S292.
[16] In S135, S176, S205, S256, S283, and S292. Strictly speaking, all the reviewers but Schröder may have reviewed the book without *reading* it. Schröder, on the other hand, studied Frege's book in great detail before reviewing it.
[17] For example, in S220.
[18] In S291.
[19] In §§14–15 above.
[20] See p. 268 of S54. For a discussion of some of the imperfections in Russell's logic see A70.

greatest logician since Aristotle,[21] while Frege died with little recognition.

§17. AFTER RUSSELL'S PARADOX

During the decade following the publication of *Basic Laws of Arithmetic* II Frege led a rather unhappy life. There is a widespread myth that Russell's Paradox had left him a disappointed and broken man; but actually, at least until 1914, he believed his logistic programme had been carried out successfully. The problem was rather that his health was not good, and in 1905 death claimed his wife,[1] leaving him to raise their young adopted son alone. Also, it is clear from his published responses[2] that Frege was irked and upset by two harsh, misguided attacks on his work—one by his colleague Johannes Thomae at Jena University,[3] and one by A. Korselt on Frege's critique of Hilbert's early views concerning axioms and definitions in geometry.[4] All these troubles left their mark, and (as Carnap reported) in 1910 "Frege looked old beyond his years".[5]

Right up to his retirement from Jena University in 1918, however, Frege remained a keen and active scholar, continuing to work on new applications of his "conceptual notation" and to study critically the views of others on the foundations of mathematics.[6] He based his university lectures upon this current research and his courses continued to be demanding upon the student, impressive, and inspiring.[7]

He was in touch by mail with other scholars, including Couturat, Darmstaedter, Dingler, Husserl, Jourdain, Löwenheim, Russell, and Vailati.[8] Through a large correspondence with Löwenheim, which unfortunately was lost during the Second World War, Frege was apparently convinced of the *possibility* of constructing an acceptable formal arithmetic *à la* Hilbert.[9]

Besides corresponding with other scholars, Frege apparently also travelled from time to time to visit them. An extant postcard on

---

[21] See, for example, "Russell Releases Life Story", *New York Times*, 19 March 1967, p. 79.

[1] I am indebted to Professor Dr. G. Uschmann and Professor Ignazio Angelelli for providing from the Jena University Archives the correct date of Frau Frege's death. The probable date given by Hermes in S128 is incorrect.

[2] F34, F35, F36, F37.   [3] S285, S286, S287.

[4] Frege's critique of Hilbert is found in F31 and F32. Korselt's attack is in S169a. Frege's response is in F34.

[5] See A34.   [6] See S253.   [7] See A34.

[8] Most of these letters can be found in the Frege Archives at Münster, Germany.

[9] See S253.

which he thanked Vailati for breakfast indicates that Frege went to Italy.[10] Perhaps he met Peano there, as well as Vailati. The last letter of the Frege–Russell correspondence (dated "Jena, 9 June 1912")[11] reveals that Frege had accepted an invitation from Russell to come to England for a mathematics conference in the summer of 1912; but he was forced to cancel the trip at the last moment because his adopted son Alfred fell ill.

Although Frege was active during this period, he published only a few things, including (1) several articles on the foundations of geometry, which arose from his correspondence with Hilbert before Russell's Paradox;[12] (2) three articles against "formalist" arithmetic in answer to the attack by his colleague Johannes Thomae.[13]

Besides the published articles on "formalist" arithmetic, he also wrote (1905–8) four unpublished essays on the same topic.[14] Other works in Frege's scientific *Nachlass* which were written in this period include (1) two incomplete manuscripts, "A Short Survey of My Logical Theories" and "Introduction to Logic",[15] which consider the same topics as the published "logical studies"; (2) some essays against Pasch, Hilbert, Korselt, Moore, and Schoenflies on paradoxes of set theory; and (3) the large manuscript (151 pages) "On Logic in Mathematics", which served as a basis for his university lectures of 1914.[16]

Frege's students had the advantage of hearing him discuss in his lectures some of the topics from these unpublished works. One of those students was Rudolf Carnap, who in the autumn of 1910 attended Frege's course "Conceptual Notation", which was an introduction to Frege's "new logic".[17] In 1913, curious about Frege's comment that his new logic could be used to construct the whole of arithmetic, Carnap attended "Conceptual Notation II":

Frege occasionally made critical remarks about other conceptions, sometimes with irony and even sarcasm. In particular he attacked the formalists, those who declared that numbers are mere symbols. . . . [He] explained various applications [of his "conceptual notation"], among them

[10] I am indebted to Professor Ignazio Angelelli for this information.

[11] Bertrand Russell very kindly showed me that letter in the summer of 1965.

[12] F31, F32, F34. The last item cited here is Frege's response to Korselt's attack mentioned above.

[13] F35, F36, F37.   [14] See S253, p. 29; also F45.

[15] "Kurze Übersicht meiner logischen Lehren" and "Einleitung in die Logik"; see S253, p. 26. (Published in F45.)

[16] All these articles are mentioned in S253. For an account of the contents of the lectures see A34. (Articles published in F45.)

[17] See A34.

some which are not contained in his publications, e.g., a definition of the continuity of a function, and of the limit of a function, the distinction between ordinary convergence and uniform convergence. All these concepts were expressible with the help of the quantifiers, which appear in his system of logic for the first time. He gave also a demonstration of the logical mistake in the ontological proof for the existence of God.[18]

In 1914 Carnap attended yet another Frege course, "Logic in Mathematics", in which Frege criticized some of the usual formulations and conceptions in mathematics:

He deplored the fact that mathematicians did not even seem to aim at the construction of a unified, well-formed *system* of mathematics, and therefore showed a lack of interest in foundations. He pointed out a certain looseness in the customary formulation of axioms, definitions, and proofs, even in works of the more prominent mathematicians. . . . He criticized in particular the lack of attention to certain fundamental distinctions, e.g., the distinction between the symbol and the symbolized, that between a logical concept and a mental image or act, and that between a function and the value of the function.[19]

A decade or two after his student years Carnap became a famous and influential scholar; and because he greatly admired Frege and had learned much from him in logic and semantics, he disseminated and further developed many Fregean ideas. It is Carnap, more than any other scholar (though perhaps Wittgenstein runs a close second), who is chiefly responsible for the present "Frege renaissance" and the growing acclaim that Frege's works are now receiving.

During the time that Carnap was a student at Jena, Frege met Wittgenstein, who later spread and developed Fregean ideas and methods. In 1910 Wittgenstein was an engineering student at Manchester University in England. There he became interested in the foundations of mathematics and read Russell's *Principles of Mathematics*, where he found an account of Frege's views. He wrote to Frege, putting forth some objections; and Frege replied with an invitation to come to Jena and discuss the matter. In 1911 he visited Frege and, besides discussing his objections, asked for advice about studying the foundations of mathematics. Frege recommended that he should go to Cambridge and study with Russell, who had just published (with Whitehead) the first volume of *Principia Mathematica*. Wittgenstein, of course, took Frege's advice.[20]

---

[18] From A34, pp. 5–6.   [19] From A34, p. 6.
[20] See S22 and A175. Russell's report in 1951 (*Mind*, vol. 60, pp. 297–8) that Wittgenstein had not met Frege at the time he came to Cambridge is mistaken.

In his study of the foundations of mathematics Wittgenstein read Frege's works and was very strongly influenced by them. Later, in the Preface to his *Tractatus*,[21] he reveals this: "I owe a great part of the stimulation of my thoughts to the great works of Frege and to the writings of my friend Mr. Bertrand Russell."

So strongly did Frege influence Wittgenstein that it is difficult to understand his works without first reading Frege. Anscombe says of the *Tractatus*, for example:

Wittgenstein's *Tractatus* has captured the interest and excited the admiration of many, yet almost all that has been published about it has been wildly irrelevant. If this has had any one cause, that cause has been the neglect of Frege and of the new direction that he gave to philosophy. In the *Tractatus* Wittgenstein assumes, and does not try to stimulate, an interest in the kind of questions that Frege wrote about; he also takes it for granted that his readers will have read Frege.[22]

Frege's influence on Wittgenstein is evident throughout the latter's work, including the later part where he rebels against his earlier views.

Sometime after 1914, as Frege approached the age of seventy and retirement from Jena University in 1918, he began to have doubts and second thoughts about his "purely logical" foundation for arithmetic. Because of these doubts he became more experimental and explorative. For example, his last published papers—"The Thought" (1918), "Negation" (1918), and "Compound Thoughts" (1923)[23]—contain some of his new explorations in logic.

Several papers from Frege's *Nachlass*[24] reveal that by 1924 he had completely given up his logistic thesis that arithmetic is a part of logic. Either he discovered that his own "way out" of Russell's Paradox did not work, or perhaps he merely came to view it as *ad hoc*. At any rate, he was apparently dissatisfied even with the repairs of Russell and Zermelo, for in 1924 he wrote "the paradoxes of set theory . . . have destroyed set theory".[25]

---

[21] A173. The English translation here is that of Anscombe in S21.

[22] From S21, p. 12.

[23] F39, F40, and F41, respectively.

[24] The papers are, "(Tagebucheintragungen über den Begriff der Zahl)", "Zahl", "Erkenntnisquellen der Mathematik und der mathematischen Naturwissenschaften", "Zahlen und Arithmetik" and "Neuer Versuch der Grundlegung der Arithmetik". They were all published recently in F45.

[25] From "Erkenntnisquellen", ibid. F 45, p. 289.

Thus Frege gave up the belief that numbers are abstract objects of logic (sets). However, he did not give up the belief that they are abstract objects of *some* sort. In searching for a new foundation for arithmetic he turned to an area of lifelong interest: geometry. He wrote:

The more I thought about it, the more convinced I became that arithmetic and geometry grew from the same foundation, indeed from the geometrical one; so that the whole of mathematics is actually geometry.[26]

By identifying numbers with points on a Gaussian plane, Frege found the abstract objects he thought he needed to give arithmetic a geometric foundation. In so doing, he gave up a belief he had held for at least fifty years (expressed as early as 1874 in his *Habilitationsschrift*[27])—the belief that arithmetic is analytic a priori knowledge rooted in logic while geometry is synthetic a priori knowledge rooted in "geometric intuition".

Unfortunately, Frege did not live to pursue his new foundations of arithmetic beyond the mere beginnings or to see the great influence and acclaim that his life's work would eventually win. In 1918 he had left his home at Forstweg 29 in Jena and retired to Haus 52 in Bad Kleinen, near his home town of Wismar; on 26 July 1925, at the age of 77, he died. His death was virtually unmarked by the scholarly world—a tragic fate for such a man, who had singlehandedly created a revolution in logic and initiated a great movement in philosophy.

---

[26] From "Zahlen und Arithmetik", ibid. F45, p. 297.   [27] F2.

EDITOR'S INTRODUCTION

THE present volume includes Frege's *Conceptual Notation* plus several works concerned with it—three related articles by Frege, six reviews (apparently the only ones) which appeared shortly after Frege's book was published, and some remarks by four distinguished contemporary scholars.[1] Taken together, these works cover an important chapter in the rise of modern logic.

Even though the *Conceptual Notation* ushered in a logical renaissance, and, as such, has been duly celebrated by historians of logic,[2] many important facts about the book have remained obscure or generally unknown. Why did Frege write his book—precisely what was its aim? What did he take as a basis for his work? How did he make the great logical discoveries which the book contains? Why did he use an unusual two-dimensional notation? To date, in spite of a growing interest in Frege, such issues have not been considered in detail. The present Introduction attempts to answer these questions and thereby provide a natural and appropriate preface to Frege's work.

1

The *Conceptual Notation* grew out of a project (henceforth called "Frege's logistic project") that Frege first set for himself about 1874. In that year he reviewed a mathematics text[3] intended to introduce students to the fundamentals of arithmetic. In the review, Frege complains that the book lacks (i) clear definitions of the basic concepts[4] of arithmetic and (ii) proofs of the fundamental laws of arithmetic.[5] These shortcomings may have spurred him to develop

---

[1] The *Conceptual Notation* is F7; the related articles are F8, F11, F12; the reviews are S135, S176, S205, S256, S283, S292; the remarks are excerpts from S54, S167, A55, A127.

[2] See Appendix II below, pp. 236–8.   [3] The review is F3.

[4] In this early period of his career, Frege used the term 'concept' (*Begriff*) rather loosely, allowing it to stand for various types of entity, both subjective and objective. (See 6 of the present Introduction.) Later (see F19) he assigned 'concept' the specific meaning of a one-argument function "whose value is always a truth-value".

[5] Frege used the term 'arithmetic' very broadly to include, for example,

such definitions and proofs himself; for, about the same time, he began an effort to do just that.

Before attempting to prove the fundamental laws of arithmetic, Frege had to decide what kind of proof would be appropriate. Since he considered arithmetic a science, the proofs had to be scientific. He believed that there are two kinds of scientifically acceptable proof[6]—those which depend upon empirical evidence, and those which proceed "purely logically" (*rein logisch*). He rejected the view, however, that proofs of arithmetical truths appeal to experience,[7] so he was left with the task of proving them "purely logically".[8]

Since the fundamental laws of arithmetic employ basic arithmetical concepts (e.g. "number"), the *concepts* had to be defined purely logically, in order to prove the *laws* purely logically. Apparently, the concepts Frege had in mind (besides that of "number") were, for example, the notion of mathematical induction, and relations such as "less than", "equal to", and "greater than". To define these, Frege chose to use the concept of "ordering-in-a-sequence"[9]—a very appropriate choice, since mathematical induction essentially involves sequential ordering; and one can define "less than", "equal to", and "greater than" in terms of occurring "before", "at the same place", or "after" in the sequence of integers.

It was apparently with ideas such as these in mind that Frege devised the following plan: first, define the notion of "ordering-in-a-sequence" (proper ancestral) purely logically;[10] then, on this basis, define the basic concepts of arithmetic; and finally, given these definitions and the laws of logic, prove the fundamental laws of arithmetic.

algebra, differential and integral calculus, and functional analysis. In the present Introduction the term is employed in this broad sense.

[6] See the Preface to F7, this volume, pp. 103–4.

[7] In F14, where he argues against J. S. Mill, Frege explains his reasons for taking this position. See also F16.

[8] As it turned out, this meant deducing them (with rules of inference provided by logic) from laws of logic, together with basic arithmetical concepts that are defined using only concepts from logic.

[9] What Frege calls the concept of "ordering-in-a-sequence" {der Begriff der Anordnung in einer Reihe} is today called the "proper ancestral of a relation" (formula 76 of the *Conceptual Notation*, p. 173 below). It plays an important role in his effort to derive arithmetic from logic. See 8 of the present Introduction and pp. 92–6 of F14.

[10] Frege achieved this first phase in Part III of F7, translated in the present volume, pp. 167–202. See also the discussion in 8 of the present Introduction, and Schröder's review below, pp. 218–32.

2

In the Preface to the *Conceptual Notation* Frege explains that the initial phase of his project was an effort "to reduce the concept of ordering-in-a-sequence to that of *logical* ordering.[11] At first, he tried to develop his arguments in German, but soon found the language inadequate. Many words were ambiguous or vague; modes of inference were numerous, obscure, and difficult to characterize precisely; implicit assumptions and intuitions could creep into arguments unnoticed, leaving "gaps" in the chains of reasoning.[12] Hence, "proofs", if they could be given at all, were loose and inconclusive. Frege, who was well schooled in geometry, was accustomed to more rigorous proofs, such as those in Euclidean geometry;[13] and he was therefore quite dissatisfied with this first effort. Consequently, he decided to develop a more precise language in which to couch his proofs; and he was determined to construct the language in such a way that the possibility of human error in reasoning would be minimized, thereby making his proofs as reliable as possible.

Since he was familiar with the work of Leibniz,[14] and he was seeking a precise, scientific language, Frege thought of Leibniz's ambitious programme to develop a precise, scientific "universal language". As C. I. Lewis describes it,

This universal medium is to be an ideographic language each single character of which will represent a single concept. It will differ from existing ideographic languages, such as Chinese, through using a combination of symbols, or some similar device, for a compound idea, instead of having a multiplicity of characters corresponding to the variety of things. So that while Chinese can hardly be learned in a lifetime, the universal characteristic may be mastered in a few weeks. The fundamental characters of the universal language will be few in number, and will represent the *"alphabet of human thought"*.[15]

Leibniz characterized his proposed language as "a certain sensible and palpable medium, which will guide the mind as do the lines

[11] F7, this volume, p. 104.
[12] See F11, the present volume, pp. 83–9.
[13] In F11, however, Frege points out that even Euclid's proofs contain "gaps". See below, p. 85.
[14] See, for example, the Preface of F7, this volume, pp. 105–6.
[15] A101, pp. 6–7. (Originally published by the University of California Press; reprinted by permission of The Regents of the University of California.)

drawn in geometry and the formulae for operations . . . in arithmetic".[16] Thus,

if we could find characters or signs appropriate for expressing all our
thoughts, as definitely and as exactly as arithmetic expresses numbers and
geometric analysis expresses lines, we could in all subjects *in so far as they
are amenable to reasoning* accomplish what is done in Arithmetic and
Geometry.

For all inquiries which depend on reasoning would be performed by the
transposition of characters and by a kind of calculus. . . .[17]

The language Leibniz proposed was to be modelled upon arithmetic and geometry—disciplines in which Frege had considerable
interest and training; and, even though Leibniz never succeeded in
his efforts to develop a "universal characteristic", Frege found the
programme attractive. If he could fulfil a less ambitious project by
developing only a portion of the Leibnizian language—that part
concerned with logic and mathematics—Frege would have the tools
required to fashion the proofs he sought to provide.

Thus, basing himself upon the Leibnizian programme for a
universal language, Frege began the development of his "conceptual
notation".

In his universal language Leibniz ruled out "equivocations and
amphibolies".[18] Frege banned ambiguity from his "conceptual
notation", requiring that every symbol keep the same meaning in
each of its occurrences throughout a given context.[19]

According to Leibniz, those using his language will make no
reasoning mistakes "provided they avoid the errors of calculation,
barbarisms, solecisms and other errors of grammar and construction".[20] In the "conceptual notation" rules of inference[21] were to be
syntactically specified, and the grammar so constituted that "mere
adherence to grammar would guarantee the formal correctness of
thought processes".[22]

[16] In a letter to Galois, 1677. Quoted in A101, p. 6.
[17] Leibniz, "Preface to the General Science" (1677), quoted in *Leibnitz
Selections*, ed. P. P. Wiener (New York: Scribner's, 1951), p. 15. (Henceforth,
this book will be called simply 'Wiener'.)
[18] See Wiener, p. 16.
[19] See F11, the present volume, p. 86.
[20] Wiener, p. 16.
[21] F7, this volume, p. 117. Frege was apparently the first clearly to distinguish
axioms from rules of inference; see A124, p. 88.
[22] F11, this volume, p. 84.

Leibniz required that there should be no "gaps" in chains of reasoning:

> To derive one truth from another, we must keep uninterruptedly to a certain chain. For as we may be sure that a chain will hold when we are sure that each separate ring is of sound material, and that it clasps . . . the one before and the one after it, so likewise, we may be sure of the accuracy of the reasoning when . . . it contains nothing doubtful, and when the form consists of a perpetual linking with no gaps.[23]

To prevent "gaps" in proofs, and guarantee that nothing could slip in unnoticed. Frege required that every assumption—no matter how trivial—should be fully expressed; and every inference in a proof must conform to a simple, firmly established and syntactically specified rule of inference, linking the derived sentence in question to given assumptions or previously derived sentences.[24]

3

In applying these rigorous standards, Frege went beyond those previously employed in geometry and arithmetic,[25] which in several other respects served as a model for his "conceptual notation". One of the things he did adopt from those two disciplines was the practice of utilizing the two-dimensionality of the writing surface to achieve perspicuity.[26] Geometric figures are obviously two-dimensional; but often proofs in arithmetic also occur as two-dimensional arrays.[27] For example, one frequently writes down a propositional expression[28] (equation, inequality, etc.) immediately below the one

[23] Leibniz, "On Wisdom" (1693), Wiener, p. 78.
[24] See F11, the present volume, p. 85.
[25] Indeed, because of these requirements, Frege achieved the first really "gapless" proofs in any discipline. His proofs are purely syntactical, requiring no intuitive steps or components. They achieve a level of rigour and formal correctness unmatched for over forty years until the works of Łukasiewicz in 1920. See S54, this volume, p. 237.
[26] See F11, this volume, p. 87 and F12, this volume, p. 97.
[27] See F11, this volume, p. 88.
[28] Terms such as 'proposition', '(declarative) sentence', and so on, have been used in different ways by various authors. (See A40, p. 26.) To avoid confusion, the present Introduction consistently employs such terms in the following way: an *expression* is a set of symbols in a given language or notation; a *propositional expression* is one which has the form of a sentence; a *sentence* is a propositional expression whose meaning is a proposition; a *proposition* (roughly Frege's "assertible content" {*beurteilbarer Inhalt*}; see **6** below) is the meaning expressed

from which it is derived:

$$x+6 = 8$$
$$x = 8-6$$
$$x = 2$$

thus achieving more perspicuity than could be attained by placing the expressions side by side:

$$x+6 = 8, \quad x = 8-6, \quad x = 2.$$

Also, if one propositional expression is derived from two (or more) previous ones, the latter are placed one below the other as before; then a line is drawn, and the derived expression is placed below it,

$$x^2 = 4$$
$$x < 0$$
$$\overline{}$$
$$x = -2.$$

The line can be read "therefore".

Frege wished to retain for his "conceptual notation" the perspicuity inherent in two-dimensional arrays;[29] and so he adopted from arithmetic the practice of writing propositional expressions one below the other and including a line for "therefore".

To interrelate propositional expressions, Frege needed logical connectives to represent connections such as 'not', 'and', 'or', and so forth. Since propositional expressions were to occur one below the other, he could add another two-dimensional aspect to his notation and further increase perspicuity by constructing figures from lines (as in geometry) to serve as the logical connectives. For example, the array

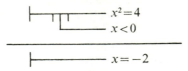

by a sentence; an *assertion* (Frege's "judgement" {*Urteil*}) is an asserted proposition and is either true or false. If, in a given context, the proposition expressed by a sentence is asserted, the sentence itself is said to be asserted in that context and either true or false.

[29] See F12, the present volume, pp. 97–8.

is an argument using Frege's connectives. In English it could be read

x is less than zero, and x squared equals four; therefore, x equals minus two.

The two-dimensional structure of arrays in Frege's notation makes them very easy to read;[30] for one can tell at a glance how the given propositional expressions are related; and in proofs one can see immediately whether a given derivation conforms to Frege's major rule of inference—a rule of detachment (*modus ponens*). This fits very nicely with his desire to minimize the possibility of mistakes.

4

Given Frege's rigorous proof standards and his two-dimensional connectives, one would indeed have the rudiments of a Leibnizian "medium, which will guide the mind as do the lines drawn in geometry"; but one would have to add, as well, some kind of notation to construct the propositional expressions that the logical connectives relate. To be sure, Frege could—and did—combine his connectives with expressions from arithmetic to form mathematical sentences.[31] His major aim, however, was to provide *purely logical* proofs of the fundamental laws of arithmetic; and to achieve this end he could not (without being circular) base his proofs upon propositional expressions from arithmetic—he had to use *purely logical* ones.

To develop a notation for purely logical propositional expressions Frege drew upon his mathematical training and proficiency. One of his major interests in mathematics was functional analysis,[32] which commonly employs letters for numerical functions and their arguments (variables);[33] for example, 'x', 'y', and 'f' in '$y = f(x)$'. Such letters enable one to express precisely simple or complex mathematical properties, relations, and operations; and, as Leibniz explained, "by making use of letters instead of . . . numbers we

[30] Unfortunately, the erroneous view that Frege's notation is difficult to read is very common. See, for example, Russell's remarks in the Preface of his *Principles of Mathematics* (S241).

[31] See F8, the present volume, pp. 204–8.

[32] Frege had taken several university courses in this field as a student (see above, pp. 3–4).

[33] Frege disapproved of using the term 'variable', because he thought (with justification) that it is often erroneously held to mean some mysteriously varying entity. He preferred simply to use the term 'letter' (see F38 or F7 [*b*], p. 10). (Frege was apparently the first to give a clear, consistent account of the notion of a variable. See S54, this volume, p. 237.)

obtain formulas in which there is some connection and order, which gives our mind a means of noticing theorems and general rules".[34]

Because of these advantages, to construct the propositional expressions he would need (that is, purely logical ones), Frege wished to employ letters for functions and their arguments. This would involve construing letters in non-numerical ways; but, as Leibniz had previously noted, such a practice was not new:

the best advantages of algebra are only samples of the art of characters whose use is not limited to numbers or magnitudes. For if these letters designated points (a common practice actually among Geometers), we could form a certain *calculus* or sort of operation which would be entirely different from Algebra and would continue to enjoy the same advantages as the latter has. . . . When these letters designate terms or notions, as in Aristotle, we obtain that part of logic which treats of the figures and moods.[35]

In the Preface to the *Conceptual Notation* Frege reveals that he developed his logical functions and arguments by taking those in arithmetic as a model.[36] Though he does not explain this comment in detail, if one keeps in mind Frege's view of logic as that scientific discipline concerned with "everything thinkable",[37] and maintains a strict analogy with arithmetic, one can derive an account of the logical functions Frege developed: Arithmetic, according to Frege, is the scientific discipline concerned with numbers; therefore the range of arguments of its functions is the numbers. Maintaining a strict analogy with this view of arithmetic, one can say that, if logic is that scientific discipline concerned with anything at all, then the range of arguments of its functions should be anything at all.[38] Thus, using functional notation analogous to that of arithmetic, but with the arguments no longer restricted to numbers, Frege could construct purely logical expressions—both propositional and non-propositional ones;[39] but, as noted above, he was mainly interested in the former;[40]

---

[34] "The Horizon of Human Doctrine" (after 1690), in Wiener, p. 74.

[35] Ibid., pp. 74–5. Aristotle used letters not only to stand for terms, but also for propositions. See, for example, *Prior Analytics* i. 15 (34^{a}5–24) and *Prior Analytics* ii. 2 (53^{b}12) or 4(57^{b}6). See also S167, pp. 92 and 96.

[36] See below, p. 104.

[37] See F16, or the quotation above, p. 32.

[38] At this early stage of his logistic project Frege apparently was not concerned with problems of semantics and ontology. (See 6 below.) For example, he did not yet introduce a distinction between "saturated" and "unsaturated" entities.

[39] See F7, the present volume, p. 127.   [40] See above, p. 61.

and so, in the *Conceptual Notation*, he limits himself to propositional expressions.[41] Because of this restriction, all functions in his "conceptual notation" are *propositional*,[42] and all non-function letters which are not in argument places of functional expressions (or part of quantifiers) are *propositional letters*.[43]

Frege's functional expressions are not only "modelled upon the formula language of arithmetic" as described above, they are also analogous in the following way. In an arithmetic propositional expression, say '$y = f(x)$', if one were to replace all the letters by symbols for particular arguments, the resulting expression would be a sentence. *Some* resulting sentences, if asserted, would be *true*—for example (replacing 'y' by '4', 'x' by '2', and '$f(\ )$' by the square function '$(\ )^2$'),

$$4 = (2)^2;$$

while others would be false—for example (replacing 'y' by '9', 'x' by '5', and '$f(\ )$' by '$(\ )^3$'),

$$9 = (5)^3.$$

Similarly, in Frege's logical propositional expressions, say 'a' or '$F(x)$', replacing all the letters by symbols for particular arguments produces sentences which, if asserted, would be true or false—for example, replacing 'a' by 'All men are mortal'; or replacing 'x' by 'Plato' and 'F' by 'is a Roman' to get 'Plato is a Roman'.

5

By introducing logical functions Frege had taken a major stride toward developing the kind of language he was seeking. Even so, he still needed an important addition to be able to apply his logical functions most effectively and express many of the propositions with which he was concerned. Since the range of arguments of his

---

[41] See F7, the present volume, p. 132.

[42] Frege himself did not use the term 'propositional function' nor a German equivalent. It is used here in the sense of "propositional function *in intension*" as defined by Church (S66, p. 257) as "a *function* for which the range of the dependent variable is composed of *propositions*". (See 6 below.) After F20, Frege used propositional functions *in extension*, i.e. ones for which the range of the dependent variable is composed of truth-values.

[43] Propositional letters in the *Conceptual Notation* stand for propositions ("assertible contents") rather than truth-values. See 7 below.

functions was the entire universe,[44] he could use them without supplementation to indicate "generality" (*Allgemeinheit*), and thereby express propositions about everything in the universe—for example, if 'Φ' stands for a given property, '$\Phi(x)$' would mean "Everything has property Φ". On the other hand, one may wish to express either

(1) Not everything has property Φ (i.e. something does not have property Φ),

or

(2) Everything is such that it is not the case that it has property Φ (i.e. nothing has property Φ).

Clearly, these two sentences differ in meaning. Merely adding a symbol for 'not' to Frege's functional expressions would not enable him to express the different meanings. The reason is that the generality (here indicated by 'everything') and the negation (here indicated by 'not') govern different parts of the expressions in question.

Let us say, with Frege,[45] that the part of the expression covered by the generality (or the negation) is the *scope* (*Gebiet*) of the generality (or the negation). If, in (1) and (2) above, the scope of the negation is indicated by '[ ]' and that of the generality by '{ }', the result is

(i) Not [everything {has property Φ}]

(ii) Everything is such that {it is not the case that [it has property Φ]}.

In (i) the scope of the generality is *included within* that of the negation, while in (ii) the reverse is the case.

As these examples illustrate, the scope of generality or negation must sometimes be limited to a *part* of an expression. This is the case even where negation is not involved—for example, in

(iii) If everything {has property Φ}, then the moon has property Φ.[46]

Many propositions with which Frege was concerned could not be expressed without a notation which clearly delimits scopes. His symbol for negation performs the task "automatically"—the intended scope of a given negation sign is unambiguously indicated by the position it occupies in the array of connective lines.[47] Frege's letters, however, occur to the right of that array, not *within* it; and

---

[44] *Not* a limited "universe of discourse", but *the* universe.

[45] See F7, the present volume, p. 131.

[46] Frege's own examples are similar to (i) and (iii) above. See F7, this volume, p. 131.

[47] See the section "Negation" in F7, the present volume, pp. 120–4.

they do not, by themselves, indicate their intended scope.[48] To over-come this difficulty, Frege introduced a generality-delimiting symbol, which is placed in the connective array in a manner similar to that of the negation sign. The symbol in question is a "concavity" (——⌣——) which can occur *within* any horizontal line (just as the negation sign can be *attached* to any horizontal line). In order to identify the letter, say ɑ, whose scope is to be indicated, that letter is placed in the concavity (——⌣ɑ——) as well as in the argument places of the appropriate function expressions.

With this device (which logicians would later call "the universal quantifier"),[49] Frege was able not only to delimit generality scopes; he also was able, by combining his "quantifier" with the negation sign, to express *particular* as well as universal propositions.[50]

Frege's universal quantifier was the first variable binding operator[51] used in logic. Here is yet another similarity between the "conceptual notation" and "the formula language of arithmetic"; for variable binding operators are used in arithmetic as well—for example, in the expressions

$$\int_0^2 x^x \, dx \quad \text{and} \quad \lim_{x \to 0} \frac{\sin x}{x},$$

the variable 'x' is bound by '$\int_0^2 (\ ) \, dx$' and '$\lim_{x \to 0}$' respectively.[52]

By combining his universal quantifier with his letters and connec-tives and adding his rules for their application, Frege produced "the most powerful and most characteristic instrument of modern logic",[53] though at that time he was not aware that he had done so. He was satisfied, however, that he had developed the Leibnizian language he needed, so he proceeded to the first phase of his logistic project.

6

The "conceptual notation" proved to be adequate for the first phase of Frege's logistic project;[54] but he would later discover the

---

[48] When Frege uses italic letters, however, they always have the entire expres-sion as the scope of their generality.
[49] The term 'quantifier' stems from C. S. Peirce. See A40, p. 288.
[50] See Frege's version of the square of opposition in F7, this volume, p. 135.
[51] For a discussion of the use of these in logic and mathematics, see A40, §6.
[52] See A40, p. 14.
[53] W. V. Quine, A127, p. vii. Quoted below, p. 236.
[54] See above, p. 10.

need for modifications and additions in order to complete the effort. In particular, he would need a carefully developed theory of meaning.

In the *Conceptual Notation* Frege gives little attention to problems of meaning. He does make linguistic or semantic distinctions where they seem appropriate or helpful; but he does not systematize his distinctions, nor even follow them consistently. For example, he distinguishes sign from thing signified (or using from mentioning an expression) by employing capital Greek letters while writing *about* his notation, but not while writing *in* it.[55] Similarly, he often places ordinary-language expressions within quotation marks when mentioning rather than using them. On the other hand, at many places Frege seems to confuse his symbols with what they stand for.[56]

Frege recognizes only one kind of meaning in the *Conceptual Notation*, which he calls the "content" (*Inhalt*) of an expression. At this early stage he does not clearly distinguish (as he will later) between *subjective* meaning (private, mental images "arising from memories of sense impressions" and "saturated with feeling"),[57] which vary from person to person and even fluctuate for the same person, and *objective* meaning, "which may be the common property of many and therefore is not a part or mode of the individual mind".[58] He does introduce a related distinction, however—his notation is to express only "conceptual content", which is that meaning necessary for logical inference.[59] Emotive connotations and rhetorical accessories are to be excluded. This restriction is a move toward the distinction between subjective and objective meaning, though there are still places in which Frege seems to confuse the two.

The major units of meaning for Frege's notation are conceptual contents of propositional expressions[60]—"assertible contents" (*beurtheilbare Inhalte*).[61] Only such contents can be asserted and thereby become "judgements" (today called "assertions").[62] Another term for "assertible contents" would be 'propositions' (*Sätze*); and,

---

[55] Since Frege introduced a distinctive notation for talking *about* his "conceptual notation", he had the beginnings of a distinction between "metalanguage" and "object language", though he does not use those terms.

[56] For a discussion of this last point and some examples see S167, p. 485.

[57] From F20 in F′47, p. 59.   [58] Ibid.

[59] See F7, the present volume, p. 113.   [60] See above, p. 62.

[61] Literally "judicable contents"; but this literal translation is misleading, since one can make judgements about *any* content. For Frege, a judgement is an *asserted* content, and only *beurtheilbare Inhalte* can be asserted; on these grounds, the term is here rendered "assertible contents".

[62] See below, p. 69.

indeed, Frege sometimes refers to them that way. Again, however, he seems to blur the distinction between subjective, mental entities— as traditional Scholastic logicians would have them[63]—and objective "thoughts", as he himself would later call them.

In explaining the meaning of his identity sign ('$\equiv$' (*Inhaltsgleichheit*)),[64] which he uses to introduce abbreviations and express some of his "laws of pure thought", Frege makes (but never uses in the *Conceptual Notation*) a semantical distinction which seems to correspond exactly to his later one between the "sense" (*Sinn*) and the "denotation" (*Bedeutung*) of a sign.[65] He treats identity as a relation between linguistic expressions, indicating that two expressions have the same conceptual content. Using an example from geometry, he gives the name 'A', which stands for a given point on a circle, and the "name" 'B', which stands for the point of intersection of the circle and a line rotating about A.

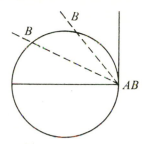

When the rotating line is perpendicular to the diameter drawn from A, then 'A' and 'B' stand for the very same point. In this example, Frege distinguishes

(1) The expression ('A' or 'B');

(2) The content of the expression (the given point);

(3) The way in which the content is determined (as the point on the circle, or as "the point of intersection . . . when the rotating line is perpendicular . . .").

This tripartite distinction apparently exactly corresponds to Frege's later one:[66]

(i) The expression ('A' or 'B');

---

[63] See A40, p. 26.
[64] See § 8 of F7, the present volume, pp. 124–6.   [65] See F20.
[66] I. Angelelli, in S5, was apparently the first to notice this point.

(ii) The *denotation* of the expression (the given point);

(iii) The *sense* of the expression; i.e. the way in which the denotation is given (as the point on the circle, or as "the point of intersection . . . when the rotating line is perpendicular . . .").

In the *Conceptual Notation* Frege does not use (3) as an aspect of meaning; but he later employed the distinction of sense and denotation to great advantage in his logistic project. At that time he also added the terms 'the True' (*das Wahre*) and 'the False' (*das Falsche*) to refer to the values of propositional letters and the denotations of true and false sentences, respectively. In the *Conceptual Notation* Frege does not have truth-values, but uses, instead, the expressions 'is affirmed' and 'is denied' to distinguish between true and false sentences.

Thus, in the *Conceptual Notation* Frege provides a set of semantic distinctions, though he does not employ them consistently or develop them carefully. Taken together, however, they do foreshadow his later semantics and indicate the direction in which he will move:

Distinctions in the 'Conceptual Notation'	Later distinctions
1 *a.* sign	1 *a.* sign
b. content	*b.* denotation
c. the way the content is determined	*c.* sense—the way the denotation is given
2 *a.* conceptual content	2 *a.* objective meaning
b. other kinds of content	*b.* subjective meaning
3 *a.* the assertible content	3 *a.* the thought
b. the judgement	*b.* the judgement
4 *a.* 'is affirmed'	4 *a.* 'the True'
b. 'is denied'	*b.* 'the False'
5 using Greek capitals and quotation marks to mention expressions	5 use-mention distinction

7

The theory of meaning in the *Conceptual Notation* is the only major aspect of that work which is not rigorously and carefully developed with an eye toward maximizing perspicuity and minimizing the chance of error. In other respects, the desire for rigour and clarity maintains constant control over developments; and this fact throws light upon several special features of Frege's notation. It explains, for example, why he uses so many different kinds of letters: for the sake of perspicuity, different letters are used when different purposes are being served.[67] When discussing the "conceptual notation", rather than employing it, Frege uses capital Greek letters, such as 'A', 'B', 'Γ', 'Φ', 'Ψ' and 'X'. In the "conceptual notation" itself he employs italic letters to express a generality when the scope of the generality (universal quantifier) is the whole of an asserted formula, and German letters when the scope is limited to part of an asserted formula. Lower-case Greek letters, such as 'α', 'β', and 'γ' mark argument places.

Since Frege distinguishes mere assertible contents from judgements,[68] he introduces some notation to clearly capture the distinction. He places a long, horizontal line, called the "content stroke", to the left of a propositional expression, say 'A', in order to denote the assertible content of 'A':

$$\text{------} \quad A.$$

This can be read "the proposition that A". When he actually *asserts* the given content, and thus expresses a judgement, he adds the "judgement stroke" to the left end of the content stroke:

$$\vdash\!\text{------} \quad A.$$

This can be read "A is a fact".[69]

The desire to preclude mistakes by achieving perspicuity and simplicity also led Frege to adopt Leibniz's strategy[70] of using in his notation the fewest and simplest basic concepts. For this reason Frege sought to find the smallest number of simple propositional connectives and rules of inference that would fill his needs.

[67] See F38 or footnote 14 of F7 (*b*).
[68] See 6 above, p. 66.
[69] In S242 Russell and Whitehead adopted the sign '$\vdash$' from Frege, calling it the "assertion sign" (p. 8) and using it with approximately Frege's sense. From this source, the "assertion sign" came into general use. After the *Conceptual Notation* Frege modified his account of the meaning of propositional expressions and changed the meaning of '$\vdash$' accordingly. See S66, "Assertion".
Some logicians (e.g. Church in A40) use the sign '$\vdash$' syntactically to indicate that a formula is a theorem in a given logistic system. This usage is entirely different from Frege's.
[70] See Wiener, pp. xxvi and 10; and also A101, pp. 6–7.

He managed to limit himself to only two connectives[71]—negation and conditionality—defining conjunction, inclusive disjunction, and exclusive disjunction in terms of these. The conditional he employed, however, turned out to be the "truth functional" or "material" conditional, which apparently had not been used by logicians since the time of ancient Greece, when Philo of Megara was its major advocate.[72] There is no evidence, however, that Frege knew of its previous use; and it seems likely that he hit upon the material conditional himself while experimenting with negation and conjunction in his effort to find the fewest suitable connectives. He apparently noticed that the combination 'not (B and not-A)' shares many logical properties with the ordinary-language expression 'if B, then A'. Indeed, when he introduces his notation for the material conditional (with B as antecedent and A as consequent),

his first account of its meaning is "not (B and not-A)".[73] Only later does he say that his "conditional stroke" can *sometimes* be read "if"; and he carefully points out that his symbol does not fully correspond to the ordinary-language "if". Even after this explanation, he continues to read the conditional stroke as "not (B and not-A)", especially while providing a justification (or meta-linguistic "proof") of a rule of inference or an axiom.[74]

While explaining the meaning of his conditional stroke, Frege employs what amounts to the truth-table method.[75] At this stage of his logistic project, however, he does not yet employ truth-values,

[71] It is not known whether Frege was aware of the possibility of using just one primitive connective, such as "non-disjunction" or "non-conjunction". The possibility was known to C. S. Peirce in the early 1880s, and first mentioned in a publication by H. M. Scheffer in 1913. See A40, pp. 134–5. Even if he knew about the possibility, it is unlikely that Frege would have used such a connective as a primitive one in his notation, since it is neither so simple nor so perspicuous as negation, conjunction, and the material conditional.

[72] See S167, pp. 128–38.

[73] Frege's way of putting it is "it is denied that A is denied and B is affirmed". See F7, this volume, p. 115.

[74] See, for example, the supporting arguments for his rule of detachment (pp. 117 and 119 below) or for some of his axioms (pp. 137 and 146 below).

[75] This seems to be the first use of the truth-table method in the history of logic. See A40, pp. 161–2. Strictly speaking Frege did not use tables that could be mechanically used regardless of interpretation. The nearest analogues in his work are interpreted meta-sentences.

which emerged only later from revisions in his theory of meaning.[76] Thus, instead of listing truth-values, Frege uses 'is affirmed' and 'is denied'.

Though he employs the material conditional as a primitive connective, Frege notes that conjunction could have been used instead, and he chose the former because it gives him a simpler, more perspicuous rule of inference.[77] That rule is *modus ponens*, which he defines purely syntactically.[78] In several places he states that it is his only rule of inference; but at one point[79] he qualifies this claim, apparently acknowledging that he does use other rules when he derives a new judgement from a single premiss. He assigns no specific names to these other rules, which today might be called "substitution", "generalization", and "confinement of quantifiers to a consequent". Frege refers to all his rules of inference as "rules for the application of our symbols",[80] a phrase which indicates their purely syntactical character.

Except for a principle which could be called "alphabetic change of bound variables",[81] Frege's substitution rules are not fully stated; so to see what he permits, one must observe his practice. His substitutions are simultaneous and are indicated by tables placed to the left of the expressions derived therefrom.[82] He does state his rule for generalization[83] and one for confinement.[84] Though he does not employ it in his deductions, he also states a principle of instantiation:

[Given a judgment with a generality sign immediately after the judgment stroke] we can always derive an arbitrary number of *judgments with less general content* by putting something different each time in place of the German letter; when we do this, the concavity in the content stroke disappears. . . .[85]

[76] See 6 above. For this reason, Frege's propositional letters in the *Conceptual Notation* actually stand for propositions ("conceptual contents"), rather than truth-values. This is one major respect in which this formulation of the propositional calculus differs from most later ones, including that in his own F23.

[77] See F7, the present volume, pp. 120 and 123.

[78] Ibid., p. 117.   [79] Ibid., p. 119.   [80] Ibid., p. 136.

[81] Stated in §11, p. 131 below. Used in the derivations of formulae 70, 116, and 118.

[82] Frege's explanation of these tables is found in §15, pp. 142–3 below.

[83] In §11, p. 132 below. Used in the derivations of formulae 97 and 109.

[84] In §11, pp. 132–3 below. A first-order version is used in the derivations of formulae 81, 96, 109, 123, and 130. A second-order version is used in the derivations of formulae 91, 93, and 95.

[85] In §11, p. 130 below.

8

In Part I of his little book Frege presents and explains his special language; in Part II[86] he begins to apply it. There, he introduces a set (he calls it a "kernel") of "judgements of pure thought" which, he says, is meant to be *complete* (*vollständig*), in the sense that, together with "the rules for the application of the symbols" (rules of inference), the "kernel" of laws must imply all the others. His plan is to derive many other laws of thought from the given ones, in order to show their interconnections and demonstrate "how some are implicitly contained in others".[87] Thus, he intends to present an axiomatic systematization of the laws of logic.[88] He notes that other complete systems are possible, for his is merely one example, which may be used, however, to facilitate the discovery of all the others.

The "kernel" of axioms for his system is the following set of nine, corresponding to his formulae (1), (2), (8), (28), (31), (41), (52), (54), and (58), respectively:

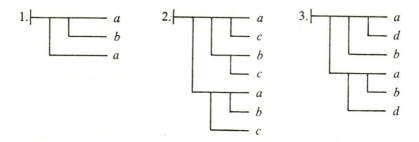

[86] Pp. 136–66 below.

[87] See below, p. 136.

[88] In the *Conceptual Notation* Frege is pioneering the development of quantificational logic. At this early stage he does not clearly distinguish first-order from second- and higher-order logic. Thus, for example, in the derivation of formula 91 he uses a second-order confinement rule, but cites a corresponding first-order one. In the derivations of formulae 77 and 93, he uses judgements from second-order logic, but cites corresponding first-order ones. The tables showing how 77 and 93 are obtained indicate that, at the time he wrote the *Conceptual Notation*, Frege thought the second-order judgements follow from the cited first-order ones in accordance with his rules of inference. Van Heijenoort (see p. 3 of F7(*b*)) takes this slip as evidence that a paradox can be generated in the system of the *Conceptual Notation*; but this seems incorrect, since the difficulty is easily solved by introducing machinery which Frege later provides to distinguish between "first-level" and "second-level" functions. In the *Conceptual Notation* Frege never confuses these two kinds of functions, though he does not yet have separate terms for them. (See below, footnotes 2 and 5, pp. 174 and 183, respectively.)

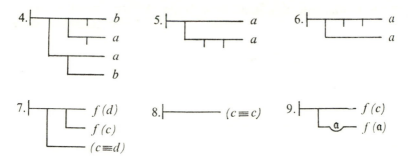

Frege treats the italic propositional letters as if they were free variables, substituting more complicated propositional expressions for them. The substitution instances, he says, are special cases "contained in" the expressions from which they are derived.[89]

Although Frege claims *completeness* for his set of axioms, he does not fully specify what this claim means, and he does not offer a proof of completeness. In 1934, however, Łukasiewicz proved that the first six axioms of Frege's "kernel" form a complete set for the first-order propositional calculus,[90] in the sense that together they imply, using two of Frege's rules of inference (*modus ponens* and (tacit) substitution), every tautology of the propositional calculus. Thus, the *Conceptual Notation* contains the first formulation of the propositional calculus as a logistic system.

Łukasiewicz also proved that the third axiom is not independent, since it can be derived from the first two using only Frege's rules of inference.[91] None of the remaining five axioms can be derived from the others.[92]

According to Kneale,[93] Frege's "kernel" of nine axioms, together with his rules of generalization and confinement, comprise a complete set for the first-order functional calculus. Thus, he also gave the first formulation of the first-order functional calculus as a logistic system.

Starting with his "kernel" of nine "judgements of pure thought", Frege derives forty-nine more, thereby providing a foundation upon which to base his "reduction of ordering-in-a-sequence to logical-ordering" (i.e. his purely logical definition of the proper ancestral).

---

[89] See §6 of F7, this volume, p. 118.   [90] See S184.   [91] Ibid.
[92] For a proof of the independence of axioms 1, 2, 4, 5, 6, see p. 21 of the English translation of S284.   [93] See S167, p. 489.

To begin the reduction itself, he indicates the very broad notion of "function" that an expression such as '$f(x, y)$' is to stand for: since f can be any binary relation or procedure you like (spatial, temporal, logical, mathematical, etc.), and x and y can be anything in the universe, '$\vdash\!\!\!-\!\!\!- f(x,y)$' can be read either

(i) No matter what x or y may be, and no matter what relation f may be, y bears the f-relation to x,

or

(ii) No matter what x or y may be, and no matter what procedure f may be, y is a result of an application of the procedure f to x.

The notion of "relation" and "procedure" are so broad here that (i) and (ii) are to be taken as equivalent in meaning.[94] Frege seems to prefer the term 'procedure', apparently nearly always having in mind his goal of eventually logically defining mathematical induction, and thus the procedure of adding one to an integer to get its successor.

The notion of "sequence" that Frege has in mind is also very broad, being simply the idea of a number of entities being interrelated by any one binary relation you like. The relation may be spatial, temporal, mathematical, logical, etc.—and the sequence determined by the relation need not be linear, such as that formed by a string of beads or the natural numbers; it might be ring-like, or have branches like a tree, some branches might merge, and so forth.

As examples of such sequences, consider the following: Given ten different entities labelled a, b, c, d, e, g, h, i, j, k, respectively; let '$\Gamma \to \Delta$' mean that Γ bears the f-relation to Δ (where Δ and Γ can be any of the entities a through k). Consider now the following "sequences":

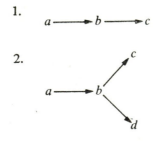

1.

$a \longrightarrow b \longrightarrow c$

2.

3.

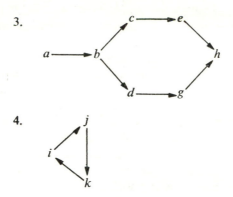

4.

Given these very broad notions of function and sequence, Frege proceeds to define what he calls "an hereditary property": if x has the property F, then every object to which x bears the f-relation also has property F; this means "F is hereditary in the f-sequence"[95] (i.e. in modern parlance, "the property F is f-hereditary").

Using this definition of 'hereditary property', Frege is able to define the "proper ancestral"[96] and the "ancestral"[97] of a relation.

In his definition of the proper ancestral, "y follows x in the f-sequence" means: for any property F, if F is hereditary in the f-sequence, and if every object to which x bears the f-relation has property F, then y has F (i.e. in modern parlance, "x is a proper f-ancestor of y").

In his definition of the ancestral, "y belongs to the f-sequence beginning with x" means: y is identical with x or follows x in the f-sequence (i.e. in modern parlance, "x is an f-ancestor of y").

Frege was the first to define these notions purely logically; and they play an important role in his later derivation of arithmetic from logic.

9

The achievements of the *Conceptual Notation* make it a monumental work in the history of logic;[98] but even Frege did not realize this at the time. He did think that the book achieved *some* advancement; and he singled out in particular the introduction of logical functions, and the demonstration of connections among the meanings

[95] See formula 69 in §24 below, p. 167.   [96] Formula 76 in §26 below, p. 173.
[97] Formula 99 in §29 below, p. 186.
[98] See Appendix II below, pp. 236–8.

of words such as 'all', 'some', 'not', 'and', and 'or'.[99] Though he was right in claiming that the introduction of functions (and the quantifiers that go with them) is an advance, he was unaware of the power and revolutionary nature of his achievements.

Perhaps for this reason, he wrote the *Conceptual Notation* as if it were just another work to be read and used by mathematicians of his day: he introduced his symbols and assumptions, presented his derivations, and left the matter at that. There was no effort to explain carefully the logistic project which his notation was intended to facilitate, no elaboration of the remark that the notation is modelled upon that of arithmetic, no explanation or defence of the very rigorous requirements he imposed upon his proofs, and no detailed discussion of the Leibnizian roots of his special language.

For these reasons Frege's book was not well received. No one understood its aim or its contents, and many were daunted or bewildered by the strange appearance of his two-dimensional formulas. Six different journals published reviews;[100] but nearly all comments were unfavourable, and those that were favourable revealed a failure on the part of the reviewers to grasp the aim and major thrust of the book.

The most important reviewers were John Venn and Ernst Schröder, who were both logicians of some stature. One would expect them to welcome the logical achievements of the *Conceptual Notation*; but instead, they both criticized the book as a clumsy effort to accomplish what Boole[101] had already achieved more elegantly. This unfortunate misconstrual was apparently caused by several factors besides the lack of detailed exegesis and justification by Frege himself. Venn and Schröder were both accustomed to thinking of logic in Boolean terms. (Venn was completing his book *Symbolic Logic*,[102] and Schröder had recently published a booklet on Boolean logic.[103]) Because of this, they must have thought immediately of Boole's algebraic formulas when they read in Frege's book that the "conceptual notation" is modelled upon arithmetic; and they must have thought of Boole's *The Laws of Thought* when they noticed that Part

---

[99] See the Preface of F7, the present volume, p. 107.

[100] The reviews are included in Appendix I below, pp. 209–35. The reception of Frege's book is discussed above, pp. 15–20.

[101] George Boole, *An Investigation of the Laws of Thought* (London, 1854).

[102] John Venn, *Symbolic Logic* (London, 1881).

[103] Ernst Schröder, *Der Operationskreis des Logikkalküls* (Leibzig: Teubner, 1877).

II of the *Conceptual Notation* deals with "laws of pure thought". Finally, the most striking components of Frege's notation, upon first sight, are the two-dimensional arrays of lines standing for the kind of propositional relations that Boole's mathematical formulas can express.

For these reasons, Venn and Schröder took the major intended contribution of Frege's book to be an analysis of propositional connectives such as 'and', 'or', and 'not'; and they focused their attention upon this aspect of the book, rather than on major contributions such as logical functions, quantifiers, and the establishment of a purely formal system.

Schröder was developing his own Boolean logic at the time, and apparently viewed Frege's notation as a would-be challenger. He published a long, captious review[104] of Frege's book, arguing that Boole's logic (and therefore his own as well) is better than the "conceptual notation", accomplishing "in a doubtlessly more adequate fashion" nearly all that Frege achieves. He characterizes Frege's two-dimensional notation as "a monstrous waste of space" that "indulges in the Japanese custom of writing vertically". He finds "absolutely nothing of value" in Frege's "reduction of ordering-in-a-sequence to logical ordering". Instead of recognizing the advantages of Frege's purely formal proofs, he labels them "pedantic". He finds "an enormous lack of systematization", though Frege's book presents the first rigorous logistic system. He claims that Frege's laws of pure thought "offer nothing especially interesting", though (as Łukasiewicz would later show)[105] they include the first complete set of axioms for the propositional calculus.

Both Venn and Schröder suggest in their reviews that Frege did not know any Boolean logic at the time he wrote the *Conceptual Notation*. In this, they seem to be right. Frege apparently took no logic as a university student;[106] and, in mathematics, all his courses were in geometry and functional analysis. He took no courses in algebra or theory of algebra—the most likely ones in mathematics in which to encounter Boolean logic. In the *Conceptual Notation* itself he mentions no Boolean logic and cites no Boolean logician. In the Preface he claims that his demonstration of the connections among the meanings of 'not', 'and', and 'or' constitute an advancement in

[104] See below, pp. 218–32.
[105] See the discussion in 8 above, p. 73.
[106] See the above discussion regarding his university studies, pp. 3–4.

logic; and thus, he did not know that Boolean logicians had previously known and used those connections.[107]

After the appearance of Schröder's review Frege apparently studied some Boolean logic, and then wrote a long, technical paper—"Boole's Calculating Logic and the 'Conceptual Notation'"[108]—comparing his own logic with that of Boole. This time he discussed the Leibnizian basis of his notation, explained its aim, and proved that he could not have used Boolean logic for his purposes. Unfortunately, this paper (and even a shorter version)[109] was rejected by all the journals to which it was submitted,[110] apparently because it was very technical and full of unusual symbols.

Three years after the appearance of his book Frege finally managed to publish an article defending his "conceptual notation"—"On the Scientific Justification of a Conceptual Notation"[111]—and he did so by making it very general, and including the kind of psychological speculation that was then popular in philosophy, logic, and mathematics. The article discusses the "softness" and inadequacy of ordinary language for scientific purposes and explains the advantages of a technical two-dimensional notation. In that same year (1882) Frege was invited to address the *Jenaische Gesellschaft für Medicin und Naturwissenschaft* and explain his scientific language. He took the opportunity to answer the objections of Schröder and compare his own logic with Boole's. The address was later published as the article "On the Aim of the 'Conceptual Notation'".[112]

10

The *Conceptual Notation* and Frege's related articles appear below in English translation. Instead of occurring chronologically, they are arranged in an order which allows the articles on the justification and aim of the "conceptual notation" to serve as an effective preface to the book itself.

Much of Frege's special terminology is explained in the paragraphs above; but a glossary and summary comments are included

---

[107] See below, p. 107.
[108] This paper was recently published in F45, pp. 9–52.
[109] This also appears in F45, pp. 53–9.
[110] See the discussion above, p. 21.
[111] This is F11, which appears below, pp. 83–9.
[112] This is F12, which appears below, pp. 90–100.

here for the reader's convenience. Unless otherwise indicated, the following renderings have been used:

Anschauung	intuition
bedeuten	mean, refer to, signify, stand for
Bedeutung	meaning, importance
begrifflicher Inhalt	conceptual content
Begriffsschrift	*Conceptual Notation*, "conceptual notation", conceptual notation
(*wird*) *bejaht*	is affirmed
Bestimmungsweise	mode of determination
beurtheilbarer Inhalt	assertible content
eindeutig	many-one
Inhalt	content
Satz	proposition
Urtheil	judgement
Umfang eines Begriffes	extension of a concept
Verneinung	negation
(*wird*) *verneint*	is denied
Vorstellung	idea
Vorstellungsverbindung	combination of ideas

Some of these renderings merit comment.

Begriffsschrift —Frege uses this term in three different ways. In the present volume, when 'conceptual notation' appears in italics, it refers to Frege's book; when it is enclosed in double quotation marks, it denotes Frege's symbolic language; when neither occurs, it means simply a language like Frege's.

Bedeutung, bedeuten —As indicated in **6** above, in the *Conceptual Notation* Frege does not yet have a carefully developed semantical theory. Thus, the present terms are very loosely used and are not contrasted with the later technical terms *Sinn* (sense) and *ausdrucken* (express), respectively.[113]

Beurtheilbarer Inhalt —Literally "judicable content" (indeed, this is how Jourdain translates this term),[114] but this literal translation is misleading, for one can make judgements about *any* content. For Frege a judgement is an asserted content; and on these grounds the present term is rendered "assertible content". Russell uses "propositional content", Geach employs "possible content of judgement";

---

[113] See F20.   [114] See F23(*a*).

and Bauer–Mengelberg suggests "content that can become a judge-ment".[115]

Previous translations of the works below are listed in the Biblio-graphy of the present volume. The strategy adopted to take full account of these was to translate Frege's works independently, then compare the present one to previous ones, accepting renderings that seem better and footnoting any major differences that remain. Frege's footnotes are marked with asterisks, while those of the present editor employ arabic numerals.

[115] See S241, F'47, and F7(*b*), respectively.

TRANSLATIONS OF
FREGE'S WORKS

ON THE SCIENTIFIC JUSTIFICATION
OF A CONCEPTUAL NOTATION[1]

TIME and again, in the more abstract regions of science, the lack of
a means of avoiding misunderstandings on the part of others, and
also errors in one's own thought, makes itself felt. Both [short-
comings] have their origin in the imperfection of language, for we do
have to use sensible symbols to think.

Our attention is directed by nature to the outside. The vivacity of
sense-impressions surpasses that of memory-images {*Erinnerungsbilder*} to such an extent that, at first, sense-impressions determine
almost by themselves the course of our ideas, as is the case in animals.
And we would scarcely ever be able to escape this dependency if the
outer world were not to some extent dependent upon us.

Even most animals, through their ability to move about, have an
influence on their sense-impressions: they can flee some, seek others.
And they can even effect changes in things. Now man has this ability
to a much greater degree; but nevertheless, the course of our ideas
{*unser Vorstellungsverlauf*} would still not gain its full freedom from
this [ability alone]: it would still be limited to that which our hand
can fashion, our voice intone, without the great invention of symbols
which call to mind {*uns gegenwärtig machen*} that which is absent,
invisible, perhaps even beyond the senses {*unsinnlich*}.[2]

I do not deny that even without symbols the perception of a thing
can gather about itself {*um sich sammeln*}[3] a group of memory-images
{*Erinnerungsbilder*}; but we could not pursue these further: a new
perception would let these images sink into darkness and allow others
to emerge. But if we produce the symbol of an idea which a perception has called to mind, we create in this way a firm, new focus about

[1 This translation was made independently of the one by J. Bartlett which
appeared in *Mind*, 73 (1964), pp. 155–60; and then the two were compared.
Wherever Bartlett's interpretation or wording seemed better, it was adopted and
duly noted. Wherever important differences of interpretation remained, they
were also noted, to give the reader the benefit of both views.]

[2 Bartlett renders this "unseeable", but here it seems to have more the sense
of "transcendental". Moving air, for example, is unseeable, but not *unsinnlich*.]

[3 Bartlett renders this "catalyse".]

which ideas gather. We then select another [idea] from these in order
to elicit *its* symbol. Thus we penetrate step by step into the inner
world of our ideas and move about there at will, using the realm of
sensibles itself {*das Sinnliche selbst*} to free ourselves from its con-
straint. Symbols have the same importance for thought that discover-
ing how to use the wind to sail against the wind had for navigation.
Thus, let no one despise symbols! A great deal depends upon
choosing them properly. And their value is not diminished by the
fact that, after long practice, we need no longer produce [external]
symbols, we need no longer speak out loud in order to think; for we
think in words nevertheless, and if not in words, then in mathematical or other symbols.

Also, without symbols we would scarcely lift ourselves to conceptual thinking. Thus, in applying the same symbol to different but
similar things, we actually no longer symbolize the individual thing,
but rather what [the similars] have in common: the concept. This
concept is first gained by symbolizing it; for since it is, in itself,
imperceptible, it requires a perceptible representative in order to
appear to us.

This does not exhaust the merits of symbols; but it may suffice to
demonstrate their indispensability. Language proves to be deficient,
however, when it comes to protecting thought from error. It does not
even meet the first requirement which we must place upon it in this
respect; namely, being unambiguous. The most dangerous cases [of
ambiguity] are those in which the meanings of a word are only
slightly different, the subtle and yet not unimportant variations. Of
the many examples [of this kind of ambiguity] only one frequently
recurring phenomenon may be mentioned here: the same word may
serve to designate a concept and a single object which falls under that
concept. Generally, no strong distinction is made between concept
and individual. "The horse" can denote a single creature; it can also
denote the species, as in the sentence: "The horse is an herbivorous
animal." Finally, horse[4] can denote a concept,[5] as in the sentence:
"This is a horse."

Language is not governed by logical laws in such a way that mere
adherence to grammar would guarantee the formal correctness of

[4 Frege did not yet use quotation marks to distinguish use from mention. His
first systematic use of that convention was in 1892 in F20. For this reason, the
word 'horse' in the above passage is not enclosed in quotation marks.]

[5 Frege is not careful here—as he will be later—to distinguish between '*the*
horse', which denotes an individual, and '*a* horse', which denotes a concept.]

thought processes {*Gedankenbewegung*}. The forms in which inference is expressed are so varied, so loose and vague, that presuppositions can easily slip in unnoticed and then be overlooked when the necessary conditions for the conclusion are enumerated. In this way, the conclusion obtains a greater generality {*grössere Allgemeinheit*}[6] than it justifiably deserves.

Even such a conscientious and rigorous writer as Euclid often makes tacit use of presuppositions which he specifies neither in his axioms and postulates nor in the premisses of the particular theorem [being proved]. Thus, in the proof of the nineteenth theorem of the first book of *The Elements* (in every triangle, the largest angle lies opposite the largest side), he tacitly uses the statements:

(1) If a line segment is not larger than a second one, the former is equal to or smaller than the latter.

(2) If an angle is the same size as a second one, the former is not larger than the latter.

(3) If an angle is smaller than a second one, the former is not larger than the latter.

Only by paying particular attention, however, can the reader become aware of the omission of these sentences, especially since they seem so close to being as fundamental as the laws of thought that they are used just like those laws themselves.

A strictly defined group of modes of inference is simply not present in [ordinary] language, so that on the basis of linguistic form we cannot distinguish between a "gapless" advance {*lückenloser Fortgang*} [in the argument] and an omission of connecting links. We can even say that the former almost never occurs in [ordinary] language, that it runs against the feel of language because it would involve an insufferable prolixity. In [ordinary] language, logical relations are almost always only hinted at—left to guessing, not actually expressed.

The only advantage that the written word has over the spoken word is permanence: [with the written word], we can review a train of thought many times without fear that it will change; and thus we can test its validity more thoroughly. In this [process of testing], since insufficient security lies in the nature of the word-language itself, the laws of logic are applied externally like a plumb-line. But even so,

[6 Bartlett renders this "greater validity".]

mistakes easily escape the eye of the examiner, especially those which arise from subtle differences in the meanings of a word. That we nevertheless find our way about reasonably well in life as well as in science we owe to the manifold ways of checking that we have at our disposal. Experience and space perception protect us from many errors. Logical rules [, externally applied,] furnish little protection, as is shown by examples from disciplines in which the means of checking begin to fail. These rules have failed to defend even great philosophers from mistakes, and have helped just as little in keeping higher mathematics free from error, because they have always remained external to content.

The shortcomings stressed [here] are rooted in a certain softness {*gewissen Weichheit*} and instability of [ordinary] language, which nevertheless is necessary for its versatility and potential for development. In this respect, [ordinary] language can be compared to the hand, which despite its adaptability to the most diverse tasks is still inadequate.[7] We build for ourselves artificial hands, tools for particular purposes, which work with more accuracy than the hand can provide. And how is this accuracy possible? Through the very stiffness and inflexibility of parts the lack of which makes the hand so dextrous. Word-language is inadequate in a similar way. We need a system of symbols {*Ganzes von Zeichen*}[8] from which every ambiguity is banned, which has a strict logical form from which the content cannot escape.

We may now ask which is preferable, audible symbols or visible ones. The former have, first of all, the advantage that their production is more independent of external circumstances. Furthermore, much can be made in particular of the close kinship of sounds to inner processes {*innere Vorgängen*}. Even their form of appearance {*die Form des Erscheinens*},[9] the temporal sequence, is the same; both are equally fleeting. In particular, sounds have a more intimate relation to the emotions {*das Gemüthsleben*}[10] than shapes and colours do; and the human voice with its boundless flexibility is able to do justice to even the most delicate combinations and variations of feelings. But no matter how valuable these advantages may be for other purposes, they have no importance for the rigour of logical deductions. Perhaps this intimate adaptability of audible symbols to

[7 Bartlett's turn of phrase.]   [8 Bartlett's translation.]
[9 Bartlett renders this "the experiential form".]
[10 Bartlett's translation.]

the physical and mental conditions of reason has just the disadvantage of keeping reason more dependent upon these.

It is completely different with visible things, especially shapes. They are generally sharply defined and clearly distinguished. This definiteness of written symbols will tend to make what is signified also more sharply defined; and just such an effect upon ideas {*die Vorstellungen*}[11] must be asked for the rigour of deduction. This can be achieved, however, only if the symbol directly {*unmittelbar*} denotes the thing [symbolized].

A further advantage of the written symbol is greater permanence and immutability. In this way, it is also similar to the concept—as it should be—and thus, of course, the more dissimilar to the restless flow of our actual thought processes {*wirkliche Gedankenbewegung*}. Written symbols offer the possibility of keeping many things in mind at the same time; and even if, at each moment, we can only concentrate upon a small part of these, we still retain a general impression of what remains, and this is immediately at our disposal whenever we need it.

The spatial relations of written symbols on a two-dimensional writing surface can be employed in far more diverse ways to express inner relationships {*innere Beziehungen*} than the mere following and preceding in one-dimensional time, and this facilitates the apprehension of that to which we wish to direct our attention. In fact, simple sequential ordering in no way corresponds to the diversity of logical relations through which thoughts are interconnected.

Thus, the very properties which set the written symbol further apart [than the spoken word] from the course of our ideas {*der Vorstellungsverlauf*} are most suited to remedy certain shortcomings of our make-up. Therefore, when it is not a question of representing natural thought as it actually took shape in reciprocal action with the word-language, but concerns instead the supplementation of the onesidedness of thinking which results from a close connection with the sense of hearing, then the written symbol will be preferable. Such a notation must be completely different from all word-languages in order to exploit the peculiar advantages of written symbols. It need hardly be mentioned that these advantages scarcely come into play at all in the written word. The relative position of the words with respect to each other on the writing surface depends to a large extent upon the length of the lines [of print] and is, thus, without importance.

[11 Bartlett renders this "imagery".]

There are, however, completely different kinds of notation which better exploit these [mentioned] advantages. The arithmetic language of formulas is a conceptual notation since it directly expresses the facts without the intervention of speech. As such, it attains a brevity which allows it to accommodate the content of a simple judgement in one line. Such contents—here equations or inequalities—as they follow from one another are written under one another. If a third follows from two others, we separate the third from the first two with a horizontal stroke, which can be read "therefore". In this way, the two-dimensionality of the writing surface is utilized for the sake of perspicuity. Here the deduction is stereotyped {*sehr einformig*}[12] being almost always based upon identical transformations of identical numbers yielding identical results. Of course, this is by no means the only method of inference in arithmetic; but where the logical progression is different, it is generally necessary to express it in words. Thus, the arithmetic language of formulas lacks expressions for logical connections; and, therefore, it does not merit the name of conceptual notation in the full sense.

Exactly the opposite holds for the symbolism for logical relations originating with Leibniz* and revived in modern times by Boole, R. Grassmann, S. Jevons, E. Schröder, and others. Here we do have the logical forms, though not entirely complete; but content is lacking. In these cases, any attempt to replace the single letters with expressions of contents, such as analytic equations, would demonstrate with the resulting imperspicuity, clumsiness—even ambiguity—of the formulas how little suited this kind of symbolism is for the construction of a true conceptual notation.

I would demand the following from a true conceptual notation: It must have simple modes of expression for the logical relations which, limited to the necessary, can be easily and surely mastered. These forms must be suitable for combining most intimately with a content. Also, such brevity must be sought that the two-dimensionality of the writing surface can be exploited for the sake of perspicuity. The symbols for denoting content are less essential. They can be easily created as required, once the general [logical] forms are available. If the analysis of a concept into its ultimate components {*letzte Bestandtheile*} does not succeed or appears unnecessary, we can be content with temporary symbols.

[12] Bartlett's translation.]
* *Non inelegans specimen demonstrandi in abstractis*. Erdm. p. 94.

It would be easy to worry unnecessarily about the feasibility of the matter.[13] It is impossible, someone might say, to advance science with a conceptual notation, for the invention of the latter already pre-supposes the completion of the former. Exactly the same apparent difficulty arises for [ordinary] language. This is supposed to have made reason possible, but how could man have invented language without reason? Research into the laws of nature employs physical instruments; but these can be produced only by means of an advanced technology, which again is based upon knowledge of the laws of nature. The [apparently vicious] circle is resolved in each case in the same way: an advance in physics results in an advance in technology, and this makes possible the construction of new instruments by means of which physics is again advanced. The application [of this example] to our case is obvious.

Now I have attempted* to supplement the formula language of arithmetic with symbols for the logical relations in order to produce —at first just for arithmetic—a conceptual notation of the kind I have presented as desirable. This does not rule out the application of my symbols to other fields. The logical relations occur everywhere, and the symbols for particular contents can be so chosen that they fit the framework of the conceptual notation. Be that as it may, a perspicuous representation of the forms of thought has, in any case, significance extending beyond mathematics. May philosophers, then, give some attention to the matter!

[13 Bartlett's turn of phrase.]
    * *Conceptual Notation, a Formula Language of Pure Thought modelled upon the Formula Language of Arithmetic*, Halle a. S., 1879.

ON THE AIM OF THE
"CONCEPTUAL NOTATION"[1]

I HAD the honour once before to give a paper[2] here about my "conceptual notation". What induces me to return to it again is the observation that its aim has frequently been misunderstood. This I gather from several reviews of my book[3] which have appeared since [I gave my last paper here]. Distorted judgements must have resulted from these reviews.

I have been rebuked for failing, among other things, to consider the achievements of Boole. Among those who make this reproach is E. Schröder in the review in the *Zeitschrift für Mathematik und Physik*, XXV. In comparing my "conceptual notation" with the Boolean formula language, he reaches the conclusion that the latter is preferable in every respect. Although this judgement can hardly please me, I am still thankful to him for the detailed review and the technical reasons for his objections, since they give me the opportunity to refute the objections and set the matter in a brighter light.

With respect to the reproach just mentioned, I wish to say first of all that the Boolean formula language, in the more than twenty years which have passed since its invention, has in no way had such a smashing success that leaving out the foundation it established would, as a matter of course, necessarily appear foolish, and that only a further development could be considered. Besides, the problems which Boole treats appear to be, for the most part, first fabricated in order to be solved with his formulas.

This reproach, however, essentially overlooks the fact that my aim was different from Boole's. I did not wish to present an abstract logic in formulas, but to express a content through written symbols in a

[1 This paper is F12 and was delivered before the *Jenaische Gesellschaft für Medicin und Naturwissenschaft* on 27 January 1882. The present translation was made independently of the one by V. H. Dudman which appeared in the *Australasian Journal of Philosophy*, 46 (1968), pp. 89–97; and then the two were compared. No important differences of interpretation were found.]

[2 F8, delivered on 24 January 1879. An English translation appeared in the present volume, pp. 204–8.]

[3 The book is F7, the reviews S135, S176, S205, S256, S283, S292. It is not clear, however, whether Frege knew of all six reviews. All these items appear in English in the present volume, pp. 101–235.]

more precise and perspicuous way than is possible with words. In fact, I wished to produce, not a mere *calculus ratiocinator*, but a *lingua characteristica* in the Leibnizian sense. In doing so, however, I recognize that deductive calculus is a necessary part of a conceptual notation. If this was misunderstood, perhaps it is because I let the abstract logical aspect stand too much in the foreground.

Now, in order to demonstrate in detail the differences in Boole's formula language and mine, I shall give first a short presentation of the former. We cannot consider all the variants which are found in Boole's predecessors and successors, since, compared to the considerable difference between my "conceptual notation" [and Boole's calculus], these others are not important.

Boole distinguishes *primary propositions* from *secondary propositions*. The former compare the extensions of concepts {*vergleichen Begriffe ihrem Umfange nach*}, the latter express relations among assertible contents {*beurtheilbare Inhalte*}. This division is insufficient since existential judgements fail to find a place.

Let us consider first *primary propositions*. Here the letters denote the extensions of concepts. Particular things as such are not signified; and this is an important deficiency in the Boolean formula language, for even if a concept covers only a single thing, a great difference still remains between it and this thing. Now the letters are combined with each other by logical multiplication and addition. If A means the extension of the concept "triangle" and B means the extension of the concept "equilateral", then the logical product

$$A.B$$

signifies the extension of the concept "equilateral triangle". The logical sum

$$A+B$$

is to be understood as the extension of the concept "triangle or equilateral".* The [use of the] expressions "product" and "sum" is justified by the existence of the following [correct] equations:

$$A.B = B.A$$
$$A(B.C) = (A.B).C$$
$$A+B = B+A$$
$$A+(B+C) = (A+B)+C$$
$$A(B+C) = AB+AC.$$

* Boole presupposes by this that the concepts A and B exclude each other, which, among others, Schröder does not.

But these points of agreement {*Übereinstimmungen*} with algebraic multiplication and addition stand opposed to large discrepancies. The following are logically sound:

$$A = A \cdot A = A \cdot A \cdot A$$
$$A = A + A = A + A + A$$

but they do not generally hold in algebra. The differences in logical and mathematical calculation have so many important consequences that solving logical equations, with which Boole principally occupies himself, has scarcely anything in common with solving algebraic equations.

Now the subordination of one concept to another can be expressed [in Boole's notation] this way:

$$A = A \cdot B.$$

For example, if A signifies the extension of the concept "mammal" and B signifies the extension of the concept "air-breathing", then the equation says: the extensions of the concepts "mammal" and "air-breathing mammal" are the same; that is, all mammals are air-breathing. The falling of an individual under a concept, which is totally different from the subordination of one concept to another, has no particular expression in Boole['s notation]; strictly speaking, none at all.

Everything thus far is already found with only superficial divergences in Leibniz, whose works in this area I dare say were unknown to Boole.

0 signifies for Boole the extension of a concept under which nothing falls; 1 means the extension of a concept under which everything that is being considered (*universe of discourse*)[4] falls. We can see that here also the meaning of these symbols, especially of 1, deviates from arithmetic. Instead of these, Leibniz has "*non ens*" and "*ens*".

$$A \cdot B = 0$$

says that the two concepts exclude each other; like, for example, "the square-root of 2" and "whole number". The equation can hold without either

$$A = 0 \quad \text{or} \quad B = 0.$$

We still need a symbol for negation other than zero in order to convert, for example, the concept "man" into the concept "not man".

[⁴ Frege's parentheses and italics.]

Writers differ from each other here. For this purpose, Schröder attaches to the letters the index 1. Others have as well a symbol for the negation of identity. I do not consider this multiplicity of negation symbols an advantage of Boolean logic.

Boole reduces *secondary propositions*—for example, hypothetical and disjunctive judgements—to *primary propositions* in a very artificial way. He interprets the judgement "if $x = 2$, then $x^2 = 4$" this way: the class of moments of time in which $x = 2$ is subordinate to the class of moments of time in which $x^2 = 4$. Thus, here again the matter amounts to the comparison of the extensions of concepts; only here these concepts are fixed more precisely as classes of moments of time in which a sentence is true. This conception has the disadvantage that time becomes involved where it should remain completely out of the matter. MacColl explains the expressions for *secondary propositions* independently of the *primary* ones. In this way, the intermingling of time is certainly avoided; but as a result, every interconnection is severed between the two parts which, according to Boole, compose logic. We proceed, then, either in *primary propositions* and use the formulas in the sense stipulated by Boole; or else, we proceed in *secondary propositions* and use the interpretations of MacColl.[5] Any [logical] transition from one kind of judgement to the other—which, to be sure, often occurs in actual thinking—is blocked; for we may not use the same symbols with a double meaning in the same context.

When we view the Boolean formula language as a whole, we discover that it is a clothing of abstract logic in the dress of algebraic symbols. It is not suited for the rendering of a content, and that is also not its purpose. But this is exactly my intention. I wish to blend together the few symbols which I introduce and the symbols already available in mathematics to form a single formula language. In it, the existing symbols [of mathematics] correspond to the word-stems of [ordinary] language; while the symbols I add to them are comparable to the suffixes and [deductive] formwords {*Formwörter*}[6] that logically interrelate the contents embedded in the stems.

For this purpose, I could not use the Boolean symbolism; for it is not feasible to have, for example, the + sign occurring in the same

[5 See the works of Hugh MacColl in: *Mathematical Questions*, 28 (1877), pp. 20–3; *Proceedings of the London Mathematical Society*, 9 (1877–8), pp. 9–20, 177–86, and 10 (1878–9), pp. 16–28; *Mind*, 5 (1880), pp. 45–60; *Philosophical Magazine*, 5th ser. 11 (1881), pp. 40–3.]
[6 Dudman renders this "particles".]

formula part of the time in the logical sense and part of the time in the arithmetical sense. The analogy between the logical and arithmetical methods of calculation, which is of value to Boole, can only bring about confusion if both are combined together. Boole's symbolic language is conceivable only in complete separation from arithmetic. Therefore, I must invent other symbols for the logical relations.

Schröder says that my "conceptual notation" has almost nothing in common with Boole's calculus of concepts, but it does with his calculus of judgements. In fact, it is one of the most important differences between my mode of interpretation {*Auffassungsweise*} and the Boolean mode—and indeed I can add the Aristotelian mode —that I do not proceed from concepts, but from judgements. But this is certainly not to say that I would not be able to express the relation of subordination between concepts.

In front of an expression for an assertible content, such as $2+3=5$, I put a horizontal stroke, the content stroke, distinguishable from the minus sign by its greater length:

$$\text{————} 2+3=5$$

I take this stroke to mean that the content which follows it is unified, so that other symbols can be related to it [as a whole].

In $\qquad$ $\text{————} 2+3=5$

absolutely no judgement is made. Thus, we can also write:

$$\text{————} 4+2=7$$

without being guilty of writing a falsehood.

If I wish to assert a content as correct {*richtig*}, I put the judgement stroke on the left end of the content stroke:

$$\vdash \text{——} 2+3=5$$

How thoroughly one is misunderstood sometimes! Through this mode of notation I meant to have a very clear distinction between the act of judging and the formation of a mere assertible content; and Rabus* accuses me of mixing up the two!

In order to express the negation of a content, I attach the negation stroke to the content stroke; for example,

$$\text{———}_{\top}\text{—} 4+2=7.$$

* *Die neuesten Bestrebungen auf dem Gebiete der Logik bei den Deutschen und die logische Frage.* Erlangen, 1880.

The falsehood of this equation, however, is not asserted in this way. A new assertible content has been formed which becomes the judgement "4+2 does not equal 7" only by adding the judgement stroke:

$$\vdash_\top 4+2=7.$$

If we wish to relate two assertible contents, A and B, to each other, we must consider the following cases:

(1) A and B

(2) A and not B

(3) not A and B

(4) not A and not B.

Now I understand by

$$\begin{array}{l}\rule{2em}{0.4pt}\top\!\!\!-\!A \\ \qquad\rule{0pt}{1em}\!\lfloor\!-\!B\end{array}$$

the negation of the third case. This stipulation may appear very artificial at first. It is not clear at first why I single out this third case in particular and express its negation by a special symbol. The reason, however, will be immediately evident from an example:

$$\vdash\!\!\top\begin{array}{l}\rule{0pt}{1em}\!-\,x^2=4 \\ \rule{0pt}{1em}\!\lfloor\!-\,x+2=4\end{array}$$

denies the case that x^2 is not equal to 4 while nevertheless $x+2$ is equal to 4. We can translate it: if $x+2=4$, then $x^2=4$. This translation reveals the importance of the relation embedded in our symbol. Indeed, the hypothetical judgement is the form of all laws of nature and of all causal connections in general. To be sure, a rendering by means of "if" is not appropriate in all cases of linguistic usage, but only if an indeterminate constituent—like x here—confers generality on the whole. Were we to replace x by 2, then one would not appropriately translate

$$\vdash\!\!\top\begin{array}{l}\rule{0pt}{1em}\!-\,2^2=4 \\ \rule{0pt}{1em}\!\lfloor\!-\,2+2=4\end{array}$$

by "If $2+2=4$, then $2^2=4$".

Now consider the combinations of conditional stroke and negation stroke in the following table:

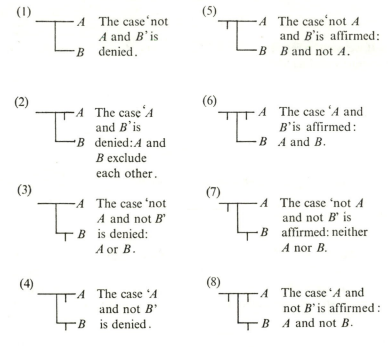

(1) ⊢A   The case 'not
         A and B' is
         B   denied.

(5) ⊢A   The case 'not A
         and B' is affirmed:
         B   B and not A.

(2) ⊢A   The case 'A
         and B' is
         B   denied: A and
             B exclude
             each other.

(6) ⊢A   The case 'A and
         B' is affirmed:
         B   A and B.

(3) ⊢A   The case 'not
         A and not B'
         B   is denied:
             A or B.

(7) ⊢A   The case 'not A
         and not B' is
         B   affirmed: neither
             A nor B.

(4) ⊢A   The case 'A
         and not B'
         B   is denied.

(8) ⊢A   The case 'A and
         not B' is affirmed:
         B   A and not B.

If we attach the negation stroke to the content strokes of the expressions on the left, we obtain the expressions next to them on the right. The denied case on the left is always affirmed on the right. The second expression arises from the first one by replacing A by the denial of A. Then in the verbal expression, the two denials of A cancel. The third expression arises from the first and the fourth from the second by the conversion of B into the denial of B. The "or" in the third case is the non-exclusive one. The exclusive "or" can be expressed this way:

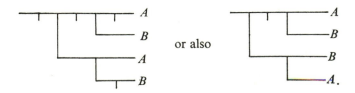

or also

I pause here to answer some objections of Schröder. He compares my representation of the exclusive "A or B" with his mode of writing

$$ab_1 + a_1 b = 1$$

and finds here, as elsewhere in my "conceptual notation", a monstrous waste of space. In fact, I cannot deny that my expression takes up more room than Schröder's, which for its part is again more spread-out than Boole's original

$$a + b = 1.$$

But this criticism is based upon the view that my "conceptual notation" is supposed to be a presentation of abstract logic. These formulas [of my "conceptual notation"] are actually only empty schemata; and in their application, one must think of whole formulas in the places of A and B—perhaps extended equations, congruences, projections. Then the matter appears completely different. The disadvantage of the waste of space of the "conceptual notation" is converted into the advantage of perspicuity; the advantage of terseness for Boole is transformed into the disadvantage of unintelligibility.[7] The "conceptual notation" makes the most of the two-dimensionality of the writing surface by allowing the assertible contents to follow one below the other while each of these extends [separately] from left to right. Thus, the separate contents are clearly separated from each other, and yet their logical relations are easily visible at a glance. For Boole, a single line, often excessively long, would result. Surely it would be unjust to charge Boole, who never

[7 For example, let A be $(a+b)(c+d) = (7+6)(4)$ and B be the equation $ac+bd+bc+ad = (7+6)(4+3)$. Then to form the exclusive disjunction of A and B, Frege could write the very perspicuous

$$(a+b)\,(c+d) = (7+6)(4)$$
$$ac+bd+bc+ad = (7+6)(4+3)$$
$$(a+b)(c+d) = (7+6)(4)$$
$$ac+bd+bc+ad = (7+6)(4+3),$$

while Schröder's version would be the unintelligible
$((a+b)(c+d) = (7+6)(4))(ac+bd+bc+ad = (7+6)(4+3))_1 + ((a+b)(c+d) = (7+6)(4))_1(ac+bd+bc+ad = (7+6)(4+3)) = 1$,
and Boole's result would be

$$((a+b)(c+d) = (7+6)(4)) + (ac+bd+bc+ad = (7+6)(4+3)) = 1.$$

The matter becomes worse and worse for Boole and Schröder as the assertible contents that replace A and B get more and more complex.]

thought of such an application of his formulas, with the easily discoverable disadvantages that arise in this way. But it would be
equally unfair to consider as a defect of the "conceptual notation"
the waste of space in the case of the mere indication of content [as
in the above case where A and B merely indicate extensive complex
contents].

Another comment of Schröder is related to what I have just said—
my formula language indulges in the Japanese custom of writing
vertically. Actually, this appears to be so, as long as one presents only
the abstract logical forms. But if one imagines replacing the single
letters with whole formulas, say arithmetical equations, he discovers
that nothing unusual is presented here; for in every arithmetical
derivation, one does not write the separate equations next to each
other, but puts them one below the other for the sake of perspicuity.

Thus, in his evaluation, Schröder proceeds throughout from [the
assumption of] an immediate comparability—which is non-existent—
of the "conceptual notation" and the Leibnizian–Boolean formula
language. He means to contribute most effectively to the correction
of opinions with the remark that the two modes of symbolization are
not essentially different because we could translate from one into
the other. But this proves nothing. If the same department of knowledge is symbolized by means of two symbol systems, then it follows
necessarily that a translation or transcription from one into the other
would be possible. Conversely, nothing more follows from this
possibility than the existence of a common department of knowledge.
The system of symbols, nevertheless, can be essentially different. We
can ask whether this translation is feasible throughout, or whether
perhaps my formal language governs a smaller region.[8]

Schröder says that my "conceptual notation" has almost nothing
in common with the Boolean calculus of concepts. From this account,
it could appear that the "conceptual notation" would not be able to
represent the subordination of concepts. An example will convince
one of the opposite. The judgement

$$\vdash\!\!\!\begin{array}{l} x^4 = 81 \\ x^2 = 9 \end{array}$$

[8 In this paragraph Frege seems to be giving too much credit to Boolean logic,
for *that* is the one which "governs a smaller region". Because of his functional
calculus and quantification Frege can express statements and logical relations
that Boolean logic cannot handle. Perhaps Frege did not yet (1882) realize what
a great advance he had achieved in logic.]

runs in words: if $x^2 = 9$, then $x^4 = 81$. Now we can call a number whose square is 9 "a square root of 9", and one whose fourth power is 81 "a fourth root of 81", and then translate: all square roots of 9 are fourth roots of 81. Here, the concept "square root of 9" is sub-ordinated to the concept "fourth root of 81". The purpose of the letter x is to make the whole judgement general in the sense that the content should hold whatever one may put in for x. A correct {*richtig*} judgement even results if, for example, we put 1 in for x:

$$\vdash\!\!\!\begin{array}{l} 1^4 = 81 \\ 1^2 = 9 \end{array}$$

for the case where $1^2 = 9$ and 1^4 does not equal 81 is to be denied since 1^2 does not equal 9.

It is sometimes necessary to confine the generality to a part of the judgement. Then I make use of German instead of italic letters, as in

$$\vdash\!\!\!\begin{array}{l} x = 0 \\ \text{\alpha}\!\!\begin{array}{l} \mathfrak{a} = x \\ \mathfrak{a}^2 = x \end{array} \end{array}$$

in words: if each square root of x is x itself, then $x = 0$. Here the concavity with the $\mathfrak{a}$ signifies that the generality expressed by $\mathfrak{a}$ should be confined to the content of

$$\begin{array}{l} \mathfrak{a} = x \\ \mathfrak{a}^2 = x. \end{array}$$

I consider this mode of notation one of the most important com-ponents of my "conceptual notation", through which it also has, as a mere presentation of logical forms, a considerable advantage over Boole's mode of notation. In this way, in place of the artificial Boolean elaboration, an organic relation between the *primary* and the *secondary propositions* is established. Schröder recognizes the advan-tage in this, when he makes the effort to establish it in the Boolean formula language. However, in so doing, he shows that he has not grasped the heart of the matter; namely, the delimitation of the scope to which the generality should extend. According to Schröder's pro-posal, the difference between

$$\begin{array}{l} x = 0 \\ \text{\alpha}\,\mathfrak{a} = x \\ \mathfrak{a}^2 = x \end{array} \quad \text{and} \quad \begin{array}{l} x = 0 \\ a = x \\ a^2 = x \end{array}$$

could not be clearly perceived. And yet the difference is so great that the latter is false while the former is true. A further disadvantage of his proposal is that it requires yet another symbol for negation.

It would lead too far afield if I were to answer all of Schröder's particular criticisms. It may suffice to have his false conception of the aim of the "conceptual notation" corrected and to show in this way the lack of cogency {*Untriftigkeit*} of at least some of his critical remarks. Had he attempted to translate some of the formulas of the third chapter of my book and those which I had the honour of presenting to you some time ago into the mode of notation which he calls better, then he would have discovered by the difficulty of the undertaking the erroneous nature of his view.

Nevertheless, I am thankful to him for the review of my book.

CONCEPTUAL NOTATION

A FORMULA LANGUAGE OF PURE THOUGHT
MODELLED UPON THE
FORMULA LANGUAGE OF ARITHMETIC
(1879)

PREFACE[1]

THE apprehension of a scientific truth proceeds, as a rule, through several stages of certainty. First guessed, perhaps, from an inadequate number of particular cases, a universal proposition becomes little by little more firmly established by obtaining, through chains of reasoning, a connection with other truths—whether conclusions which find confirmation in some other way are derived from it; or, conversely, whether it comes to be seen as a conclusion from already established propositions. Thus, on the one hand, we can ask by what path a proposition has been gradually established; or, on the other hand, in what way it is finally most firmly establishable. Perhaps the former question must be answered differently for different people. The latter [question] is more definite, and its answer is connected with the inner nature of the proposition under consideration.

The firmest method of proof {*Beweisführung*} is obviously the purely logical one, which, disregarding the particular characteristics of things {*die besondere Beschaffenheit der Dinge*},[2] is based solely upon the laws on which all knowledge rests. Accordingly, we divide all truths which require a proof into two kinds: the proof of the first kind can proceed purely logically, while that of the second kind must be supported by empirical facts. It is quite possible, however, for a proposition to be of the first sort and still be one that could never come to the consciousness of a human mind without activity of the senses* {*Sinnesthätigkeit*}. Therefore, not the psychological mode of origin, but the most perfect method of proof {*Beweisführung*} underlies the classification.

[1 This English translation was complete before the appearance of the English translation by Stefan Bauer-Mengelberg (see F7 in the bibliography below) and independent of the translation of part of Chapter 1 by Peter Geach. Later, to give the reader the benefit of several interpretations, the three translations were compared; and any important differences were noted in the footnotes of the present work. At a few places Geach's or Bauer-Mengelberg's interpretations or turns of phrase seemed better than those of the present translator, and so they were adopted and credited in the footnotes.]

[2 Bauer-Mengelberg renders this "the particular characteristics of objects".]

* Since without sense perception no mental development is possible for beings known to us, the latter point holds for all judgements.

Now, while considering the question to which of these two kinds [of truths] do judgements of arithmetic belong, I had first to test how far one could get in arithmetic by means of logical deductions alone, supported only by the laws of thought, which transcend all particulars. The procedure in this effort was this: I sought first to reduce the concept of ordering-in-a-sequence to the notion of *logical* ordering, in order to advance from here to the concept of number. So that something intuitive {*etwas Anschauliches*} could not squeeze in unnoticed here, it was most important to keep the chain of reasoning free of gaps. As I endeavoured to fulfil this requirement most rigorously, I found an obstacle in the inadequacy of the language; despite all the unwieldiness of the expressions, the more complex the relations became, the less precision—which my purpose required—could be obtained. From this deficiency arose the idea of the "conceptual notation" presented here. Thus, its chief purpose should be to test in the most reliable manner the validity of a chain of reasoning and expose each presupposition which tends to creep in unnoticed, so that its source can be investigated. For this reason, I have omitted the expression of everything which is without importance for the chain of inference {*Schlussfolge*}. In §3, I have designated by *conceptual content* {*begrifflicher Inhalt*} that which is of sole importance for me. Hence, this must always be kept in mind if one wishes to grasp correctly the nature of my formula language. Also, the name "Conceptual Notation" resulted from this. Since I limited myself, for the present, to the expression of relations which are independent of the particular state of things, I was also able to use the expression "formula language of pure thought". The modelling upon the formula language of arithmetic to which I have alluded in the title refers more to the fundamental ideas than to the detailed structure. The farthest thing from my mind was any effort to establish an artificial similarity through the interpretation of a concept as the sum of its characteristic marks {*Merkmale*}.[3] The most immediate point of contact[4] between my formula language and that of arithmetic is in the way letters are used.

I believe I can make the relation of my "conceptual notation" to ordinary language {*Sprache des Lebens*} clearest if I compare it to

[3 With this rendering of "*Merkmale*" I follow Furth in F50. Bauer-Mengelberg uses merely "marks". For Frege on characteristic marks see F14, §53.
Frege's remark here seems to be an allusion to Leibniz (*Non inelegans specimen demonstrandi in abstractis*), whose work in logic Frege apparently knew well.]

[4 Bauer-Mengelberg's turn of phrase.]

the relation of the microscope to the eye. The latter, because of the range of its applicability and because of the ease with which it can adapt itself to the most varied circumstances, has a great superiority over the microscope. Of course, viewed as an optical instrument it reveals many imperfections, which usually remain unnoticed only because of its intimate connection with mental life. But as soon as scientific purposes place strong requirements upon sharpness of resolution, the eye proves to be inadequate. On the other hand, the microscope is perfectly suited for just such purposes; but, for this very reason, it is useless for all others.

Similarly, this "conceptual notation" is devised for particular scientific purposes; and therefore one may not condemn it because it is useless for other purposes. Even if it fulfils its purposes in some measure, one may still fail to find new truths in my work. I would nevertheless take comfort in the conviction that an improvement in method also advances science. Bacon, after all, held that it is more important to invent a means by which everything can be discovered easily than to discover some particular thing; and, in fact, all great scientific advances in recent times have had their origin in an improvement of method.

Leibniz also recognized—perhaps overestimated—the advantages of an adequate method of notation {*Bezeichnungsweise*}. His idea of a universal characteristic, a *calculus philosophicus* or *ratiocinator*,* was too ambitious for the effort to realize it to go beyond the mere preparatory steps. The enthusiasm which overcomes its [would be] creator when he considers what an immense increase in the mental power of mankind would result from a method of notation which fits things themselves {*die Sachen selbst*} lets him underestimate the difficulty which such an undertaking confronts. But even if this high aim cannot be attained in one try, we still need not give up hope for a slow, stepwise approximation. If a problem in its complete generality appears unsolvable, we have to limit it provisionally; then, perhaps, it will be mastered with a gradual advance. We can view the symbols of arithmetic, geometry, and chemistry as realizations of the Leibnizian idea in particular areas. The "conceptual notation" offered here adds a new domain to these; indeed, the one situated in the middle adjoining all the others. Thus, from this starting point,

---

* On that point see Trendelenburg, *Historische Beiträge zur Philosophie*, Volume 3 [(1867) "Über Leibnizes Entwurf einer allgemeinen Charakteristik", pp. 1–47.]

with the greatest expectation of success, we can begin to fill in the
gaps in the existing formula languages, connect their hitherto separate
domains to the province of a single formula language and extend it
to fields which up to now have lacked such a language.

I am sure that my "conceptual notation" can be successfully
applied wherever a special value must be placed upon the validity of
proofs, as in laying the foundation of the differential and integral
calculus.

It appears to me to be still easier to extend the area of application
of this formula language to geometry. We should only have to add
a few symbols for the intuitive relations that occur there. In this way,
we should acquire a kind of *analysis situs*.

The transition to pure kinematics and further to mechanics and
physics might follow here. In the latter fields, where besides necessity
of thought {*die Denknotwendigkeit*},[5] physical necessity {*die Natur-
notwendigkeit*}[6] asserts itself, a further development of the mode of
notation with the advancement of knowledge is easiest to foresee.
But this is no reason to wait until such transformations appear to
have become impossible.

If it is a task of philosophy to break the power of the word over
the human mind, uncovering illusions which through the use of
language often almost unavoidably arise concerning the relations of
concepts, freeing thought from that which only the nature of the
linguistic means of expression attaches to it, then my "conceptual
notation", further developed for these purposes, can become a useful
tool for philosophers. Certainly, it also does not reproduce ideas in
pure form either, and this is probably inevitable for a means of
thought expression outside of the mind {*bei einem äussern Darstel-
lungsmittel*};[7] but on the one hand, we can limit these discrepancies
to the unavoidable and harmless; and on the other hand, merely
because they are of a completely different kind from those [discrepan-
cies] peculiar to [ordinary] language, they provide a protection
against a onesided influence of one such means of expression.

The mere invention of this "conceptual notation", it seems to me,
has advanced logic. I hope that logicians, if they do not allow
themselves to be frightened off by the first impression of unfamiliarity,
will not refuse their assent to the innovations to which I have been

[5 Bauer-Mengelberg renders this "rational necessity".]
[6 Bauer-Mengelberg renders this "empirical necessity".]
[7 Bauer-Mengelberg renders this "by concrete means".]

driven by a necessity inherent in the subject matter itself. These deviations from the traditional find their justification in the fact that logic up to now has always confined itself too closely to language and grammar. In particular, I believe that the replacement of the concepts of *subject* and *predicate* by *argument* and *function* will prove itself in the long run. It is easy to see how regarding a content as a function of an argument leads to the formation of concepts. Furthermore, the demonstration of the connection between the meanings of the words: if, and, not, or, there exists, some, all, and so forth, may deserve notice.

Only the following further things require mention here:

The restriction, declared in §6, to a single mode of inference is justified by the fact that in laying the *foundation* of such a conceptual notation the primitive components must be chosen as simple as possible if perspicuity and order are to be created. This does not preclude the possibility that, *later*, transitions from several judgements to a new one, which are possible by this single mode of inference in only an indirect way, be converted into direct ways for the sake of abbreviation. Indeed, this may be advisable in a later application. In this way, then, further modes of inference would arise.

I noticed only later that formulas (31) and (41) can be combined into the single formula

$$\vdash\!- \left(\,{\sqcap\!\!\!\sqcap}\,\, a \equiv a \right)$$

which makes even more simplifications possible.

Arithmetic, as I said at the beginning, was the starting point of the train of thought which led me to my "conceptual notation". I intend, therefore, to apply it to this science first, trying to analyse its concepts further and provide a deeper foundation for its theorems. For the present, I have presented in the third chapter some things which move in that direction. Further pursuit of the suggested course— the elucidation of the concepts of number, magnitude, and so forth— is to be the subject of further investigations which I shall produce immediately after this book.[8]

Jena, 18 December 1878

[8 These "further investigations" are those contained in F14, but their appearance was delayed several years by a poor reception of the *Conceptual Notation*.]

CONTENTS OF THE *CONCEPTUAL NOTATION*

I. DEFINITION OF THE SYMBOLS

II. REPRESENTATION AND DERIVATION OF SOME JUDGEMENTS OF PURE THOUGHT

III. SOME TOPICS FROM A GENERAL THEORY OF SEQUENCES

I. DEFINITION OF THE SYMBOLS

§1. The symbols customarily used in the general theory of magnitudes fall into two kinds. The first consists of the letters, each of which represents either a number left undetermined or a function left undetermined. This indeterminateness makes it possible to use letters for the expression of the general validity of propositions, as in

$$(a+b)c = ac+bc.$$

The other kind consists of such symbols as $+$, $-$, $\sqrt{}$, 0, 1, 2; each of which has its own specific meaning.

I adopt this fundamental idea of distinguishing two kinds of symbols, which unfortunately is not strictly carried through in the theory of magnitudes,* *in order to use it for the more inclusive domain of pure thought in general.* I therefore divide all the symbols I employ into *those which one can take to signify various things* and *those which have a completely fixed sense.* The first are the *letters,* and these are to serve mainly for the expression of *generality.* But we must insist that a letter, for all its indeterminateness, should *retain* throughout the same context the meaning which we first gave it [in that context].

THE JUDGEMENT

§2. A judgement[1] will always be expressed with the aid of the symbol

which stands to the left of the symbol or combination of symbols giving the content {*Inhalt*} of the judgement. If we omit the small vertical stroke at the left end of the horizontal one, then the judgement is to be transformed into a *mere combination of ideas* {*blosse Vorstellungsverbindung*} of which the writer does not state whether or not he acknowledges its truth. For example, let

 A

---

* Consider 1, log, sin, lim.

[1 'Judgement' here corresponds to the more modern term 'assertion'. Frege's symbol '├———' is today called the "assertion sign".]

mean the judgement: "Opposite magnetic poles attract each other."*

Then   ——— A

will not express this judgement, but should simply evoke in the reader the idea of the reciprocal attraction of opposite magnetic poles, perhaps, say, in order to derive some conclusions from it and with these test the correctness of the thought. We paraphrase in this case by means of the words "*the circumstance that*" or "*the proposition that*".

Not every content can become a judgement by placing |———
before its symbol; for example, the idea "house" cannot. We therefore distinguish *assertible* and *unassertible* contents** {*beurtheilbare und unbeurtheilbare Inhalte*}.

The horizontal stroke, which is part of the symbol |———, *ties the symbols which follow it into a whole; and the assertion, which is expressed by means of the vertical stroke at the left end of the horizontal one, relates to this whole.* Let us call the horizontal stroke the *content stroke*, the vertical one the *judgement stroke*. The content stroke serves also to relate any sign to the whole formed by the symbols that follow the stroke. *Whatever follows the content stroke must always have an assertible content.*

§3. A distinction between *subject* and *predicate* does *not occur* in my way of representing a judgement. To justify this, I note that the contents of two judgements can differ in two ways: first, it may be the case that [all] the consequences which can be derived from the first judgement combined with certain others can always be derived also from the second judgement combined with the same others; secondly, this may not be the case. The two propositions, "At Plataea the Greeks defeated the Persians." and "At Plataea the Persians were defeated by the Greeks.", differ in the first way. Even if one can perceive a slight difference in sense, the agreement [of

---

* I use capital Greek letters [in this case capital *alpha*] as abbreviations to which the reader may attribute an appropriate sense if I do not specifically define them.

** On the other hand, the circumstance that there are houses (or there is a house) would be an assertible content. (See §12.) But the idea "house" is only a part of this. In the proposition, "Priam's house was made of wood.", we could not put "the circumstance that there is a house" in place of "house".—For an example of another kind of unassertible content, see [the passage following] formula 81.

sense] still predominates. Now I call the part of the content which is the *same* in both the *conceptual content {begrifflicher Inhalt}*. Since *only this* is meaningful {*von Bedeutung ist*} for [our] "conceptual notation", we need not distinguish between propositions which have the same conceptual content. If one says, "The subject is the concept with which the judgement is concerned.", this applies also to the object. Therefore, we can say only: "The subject is the concept with which the judgement is chiefly concerned." In [ordinary] language, the subject-place has the significance {*Bedeutung*} in the word-order of a *special* place where one puts what he wishes the listener to particularly heed. (See also §9.) This can serve, for instance, to indicate a relation of this judgement to others, thus facilitating for the listener an understanding of the whole context. Now all aspects {*Erscheinungen*}[2] of [ordinary] language which result only from the interaction of speaker and listener—for example, when the speaker considers the listener's expectations and tries to put them on the right track even before speaking a [complete] sentence—have nothing corresponding to them in my formula language, because here the only thing considered in a judgement is that which influences its *possible consequences*. Everything necessary for a correct inference is fully expressed; but what is not necessary usually is not indicated; *nothing is left to guessing*. In this I strictly follow the example of the formula language of mathematics, in which, also, one can distinguish subject and predicate only by doing violence [to the language]. We can imagine a language in which the proposition, "Archimedes perished at the conquest of Syracuse.", would be expressed in the following way: "The violent death of Archimedes at the conquest of Syracuse is a fact." Even here, if one wishes, he can distinguish subject and predicate; but the subject contains the whole content, and the predicate serves only to present this as a judgement. *Such a language would have only a single predicate for all judgements; namely, "is a fact"*. We see that here we cannot speak of subject and predicate in the usual sense. *Our "conceptual notation" is such a language, and the symbol* ⊢——— *is its common predicate for all judgements.*

In my first draft of a formula language, I was misled by the example of [ordinary] language into forming judgements by combining subject and predicate. I soon became convinced, however, that this was an obstacle to my special goal and led only to useless prolixity.

[2 Bauer-Mengelberg renders this "peculiarities".]

§4. The following remarks are intended to explain the significance, for our purposes, of the distinctions which people make with regard to judgements.

People distinguish *universal* and *particular* judgements: this is really not a distinction between judgements, but between contents. *They should say, "a judgement with a universal content", "a judgement with a particular content".* These properties belong to the content even when it is put forth, not as a judgement, but as an [unasserted] proposition. (See §2.)

The same holds for negation. For example, in an indirect proof we say, "Suppose that the line segments *AB* and *CD* were not equal." Here the content—that line segments *AB* and *CD* are not equal—contains a negation; but this content, although it could be a judgement, is not presented as a judgement. Negation attaches therefore to the content, whether or not it occurs as a judgement. I therefore consider it more appropriate to regard negation as a characteristic {*Merkmal*} of an *assertible content*.

The distinction of categorical, hypothetical, and disjunctive judgements appears to me to have only a grammatical significance.*

The apodictic judgement is distinguished from the assertoric in that the apodictic suggests the existence of general judgements from which the proposition can be inferred, while the assertoric lacks such an indication. If I call a proposition necessary, I thereby give a hint about my grounds for judgement. *But since this does not affect the conceptual content of the judgement, the apodictic form of judgement has for us no significance.*

If a proposition is presented as possible, the speaker is either refraining from judgement and indicating that he knows no laws from which the negation [of the proposition] would follow; or else he is saying that the universal negation of the proposition is false. In the latter case, we have what is usually called a *particular affirmative judgement.* (See §12.) "It is possible that the earth will someday collide with another heavenly body." is an example of the first case; and "A cold can result in death." is an [example of] the second case.

CONDITIONALITY

§5. If *A* and *B* stand for assertible contents (§2), there are the following four possibilities:

(1) A is affirmed and B is affirmed

* The reason for this will be brought out by the whole of this work.

(2) *A* is affirmed and *B* is denied

(3) *A* is denied and *B* is affirmed

(4) *A* is denied and *B* is denied.

Now,

stands for the judgement that *the third of these possibilities does not occur, but one of the other three does.* Thus, the denial of

signifies that the third possibility occurs, that therefore *A* is denied and *B* is affirmed.

From among the cases in which

is affirmed, we stress the following:

(1) *A* must be affirmed. Then the content of *B* is entirely immaterial. For example, let |——— *A* stand for $3 \times 7 = 21$ and let *B* stand for the circumstance that the sun is shining. Here only the first two of the four cases mentioned are possible. There need not exist a causal connection between the two contents.

(2) *B* is to be denied. Then the content of *A* is immaterial. For example, let *B* stand for the circumstance that perpetual motion is possible, and *A* the circumstance that the universe is infinite. Here only the second and fourth of the four cases are possible. There need be no causal connection between *A* and *B*.

(3) We can make the judgement

without knowing whether *A* and *B* are to be affirmed or denied. For example, let *B* stand for the circumstance that the moon is in quadrature [with the sun], and *A* the circumstance that it appears as a semicircle. In this case, we can translate with the aid of the conjunction "if": "If the moon is in quadrature [with the sun], it appears as a semicircle." The causal connection implicit in the word "if", however, is not expressed by our symbols, although a judgement of this kind can be made only on the basis of such a connection; for this connection is something general, but at this point we do not yet have an expression for generality. (See §12.)

Let the vertical stroke which connects the two horizontal ones be called the *conditional stroke*. The part of the upper horizontal stroke situated to the left of the conditional stroke is the content stroke for the meaning, just explained, of the symbol combination

to this is attached every symbol which is intended to relate to the content of the expression as a whole. The part of the horizontal stroke lying between A and the conditional stroke is the content stroke of A. The horizontal stroke to the left of B is the content stroke of B.

Accordingly, it is easy to see that

denies the case in which A is denied and B and Γ are affirmed. We must think of this as constructed from

$$\overline{}\!\begin{array}{l}\rule[0.3em]{1em}{0.05em}A\\\rule[0.3em]{1em}{0.05em}B\end{array}$$

and Γ in the same way as

$$\overline{}\!\begin{array}{l}\rule[0.3em]{1em}{0.05em}A\\\rule[0.3em]{1em}{0.05em}B\end{array}$$

is constructed from A and B. Therefore, we have first the denial of the case in which

$$\overline{}\!\begin{array}{l}\rule[0.3em]{1em}{0.05em}A\\\rule[0.3em]{1em}{0.05em}B\end{array}$$

is denied and Γ is affirmed. But the denial of

$$\overline{}\!\begin{array}{l}\rule[0.3em]{1em}{0.05em}A\\\rule[0.3em]{1em}{0.05em}B\end{array}$$

means that A is denied and B is affirmed. From this is obtained what is given above. If a causal connection is present, we can also say, "A is the necessary consequence of B and Γ."; or, "If the circumstances B and Γ occur, then A occurs also."

We can see just as easily that

denies the case in which B is affirmed, but A and Γ are denied.[3] If we assume a causal connection between A and B, we can translate [the formula]: "If A is the necessary consequence of B, we can infer that Γ occurs."

§6. A result of the definition [of the conditional stroke] given in §5 is that from the two judgements

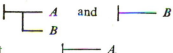

the new judgement ⊢——— A.

follows. Of the four cases enumerated above, the third is excluded by

but the second and fourth [cases are excluded] by

⊢——— B

so that only the first [case] remains.

We could write this inference perhaps this way:

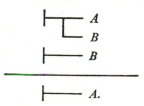

⊢——— A.

[3 There is an oversight here which was apparently first pointed out by Schröder in his review of the present work. (See this volume, p. 225.) None of the other five reviewers caught the slip.]

This would be laborious if long expressions stood in the places of *A* and *B*, because each of them would have to be written twice. I therefore use the following abbreviation: Each judgement which occurs in the context of a proof is labelled with a number which is placed to the right of the judgement at its first occurrence. Now, suppose for example that the judgement

—or one containing it as a special case—has been labelled with X. Then I write the inference this way:

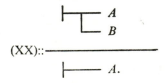

Here it is left to the reader to construct the judgement

$$\vdash\!\!\!\begin{array}{l} A \\ B \end{array}$$

from $\vdash\!\!\!-\!\!\!- B$ and $\vdash\!\!\!-\!\!\!- A$, and to see if it tallies with the cited judgement X. {*mit dem angeführten Urtheile* X *stimmt.*}[4]

   If, for example, the judgement $\vdash\!\!\!-\!\!\!- B$ was labelled by XX, then I also write the same inference this way:

$$(XX)::\!\!\dfrac{\vdash\!\!\!\begin{array}{l} A \\ B \end{array}}{\vdash\!\!\!-\!\!\!- A.}$$

Here the double colon indicates that $\vdash\!\!\!-\!\!\!- B$, which is cited only

[4 Bauer-Mengelberg renders this "and to see whether it is the judgement X above". Now this is not strictly correct, because the judgement which the reader constructs need not be X itself, but only a judgement which X "contains" as a special case. By this Frege means that the constructed sentence may also be *either a substitution instance or an instantiation of the cited judgement* X. That is why Frege uses the phrase '*tallies with* the cited judgement X' instead of merely '*is* the cited judgement X'.

   In fact, in nearly every proof in the whole *Conceptual Notation*, the judgement left for the reader to construct is not the one which Frege cites, but a substitution instance of it; and Frege indicates with a little table under the citation how to construct the substitution instance. See §13.]

by means of XX, must be formed, by a method other than the one above, from the two judgements which are written out.

Further, if, say, the judgement ├───── *Γ* were labelled with XXX, I would abbreviate the two inferences[5]

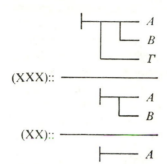

(XXX):: ─────────────

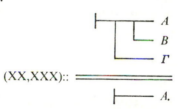

(XX):: ─────────────

├───── *A*

even more like this:

(XX,XXX):: ═════════════

├───── *A*.

In logic people enumerate, following Aristotle, a whole series of modes of inference. I use just this one—at least in all cases where a new judgement is derived from more than one single judgement.[6] We can, of course, express the truth implicit in another mode of inference in one judgement of the form: if *M* holds and *N* holds, then *Λ* holds as well; in symbols:

From this judgement plus ├───── *N* and ├───── *M*, ├───── *Λ* follows as above. In this way, an inference using any mode of inference can be reduced to our case. Accordingly, since it is possible to manage with a single mode of inference, perspicuity demands that we do so. Otherwise, there would be no reason to stop with the Aristotelian modes of inference; instead, we could go on adding new ones indefinitely: we could make a special mode of inference of each of the judgements expressed in formulas in §§13 to 22. *This restriction to a single mode of inference, however, is in no way intended to express a psychological proposition, but merely to settle the question of the most expedient form* [*of our "conceptual notation"*]. Some of the judgements that replace Aristotelian modes of inference will be presented in §22 (formulas 59, 62, 65).

NEGATION

§7. If a small vertical stroke is attached to the underside of the content stroke, this is to express the circumstance that *the content does not occur*. Thus, for example,

means: "*A* does not occur." I call this small vertical stroke the *negation stroke*. The part of the horizontal stroke to the right of the negation stroke is the content stroke of *A*; while the part to the left of the negation stroke is the content stroke of the negation of *A*. Here, as in other places in the "conceptual notation", without the judgement stroke, no judgement is made.

calls upon us merely to form the idea that *A* does not occur, without expressing whether this idea is true.

We now consider some cases in which the symbols for conditionality and negation are combined.

means: "The case in which *B* is to be affirmed and the negation of *A* is to be denied does not occur." In other words, "The possibility of affirming both *A* and *B* does not exist." Therefore, only the following three cases remain:

> *A* is affirmed and *B* is denied
>
> *A* is denied and *B* is affirmed
>
> *A* is denied and *B* is denied.

In view of the preceding, it is easy to determine the significance of each of the three parts of the horizontal stroke to the left of *A*.[7]

means: "The case in which *A* is denied and the negation of *B* is affirmed does not obtain."; or, "*A* and *B* cannot both be denied." Only the following possibilities remain:

> *A* is affirmed and *B* is affirmed
>
> *A* is affirmed and *B* is denied
>
> *A* is denied and *B* is affirmed.

A and *B* together exhaust all the possibilities. Now the words "or" and "either—or" are used in two ways:

> "*A* or *B*"

means, first, just the same as

thus, that nothing is conceivable other than *A* and *B*. For example: If a quantity of gas is heated, its volume or its pressure increases. In its second use, the expression

> "*A* or *B*"

unites the meanings of

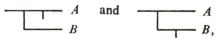

so that, first, there is no third possibility outside of *A* and *B*; and

---

[7 Bauer-Mengelberg's turn of phrase.]

secondly, A and B are mutually exclusive. Of the [original] four possibilities, then, only the following two remain:

A is affirmed and B is denied

A is denied and B is affirmed.

Of the two uses for the expression "A or B", the first, in which the coexistence of A and B is not excluded, is the more important; and *we shall use the word "or" with this meaning*. Perhaps it is appropriate to make this distinction between "or" and "either—or" that only the latter shall have the secondary meaning of mutual exclusion. We can then translate

$$\begin{array}{l} \rule{1cm}{0.4pt}\ A \\ \rule{1cm}{0.4pt}\ B \end{array}$$

by "A or B". Similarly,

$$\begin{array}{l} \rule{1.2cm}{0.4pt}\ A \\ \qquad\rule{0.6cm}{0.4pt}\ B \\ \qquad\rule{0.6cm}{0.4pt}\ \Gamma \end{array}$$

has the meaning of "A or B or Γ".

means

$$\begin{array}{l} \vdash\!\!\rule{1cm}{0.4pt}\ A \\ \qquad\rule{0.6cm}{0.4pt}\ B \end{array}$$

$$\text{``}\begin{array}{l} \rule{1cm}{0.4pt}\ A \\ \qquad\rule{0.6cm}{0.4pt}\ B \end{array}$$

is denied"; or, "the case in which A and B are both affirmed occurs". Conversely, the three possibilities left open by

$$\begin{array}{l} \rule{1cm}{0.4pt}\ A \\ \qquad\rule{0.6cm}{0.4pt}\ B \end{array}$$

are excluded. Accordingly, we can translate

$$\begin{array}{l} \vdash\!\!\rule{1cm}{0.4pt}\ A \\ \qquad\rule{0.6cm}{0.4pt}\ B \end{array}$$

by: "Both A and B are facts." Also, we can easily see that

$$\begin{array}{l} \rule{1cm}{0.4pt}\ A \\ \qquad\rule{0.6cm}{0.4pt}\ B \\ \qquad\rule{1cm}{0.4pt}\ \Gamma \end{array}$$

can be rendered by: "A and B and Γ". If we wish to represent "either A or B" in symbols with the secondary meaning of mutual exclusion, we must express "⊤⊤⊏ A and ⊤⊏ A." This gives B B

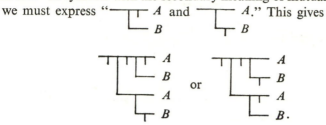

or

Instead of expressing "and" by means of the symbols for conditionality and negation, as is done here, we could, conversely, represent conditionality by means of a symbol for "and" and the symbol for negation. We could introduce, say,

$$\left\{ \begin{array}{c} \Gamma \\ \varDelta \end{array} \right.$$

as the symbol for the combined content of Γ and $\varDelta$, and then render

$$\mathsf{T}\!\!\!\!\mathsf{L}\begin{array}{c} A \\ B, \end{array}$$

by

$$\mathsf{T}\!\!\!\left\{ \mathsf{T}\begin{array}{c} A \\ B. \end{array} \right.$$

I chose the other way because deduction seemed to me to be expressed more simply that way. The distinction between "and" and "but" is the kind that is not expressed in this "conceptual notation". The speaker uses "but" when he wishes to give a hint that what follows is different from what one might at first suppose.

$$\mathsf{H}\!\!\!\!\mathsf{T}\begin{array}{c} A \\ B \end{array}$$

means: "Of the four possibilities, the third, namely that A is denied and B affirmed, occurs." Thus, we can translate [this formula by]:

"B and (but) not A occurs."

We can translate the symbol combination

in the same way.

means: "The case in which *A* and *B* are both denied occurs." We can thus translate [this formula by]:

"Neither *A* nor *B* is a fact."

Obviously, the words "or" ,"and", "neither—nor" are here considered only in so far as they combine *assertible* contents.

IDENTITY OF CONTENT

§8. Identity of content differs from conditionality and negation by relating to names, not to contents. Although symbols are usually only representatives of their contents—so that each combination [of symbols usually] expresses only a relation between their contents—they at once appear *in propria persona*[8] as soon as they are combined by the symbol for identity of content, for this signifies the circumstance that the two names have the same content. Thus, with the introduction of a symbol for identity of content, a bifurcation is necessarily introduced into the meaning of every symbol, the same symbols standing at times for their contents, at times for themselves. This gives the impression, at first, that what we are dealing with pertains merely to the *expression* and *not to the thought*,[9] and that we have absolutely no need for different symbols of the same content, and thus no [need for a] symbol for identity of content either. To show the falsity of this appearance, I choose the following example from geometry: Let a straight line rotate about a fixed point *A* on the circumference of a circle. When the straight line forms a diameter [of the circle], let us call the end [of the diameter] opposite *A* the point *B* corresponding to this position [of the straight line]. Then let us go on to call the point of intersection of the two lines [that is, the circumference and the straight line] the point *B* corresponding to the

[8 Geach's translation.]   [9 Bauer-Mengelberg's turn of phrase.]

position of the straight line at any given time. This [point *B*] is such that it follows the rule that continuous changes in the position of the straight line must always correspond to continuous changes in the position of *B*.

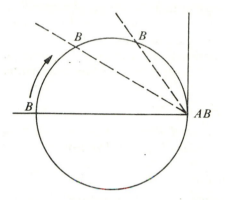

[As the line turns in the direction of the arrow, *B* moves towards *A*, till they coincide.[10]]

Therefore, the name *B* denotes something undetermined as long as the corresponding position of the straight line is not yet specified. We can now ask: What point corresponds to the position of the straight line when it is perpendicular to the diameter? The answer will be: The point *A*. Thus, in this case, the name *B* has the same content as the name *A*; and yet we could not have used only one name from the beginning since the justification for doing so is first given by our answer. The same point is determined in two ways:

(1) Directly through perception.

(2) As the point *B* corresponding to the [rotating] straight line's being perpendicular to the diameter.

A separate name corresponds to each of these two modes of determination {*Bestimmungsweisen*}. Thus, the need of a symbol for identity of content rests upon the following fact: the same content can be fully determined in different ways; but, that the *same content*, in a particular case, is actually given by *two {different} modes of determination* is the content of a *judgement*. Before this [judgement] can be made, we must supply two different names, corresponding to the two [different] modes of determination, for the thing thus determined. But the judgement requires for its expression a symbol for

[10 Here I follow Geach in including a diagram to aid the reader.]

identity of content to combine the two names. It follows from this that different names for the same content are not always merely an indifferent matter of form; but rather, if they are associated with different modes of determination, they concern the very heart of the matter.[11] In this case, the judgement as to identity of content[12] is, in Kant's sense synthetic. A more superficial reason for the introduction of a symbol for identity of content is that it is occasionally convenient to introduce an abbreviation for a lengthy expression. We must then express identity of content between the abbreviation and the original form.

Now, let $\vdash\!\!\!-\!\!\!- (A \equiv B)$

mean: *the symbol A and the symbol B have the same conceptual content, so that we can always replace A by B and* vice versa.

THE FUNCTION

§9. Let us suppose that the circumstance that hydrogen is lighter than carbon dioxide is expressed in our formula language. Then, in place of the symbol for hydrogen, we can insert the symbol for oxygen or for nitrogen. By this means, the sense is altered in such a way that "oxygen" or "nitrogen" enters into the relations in which "hydrogen" stood before. If we think of an expression as variable in this way, it divides into [1] a constant component which represents the totality of the relations and [2] the symbol which is regarded as replaceable by others and which denotes the object which stands in these relations. I call the first component a function, the second its argument. This distinction has nothing to do with the conceptual content, but only with our way of viewing it. Although, in the mode of consideration just indicated, "hydrogen" was the argument and "being lighter than carbon dioxide" the function, we can also apprehend the same conceptual content in such a way that "carbon dioxide" becomes the argument and "being heavier than hydrogen" the function. In this case we need only think of "carbon dioxide" as replaceable by other ideas like "hydrogen chloride gas" or "ammonia".

"The circumstance that carbon dioxide is heavier than hydrogen" and

"the circumstance that carbon dioxide is heavier than oxygen"

[11 Bauer-Mengelberg's turn of phrase.]   [12 Geach's turn of phrase.]

are the same function with different arguments if we regard "hydrogen" and "oxygen" as arguments. On the other hand, they are different functions of the same argument if we consider "carbon dioxide" as the argument.

Consider now as our example: "the circumstance that the centre of mass of the solar system has no acceleration, if only internal forces act on the solar system". Here, "solar system" occurs in two places. We can thus consider this as a function of the argument "solar system" in various ways, according as we think of "solar system" as replaceable by other arguments at the first or the second or at both places—but in the last case, replaceable by the same thing both times. These three functions are all different. The proposition that Cato killed Cato shows the same thing. Here, if we think of "Cato" as replaceable at the first occurrence, then "killing Cato" is the function. If we think of "Cato" as replaceable at the second occurrence, then "being killed by Cato" is the function. Finally, if we think of "Cato" as replaceable at both occurrences, then "killing oneself" is the function.

We now express the matter generally:

If, in an expression (whose content need not be assertible), a simple or a complex symbol occurs in one or more places and we imagine it as replaceable by another [symbol] (but the same one each time) at all or some of these places, then we call the part of the expression that shows itself invariant [under such replacement] a function and the replaceable part its argument.

Since, according to this account, something can occur as an argument and also at places in the function where it is not regarded as replaceable, we distinguish between argument-places and other places in the function.

Let me warn here against an illusion to which the use of [ordinary] language easily gives rise. If we compare the two propositions:

"The number 20 can be represented as the sum of four squares."

and

"Every positive integer can be represented as the sum of four squares."

it appears possible to consider "being representable as the sum of four squares" as a function whose argument is "the number 20" one time, and "every positive integer" the other time. We can discern the error of this view from the observation that "the number 20" and "every positive integer" are not concepts of the same rank {*gleichen Ranges*}. What is asserted of the number 20 cannot be asserted in the same sense of [the concept] "every positive integer"; though, of course, in some circumstances it may be asserted of every positive integer. The expression "every positive integer" by itself, unlike [the expression] "the number 20", yields no independent {*selbständige*} idea; it acquires a sense only in the context of a sentence.

For us, the different ways in which the same conceptual content can be considered as a function of this or that argument have no importance so long as function and argument are completely determinate. But if the argument becomes *indeterminate,* as in the judgement: "Whatever arbitrary positive integer we take as argument for 'being representable as the sum of four squares', the [resulting] proposition is always true.", then the distinction between function and argument acquires a *substantive*[13] {*inhaltlich*} significance. It can also happen that, conversely, the argument is determinate, but the function is indeterminate. In both cases, through the opposition of the *determinate* and the *indeterminate* or the *more* and the *less determinate,* the whole splits up into *function* and *argument* according to its own content, and not just according to our way of looking at it.

If we imagine that in a function a symbol, which has so far been regarded as not replaceable,* is now replaceable at some or all of the places where it occurs, we then obtain, by considering it in this way, a function with another argument besides the one it had before. In this way, *functions of two or more arguments* arise. Thus, for example, "the circumstance that hydrogen is lighter than carbon dioxide" can be considered a function of the two arguments "hydrogen" and "carbon dioxide".

In the mind of the speaker, the subject is usually the principal argument; the next in importance often appears as the object. [Ordinary] language, through the choice of [grammatical] forms or of words, for example,

active—passive   heavier—lighter   give—receive

[13] Following Bauer-Mengelberg.]

* We can also consider a symbol already previously regarded as replaceable [at some places] as now further replaceable at those positions where it was previously considered constant.

is free to permit, at will, this or that component of the sentence to appear as the principal argument; however, this freedom is limited by the scarcity of words.

§10. *In order to express an indeterminate function of the argument A, we put A in parentheses following a letter*, for example:

$$\Phi(A).$$

Similarly, $\qquad\qquad \Psi(A, B)$

represents a function (not more explicitly determined) of the two arguments A and B. Here, the places of A and B in the parentheses represent the positions that A and B occupy in the function, regardless of whether A or B each occupies one place or more [in that function]. *Thus, in general,* $\qquad \Psi(A, B) \quad and \quad \Psi(B, A)$

are different.

Indeterminate functions of more [than two] arguments are expressed in a corresponding way.

We can read $\qquad \vdash\!\!\!\!-\!\!\!-\ \Phi(A)$

as: "A has the property Φ."

$$\vdash\!\!\!\!-\!\!\!-\ \Psi(A,B)$$

can be translated by "B stands in the Ψ-relation to A."[14] or "B is a result of an application of the procedure Ψ to the object A."

Since the symbol Φ occurs at a place in the expression

$$\Phi(A)$$

and since we can think of it as replaced by other symbols [such as] Ψ, X—which then express other functions of the argument A—we can consider $\Phi(A)$ as a function of the argument Φ. This shows quite clearly that the concept of function in analysis, which I have in general followed, is far more restricted than the one developed here.

[14 Current usage would read it differently, namely, "A stands in the Ψ relation to B"; and indeed by the time (1893) he wrote §4 of F23, Frege had also adopted that reading.]

§11. In the expression of a judgement we can always regard the combination of symbols to the right of ├────── as a function of one of the symbols occurring in it. *If we replace this argument by a German letter and introduce in the content stroke a concavity containing the same German letter, as in*

$$\vdash\!\!\!\overset{\mathfrak{a}}{\smile}\!\!\!- \; \varPhi(\mathfrak{a})$$

then this stands for the judgement that the function is a fact whatever we may take as its argument. Since a letter which is used as a function symbol, like $\varPhi$ in $\varPhi(A)$, can itself be considered as the argument of a function, it can be replaced by a German letter in the manner just specified. The meaning of a German letter is subject only to the obvious restrictions that [1] the assertibility (§2) of a combination of symbols following the content stroke must remain intact, and [2] if the German letter appears as a function symbol, this circumstance must be taken into account. *All other conditions that must be imposed upon what may be put in for a German letter are to be included in the judgement.* Thus, from such a judgement, we can always derive an arbitrary number of *judgements with less general content* by putting something different each time in place of the German letter; when we do this, the concavity in the content stroke disappears again.

The horizontal stroke situated left of the concavity in

$$\vdash\!\!\!\overset{\mathfrak{a}}{\smile}\!\!\!- \; \varPhi(\mathfrak{a})$$

is the content stroke of [the assertible content] that $\varPhi(\mathfrak{a})$ holds, whatever we may put in the place of $\mathfrak{a}$. The horizontal stroke to the right of the concavity is the content stroke of $\varPhi(\mathfrak{a})$, and here we must think of $\mathfrak{a}$ as replaced by something definite.

After what has been said above about the significance of the judgement stroke, it is easy to see what an expression like

$$\overset{\mathfrak{a}}{\smile}\!\!\!- \; X(\mathfrak{a})$$

means. This can occur as part of a judgement like

$$\vdash_{\!\!\top}\!\!\overset{\mathfrak{a}}{\smile}\!\!- \; X(\mathfrak{a}), \qquad \vdash_{\!\!\!\!\!\!\!\underset{\smile_{\mathfrak{a}}}{\rule{0pt}{1.2em}}}\!\!\!\!\!\!\begin{array}{l} A \\[0.3em] X(\mathfrak{a}). \end{array}$$

It is obvious that, unlike

$$\vdash\!\!\!-\!\!\!\!{}^{\mathfrak{a}}\!\!\!-\!\!\!-\ \ \varPhi(\mathfrak{a})$$

these judgements cannot be used to derive less general judgements by replacing $\mathfrak{a}$ by something definite. By means of $\vdash\!\!\!\top\!\!\!-\!\!{}^{\mathfrak{a}}\!\!\!-\!\!\!- X(\mathfrak{a})$, it is denied that $X(\mathfrak{a})$ is always a fact whatever we may put in place of $\mathfrak{a}$. This in no way denies that we can specify a meaning $\varDelta$ such that $X(\varDelta)$ would be a fact.

$$
\vdash\!\!\!\!\begin{array}{l}\rule[0.5ex]{1.2em}{0.4pt}\ A\\ \rule[-0.5ex]{0.4pt}{1.2em}\!\!\!-\!\!{}^{\mathfrak{a}}\!\!\!-\ X(\mathfrak{a})\end{array}
$$

means that the case in which $\rule{1em}{0.4pt}{}^{\mathfrak{a}}\!\!\!\rule{1em}{0.4pt}\ X(\mathfrak{a})$ is affirmed and A is denied does not occur. But this in no way denies the occurrence of the case in which $X(\varDelta)$ is affirmed and A denied; for as we have just seen, $X(\varDelta)$ can be affirmed and yet $\rule{1em}{0.4pt}{}^{\mathfrak{a}}\!\!\!\rule{1em}{0.4pt}\ X(\mathfrak{a})$ denied. Thus, here also we cannot arbitrarily substitute for $\mathfrak{a}$ without jeopardizing the truth of the judgement. This explains why the concavity with the German letter written in it is necessary: *it delimits the scope {Gebiet} of the generality signified by the letter. The German letter retains its significance only within its scope.* The same German letter can occur in various scopes in one judgement without the meaning that we may ascribe to it in one scope extending to [any of] the other scopes. The scope of one German letter can include that of another, as is shown by the example

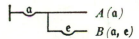

In this case, *different* letters must be chosen; we may not replace $\mathfrak{e}$ by $\mathfrak{a}$. Naturally, it is permitted to replace one German letter throughout its scope by another particular one provided that there are still different letters standing where different letters stood before. This has no effect on the content. *Other substitutions are permitted only if the concavity follows immediately after the judgement stroke* so that the content of the whole judgement constitutes the scope of the German letter. Since, accordingly, this is a specially important {*ausgezeichnet*}[15] case, I shall introduce the following abbreviation for it: *An italic letter is always to have as its scope the content of the*

[15 Geach's translation.]

whole judgement, and this need not be signified by a concavity in the content stroke. If an italic letter occurs in an expression which is not preceded by a judgement stroke[16] then this expression has no sense {*ist sinnlos*}. *An italic letter may always be replaced by a German letter which does not yet occur in the judgement*; when this is done, the concavity must be placed immediately after the judgement stroke. For example, instead of

$$\vdash\!\!\!\!\!\!-\!\!\!-\ X\,(a)$$

we may put

$$\vdash\!\!-\!\!\cup\!\!^{a}\!\!-\!\!-\ X\,(\mathfrak{a})$$

if *a* occurs only in the argument places of $X(a)$.

   It is also obvious that from

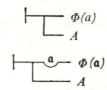

we can derive

$$\vdash\!\!-\!\!\cup\!\!^{a}\!\!-\ \varPhi\,(\mathfrak{a})$$
$$ A$$

if A is an expression in which a does not occur and a stands only in argument places of $\varPhi(a)$. If $-\!\!\cup^{a}\!\!- \varPhi(\mathfrak{a})$ is denied, then we must be able to specify a meaning for *a* such that $\varPhi(a)$ is denied. Thus, if $-\!\!\cup^{a}\!\!- \varPhi(\mathfrak{a})$ were denied and *A* affirmed, then we should have to be able to specify a meaning for *a* such that *A* would be affirmed and $\varPhi(a)$ denied. But because of

$$\vdash\!\!-\!\!\!\top\!\!-\ \varPhi\,(a)$$
$$A$$

we cannot do this; for this [formula] means that, whatever *a* may be, the case in which $\varPhi(a)$ would be denied and *A* affirmed is excluded.

[16 In order to introduce this abbreviation, Frege does not have to insist that the *judgement stroke* should precede every expression containing an italic letter; he need only insist that the *content stroke* should precede such an expression. The abbreviation essentially involves Frege's notation for quantification which employs a concavity in the content stroke, and therefore *requires the presence of the content stroke*. The *judgement stroke*, however, is not essentially involved here. Thus, the statement introducing the abbreviation could run something like: "*An italic letter is always to have as its scope the assertible content of the entire symbol combination in which that italic letter appears.*" Finally, the restriction could read: "If an italic letter occurs in an expression which is not preceded by the *content stroke* then this expression has no sense."]

Thus, we cannot deny ——𝖺—— $\Phi(a)$ and affirm A; that is:

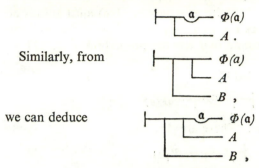

Similarly, from

we can deduce

if a does not occur in A or B and $\Phi(a)$ contains a only in argument places. This case can be reduced to the preceding one, since instead of

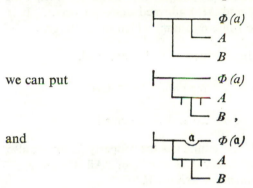

we can put

and

can be converted again into

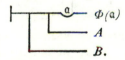

A similar treatment holds when there are still more conditional strokes.

§12. We now consider some combinations of symbols.

$$\vdash \!\!-\!\!-\!\!\overset{\mathfrak{a}}{\smile}\!\!-\!\! X(\mathfrak{a})$$

means that we can find something, say $\varDelta$, such that $X(\varDelta)$ would be denied. We can thus translate it: "There are some things which do not have the property X."

The sense of   ⊢—α—⊤— $X(α)$

is different. This means: "Whatever α may be, $X(α)$ must always be denied."; or: "There does not exist something having the property X."; or, if we call something that has the property X a X: "There is no X."

—α—⊤— $Λ(α)$ is denied by

⊢—⊤—α—⊤— $Λ(α)$.

Thus, we can translate it: "There are $Λ$'s."*

⊢—α—⊏ $P(α)$
           ⌞ $X(α)$

means: "Whatever may be put in place of α, the case in which $P(α)$ would have to be denied and $X(α)$ affirmed does not occur." It is thus possible here that for some meanings which we could give to α,

    $P(α)$ would have to be affirmed and $X(α)$ affirmed,
for others
    $P(α)$ would have to be affirmed and $X(α)$ denied,
for still others
    $P(α)$ would have to be denied and $X(α)$ denied.

We can thus translate: "If something has the property X, then it also has the property P.", or "Every X is a P.", or "All X's are P's." *This is how causal connections are expressed.*

⊢—α—⊤ $P(α)$
           ⌞ $Ψ(α)$

means: "A meaning cannot be given to α such that $P(α)$ and $Ψ(α)$ could both be affirmed." Thus, we could translate: "What has the property $Ψ$ does not have the property P.", or "No $Ψ$ is a P."

⊢—⊤—α—⊤ $P(α)$
            ⌞ $Λ(α)$

* This must be understood to include the case "There exists one $Λ$." For example, if $Λ(x)$ signifies the circumstance that x is a house, then

⊢—⊤—α—⊤— $Λ(α)$

means: "There are houses or is at least one house." See §2, [Frege's] second footnote.

denies $\overset{a}{\rule{0pt}{0pt}}\rule[0.5ex]{1.2em}{0.4pt}$ $P(a)$ and can thus be rendered as: "Some Λ's
$\Lambda(a)$

are not P's."

$\rule[0.5ex]{2em}{0.4pt}\overset{a}{\rule{0pt}{0pt}}\rule[0.5ex]{1em}{0.4pt}$ $P(a)$
$M(a)$

denies that no M is a P and thus means: "Some* M's are P's.", or
"It is possible for a M to be a P."

Thus we obtain the square of logical opposition:

$\rule[0.5ex]{2em}{0.4pt}\overset{a}{\rule{0pt}{0pt}}\rule[0.5ex]{1em}{0.4pt}$ $P(a)$ CONTRARY $\rule[0.5ex]{2em}{0.4pt}\overset{a}{\rule{0pt}{0pt}}\rule[0.5ex]{1em}{0.4pt}$ $P(a)$
$X(a)$ $X(a)$

```
S                                               S
U     C                                 Y       U
B       O                           R           B
A         N                     O               A
L           T               T                   L
T             R           C                     T
E               A   I                           E
                    D                           
E               A   I                           E
R             R           C                     R
N           T               T                   N
A         N                     O               A
T       O                           R           T
E     C                                 Y       E
```

$\rule[0.5ex]{2em}{0.4pt}\overset{a}{\rule{0pt}{0pt}}\rule[0.5ex]{1em}{0.4pt}$ $P(a)$ [SUB] CONTRARY $\rule[0.5ex]{2em}{0.4pt}\overset{a}{\rule{0pt}{0pt}}\rule[0.5ex]{1em}{0.4pt}$ $P(a)$
$X(a)$ $X(a)$

* The word "some" must always be understood here to include the case "one".
In a more lengthy manner, we could say: "some, or at least one."

II. REPRESENTATION AND DERIVATION OF SOME JUDGEMENTS OF PURE THOUGHT

§13. We have already introduced in the first chapter several principles of [pure] thought in order to transform them into rules for the application of our symbols. These rules and the laws to which they correspond cannot be expressed in our "conceptual notation" because they form its basis. Now in this chapter, some judgements of pure thought which *can* be expressed in the "conceptual notation" are to be stated in symbols. It seems natural to deduce the more complex of these judgements from the simpler ones—not to make them more certain, which generally would be unnecessary, but to bring out the relations of the judgements to one another. Merely knowing the laws is obviously not the same as also understanding how some are implicitly contained in others. In this way, we obtain a small number of laws in which (if we add the laws contained in the rules) is included, though in embryonic form, the content of all of them. And it is an advantage of the deductive mode of presentation that it teaches us to recognize this [undeveloped] kernel [of content]. Because we cannot enumerate all of the boundless number of laws that can be established, we can attain completeness only by a search for those which, *potentially*, imply all the others. Now, of course, it must be admitted that the reduction is possible in other ways besides this particular one. Thus, one such mode of presentation will not elucidate all the interconnections of the laws of thought. Perhaps there is yet another series of judgements from which (with the addition of those contained in the rules) all the laws of thought can be derived. Even so, such a quantity of interconnections is displayed by the mode of reduction given here that every other derivation will be much facilitated.

Nine propositions form the kernel in the following presentation. Three of these—formulas 1, 2, and 8—require for their expression (except for the letters) only the symbol for conditionality. Three— formulas 28, 31, and 41—contain in addition the symbol for negation. Two—formulas 52 and 54—contain the symbol for identity of content; and in one—formula 58—the concavity in the content stroke is used.

The following derivation would tire the reader if he were to trace it in all its details. Its purpose is only to keep in readiness the answer to any question about the derivation of a law.

§14.

$$\begin{array}{l} a \\ b \\ a \end{array} \tag{1}$$

says: "The case in which a is denied, b is affirmed and a is affirmed is excluded." This is obvious since a cannot be denied and affirmed at the same time. We can also express the judgement in words this way: "If a proposition a holds, it holds also in case an arbitrary proposition b holds." For example, let a stand for the proposition that the sum of the angles of the triangle ABC is two right angles and b stand for the proposition that the angle ABC is a right angle. Then we obtain the judgement: "If the sum of the angles in the triangle ABC is two right angles, this holds also for the case in which the angle ABC is a right angle."

The (1) to the right of $\begin{array}{l} a \\ b \\ a \end{array}$ is the number for this formula.

$$\begin{array}{l} a \\ c \\ b \\ c \\ a \\ b \\ c \end{array} \tag{2}$$

means: "The case in which

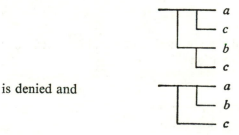

is denied and

is affirmed does not occur." But

means the circumstance that the case in which *a* is denied, *b* is affirmed, and *c* is affirmed is excluded. The denial of

says that ⌐⌐ *a* is denied and ⌐⌐ *b* is affirmed. But the
denial of ⌐⌐ *a* means that *a* is denied and *c* is affirmed.
Thus, the denial of

means that *a* is denied, *c* is affirmed, and ⌐⌐ *b* is affirmed. But,
from the affirmation of ⌐⌐ *b* and *c*, the affirmation of *b* follows.
That is why the denial of

implies the denial of *a* and the affirmation of *b* and *c*. Exactly this
case is excluded by the affirmation of

Therefore, the case in which

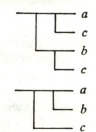

is denied and

is affirmed cannot occur; and the judgement

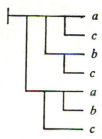

asserts this. For the case in which causal connections are present, we can also express it this way:

"If a proposition (*a*) is the necessary consequence of two propositions (*b* and *c*), that is if

and if the first of them (*b*) is again the necessary consequence of the other (*c*), then the proposition (*a*) is the necessary consequence of the last proposition (*c*) alone."

For example, let

c mean that in a sequence of numbers *Z* each succeeding term is greater than the preceding one.

b mean that a term *M* is greater than a term *L*.

a mean that the term *N* is greater than *L*.

Then we obtain the following judgement:

"If from the proposition that in the number sequence Z each succeeding term is greater than the preceding one and that a term M is greater than a term L, it can be inferred that the term N is greater than L; and if from the proposition that in the number sequence Z each succeeding term is greater than the preceding one it follows that M is greater than L; then the proposition that N is greater than L can be inferred from the proposition that each succeeding term in the number sequence Z is greater than the preceding one."

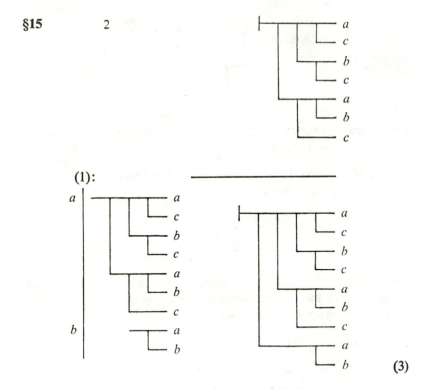

§15   2

(1):

(3)

The 2 on the left means that formula (2) stands to its right. The inference which brings about the transition from (2) and (1) to (3) is expressed in an abbreviated fashion as in §6. In full it would be written this way:

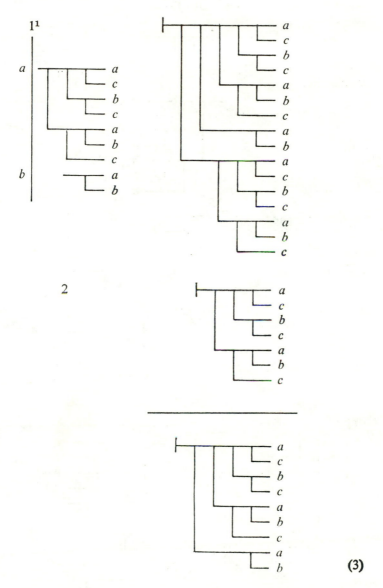

(3)

[¹ In the original German text, Frege forgot to include this table.]

Now the little table under the 1 serves to make proposition (1) more easily recognizable in the more complex form in which it appears here. It says that in [the judgement]

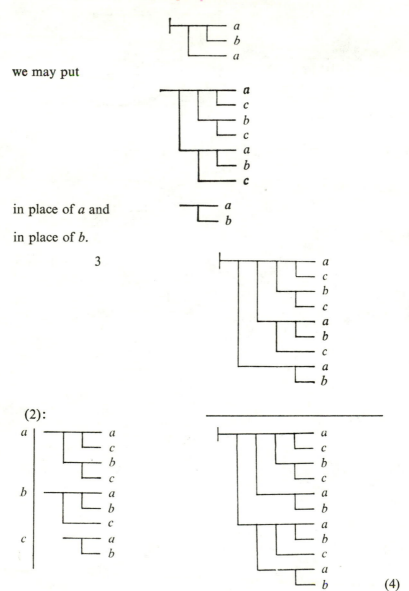

we may put

in place of *a* and

in place of *b*.

3

(2):

(4)

The table under (2) means that in

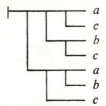

we may put in the places of *a*, *b*, *c* the expressions standing to their right. From this, we obtain

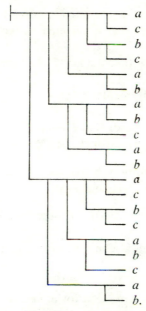

We can easily see how (4) follows from this and (3).

4

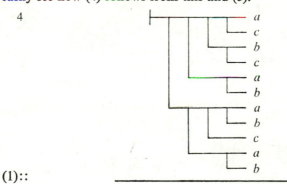

(1)::

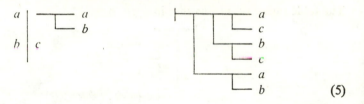

(5)

The significance of the double colon is explained in §6. As an example of (5), let

> *a* be the circumstance that the piece of iron *E* becomes magnetized,
> *b* be the circumstance that a galvanic current flows through the wire *D*,
> *c* be the circumstance that the key *T* is depressed.

We then obtain the judgement:

> "If the proposition holds that *E* becomes magnetized as soon as a galvanic current flows through *D*;
>
> if further the proposition holds that a galvanic current flows through *D* as soon as *T* is depressed;
>
> then *E* becomes magnetized if *T* is depressed."

If we assume that causal connections are present, we can express (5) this way:

> "If *b* is a sufficient condition for *a*, and if *c* is a sufficient condition for *b*, then *c* is a sufficient condition for *a*."

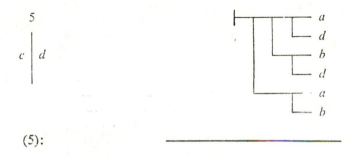

(5):

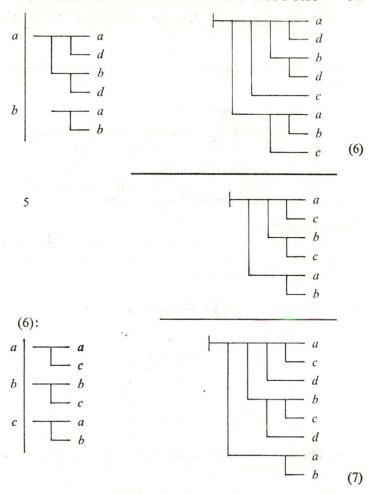

(6)

5

(6):

(7)

This proposition differs from (5) only in that it has two conditions c and d in place of the one condition c.

As an example of (7), let

d mean the circumstance that the piston K of an air pump is moved from its leftmost position to its rightmost position;

c mean the circumstance that the stopcock S^2 is in position I;

[2 Frege labelled the stopcock with 'H', but it has been changed to 'S' here for the sake of clarity, since Frege also used 'H' for the height of the barometer.]

b mean the circumstance that the density D of the air in the cylinder of the air pump is halved;

a mean the circumstance that the height H of a barometer connected to the cylinder of the air pump falls to half of its former height.

Then we obtain the judgement:

"If the proposition holds that the height H of the barometer falls to half as soon as the density D of the air is halved;

if further the proposition holds that the density D is halved if the piston K is moved from its leftmost position to its rightmost position and if the stopcock S is in position I;

then it follows that

the height H of the barometer sinks to half if the piston K is moved from its leftmost position to its rightmost position while the stopcock S is in position I."

§16.

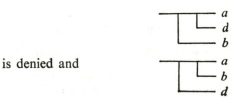

(8)

means [the circumstance] that the case in which *a* is denied, but *b* and *d* are affirmed does not occur;

means the same; and (8) says that the case in which

is denied and

is affirmed is excluded. This can also be expressed thus: "If a proposition is the consequence of two conditions, their order is immaterial."

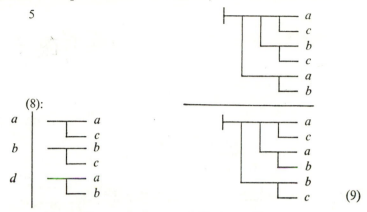

This proposition differs only immaterially from (5).

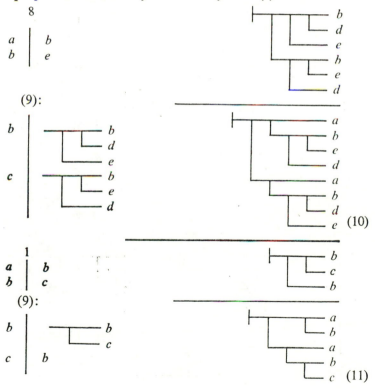

We can translate this formula thus: "If the proposition that b occurs or c does not occur is a sufficient condition for a, then b alone is a sufficient condition for a."

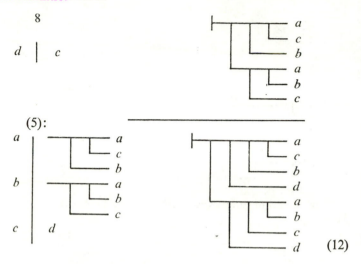

Propositions (12)–(17) and (22) show how, when several conditions are present. their order can be altered.

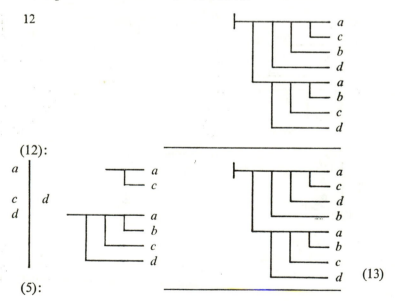

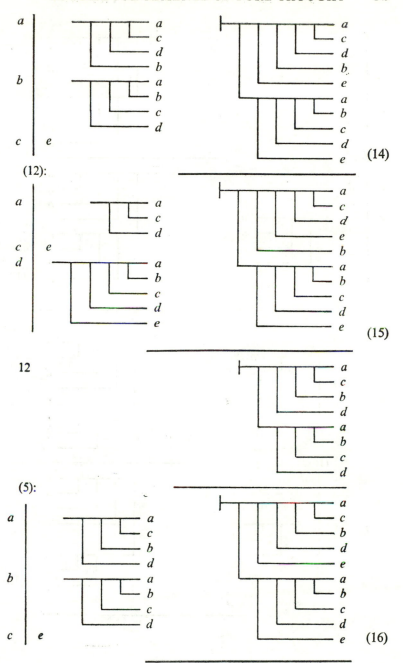

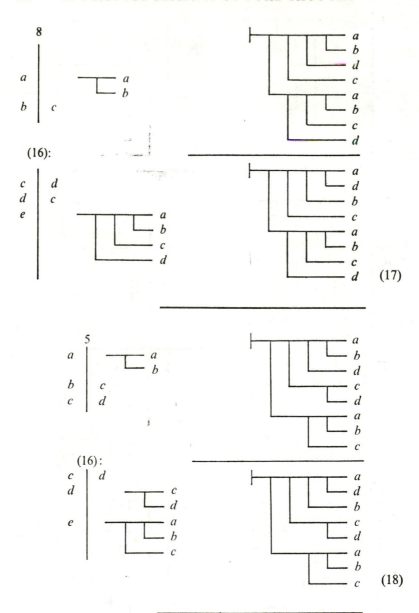

(16):

(17)

(16):

(18)

9

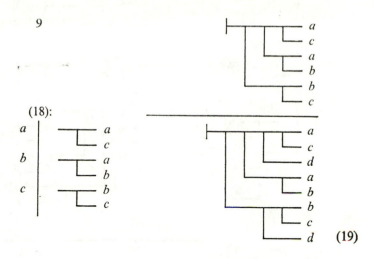

This proposition differs only immaterially from (7).

19

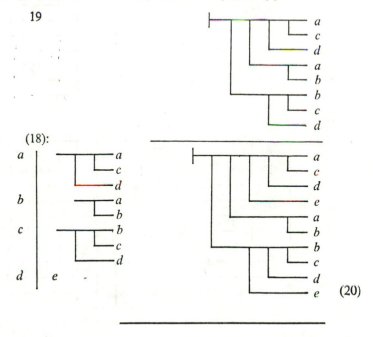

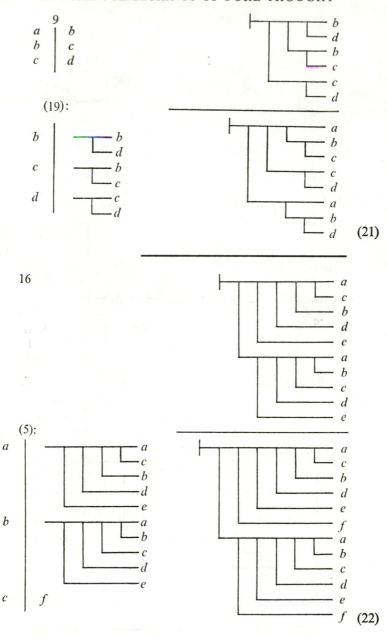

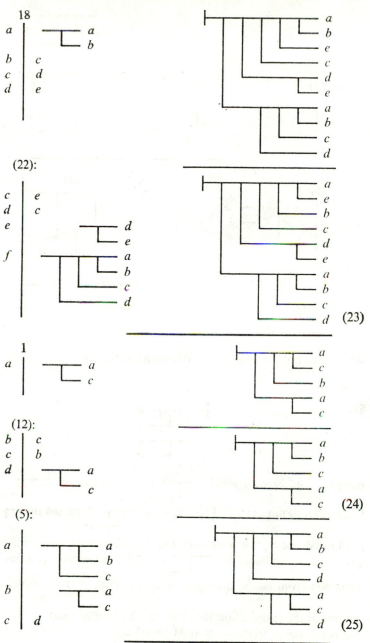

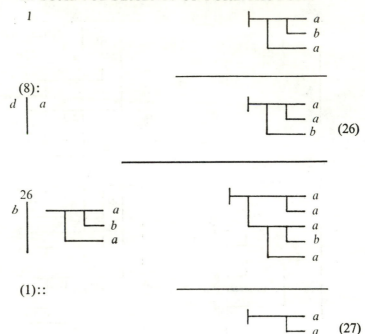

1

$(8):$

$d \mid a$

(26)

26

$b \mid$

$(1)::$

(27)

We cannot (at the same time) affirm and deny a.

§17.

(28)

means: "The case in which ⌐⊤ b is denied and ⌐⊤ a is affirmed does not occur." The denial of ⌐⊤ b means that ⊤ a is affirmed and ⊤ b is denied; that is, a is denied and b affirmed. This case is excluded by ⌐⊤ a. This judgement justifies the transition from *modus ponens* to *modus tollens*. For example, let

  b mean the proposition that the man M is alive; and
  a mean the proposition that M breathes.

Then we have the judgement:

"If from the circumstance that M is alive his breathing can be inferred, then from the circumstance that he does not breathe his death can be inferred."

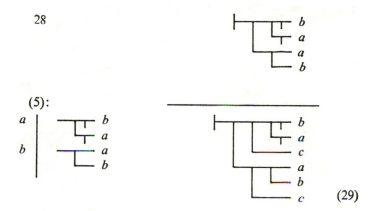

If b and c [together] are sufficient conditions for a, then from the denial of a and the affirmation of one of the conditions (c), the denial of the other condition can be inferred.

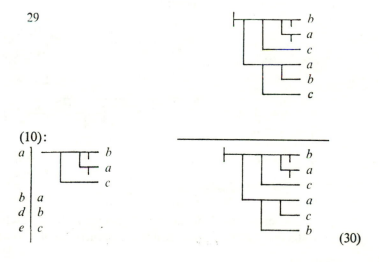

§18.

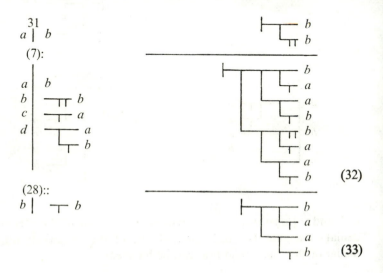

(31)

$\top\top$ a means the denial of the denial, hence the affirmation of a. Therefore, a cannot be denied and (at the same time) $\top\top$ a affirmed. *Duplex negatio affirmat.* The denial of denial is affirmation.

(32)

(33)

If a or b occurs, then b or a occurs.

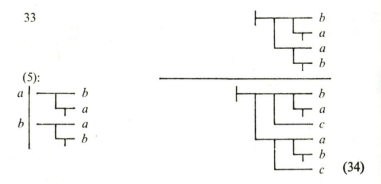

(34)

If the occurrence of the circumstance c together with the exclusion of the obstacle b has as a consequence the occurrence of a, then the occurrence of the obstacle *b* can be inferred from the non-occurrence of *a* together with the occurrence of *c*.

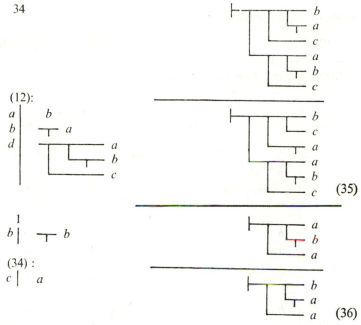

(35)

(36)

The case in which *b* is denied, ⊤ *a* is affirmed and *a* is affirmed does not occur. We can express this thus: "If *a* occurs, then one of *a* or *b* occurs."

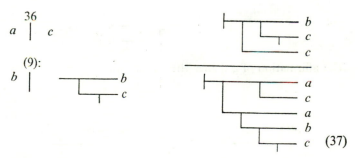

(37)

If *a* is the necessary consequence of the occurrence of *b* or *c*, then *a* is the necessary consequence of *c* alone. For example, let

   b mean the circumstance that the first factor of a product P becomes 0;

c mean the circumstance that the second factor of P becomes 0;
a mean the circumstance that the product P becomes 0.

Then we have the judgement:

"If the product P becomes 0 in case the first or the second factor becomes 0, then the vanishing of the product can be inferred from the vanishing of the second factor."

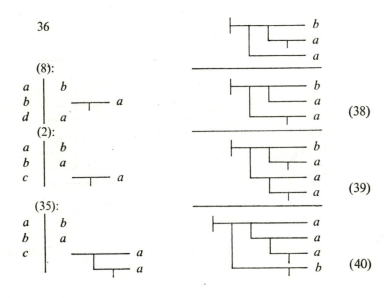

§19.

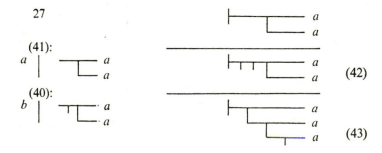

The affirmation of a denies the denial of a.

If the choice is only between a and a, then a occurs. For example, [suppose] we have to distinguish two cases which [together] exhaust all the possibilities. In pursuing the first, we arrive at the result that a occurs; the same [is the result] if we pursue the second [case]. Then the proposition a holds.

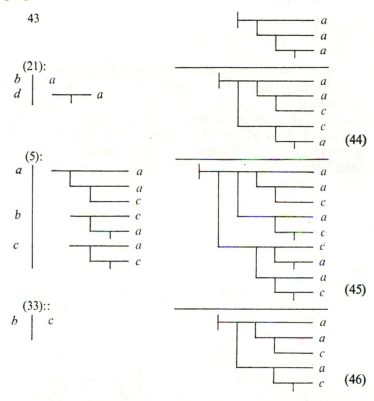

If a holds not only if c occurs, but also if c does not occur, then a holds. Another way of expressing it is: "If a or c occurs, and if the occurrence of c has a as a necessary consequence, then a occurs."

(21):

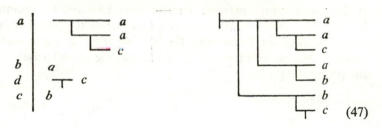

(47)

We can express this proposition this way: "If not only c, but also b is a sufficient condition for a, and if b or c occurs, then the proposition a holds." This judgement is used where two cases are to be distinguished in one proof. Where more cases occur, we can always reduce them to two by considering one of the cases as the first and the totality of the remaining cases as the second. We can divide the latter into two cases again and continue on in this manner as long as divisions are still possible.

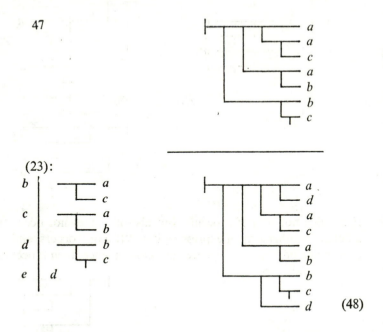

(48)

If d is a sufficient condition for the occurrence of b or c, and if not only b but also c is a sufficient condition for a, then d is a sufficient condition for *a*. The derivation of formula (101) offers an example of the application [of this judgement].

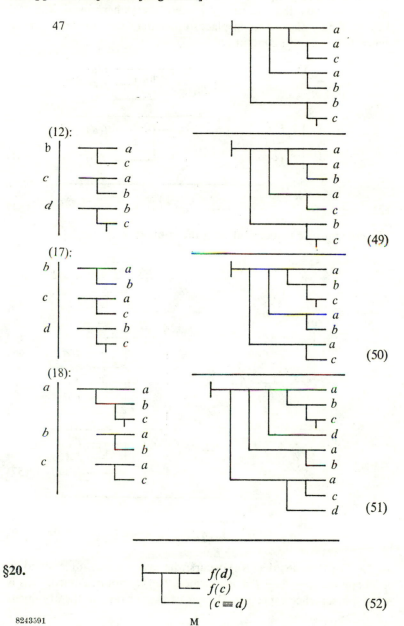

§20.

8243591   M

The case in which the content of c is identical with the content of d and in which $f(c)$ is affirmed and $f(d)$ denied does not occur. This proposition says that we may replace c everywhere by d, if $c \equiv d$. In $f(c)$, c may also occur in places other than the argument places. Thus, $f(d)$ may still contain c.

$$52$$

$$\begin{array}{c|c}
(8): & \\
a & f(d) \\
b & f(c) \\
d & (c\equiv d)
\end{array}$$

(53)

§21.
$$\vdash \quad (c\equiv c) \tag{54}$$

The content of c is identical with the content of c.

$$54$$

$$\begin{array}{c|c}
(53): & \\
f(A) & (A\equiv c)
\end{array}$$

(55)

$$\begin{array}{c|c}
(9): & \\
b & (d\equiv c) \\
c & (c\equiv d) \\
a & f(c) \\
 & f(d)
\end{array}$$

(56)

$$\begin{array}{c|c}
(52):: & \\
d & c \\
c & d
\end{array}$$

(57)

§22.

(58)

$—\!a\!— f(a)$ means that $f(a)$ occurs whatever we may understand by a. Therefore, if $—\!a\!— f(a)$ is affirmed, $f(c)$ cannot be denied. This is what our sentence expresses. Here, a can occur only in the argument places of f because this function occurs also outside the scope of $\mathfrak{a}$ in the judgement.

58

$f(A)$ ⎪ ┬─── $f(A)$
            └── $g(A)$

c ⎪ b

(30):

a ⎪ $f(b)$
c ⎪ $g(b)$
b ⎪ ─ᵃ┬── $f(\mathfrak{a})$
          └── $g(\mathfrak{a})$

┬─────── $f(b)$
│   └── $g(b)$
└─ᵃ┬── $f(\mathfrak{a})$
    └── $g(\mathfrak{a})$

┬──ᵃ┬── $f(\mathfrak{a})$
│   └── $g(\mathfrak{a})$
└─┬── $f(b)$
   └── $g(b)$ (59)

For example, let

> b mean an ostrich; that is, an individual animal belonging to this species;
>
> $g(A)$ mean "A is a bird.";
>
> $f(A)$ mean "A can fly."

Then we have the judgement:

> "If this ostrich is a bird and cannot fly, then it follows that some (see §12, [Frege's] 2nd footnote) birds cannot fly.

We see how this judgement replaces one mode of inference, namely Felapton or Fesapo, which are not differentiated here since no subject is distinguished [because of the nature of our "conceptual notation"].

58

$f(A)$ ⎪ ──┬── $f(A)$
          ├── $g(A)$
          └── $h(A)$

c ⎪ b

(12):

a ⎪ $f(b)$
b ⎪ $g(b)$
c ⎪ $h(b)$
d ⎪ ᵃ┬── $f(\mathfrak{a})$
    ├── $g(\mathfrak{a})$
    └── $h(\mathfrak{a})$

┬─────── $f(b)$
│   ├── $g(b)$
│   └── $h(b)$
└─ᵃ┬── $f(\mathfrak{a})$
    ├── $g(\mathfrak{a})$
    └── $h(\mathfrak{a})$

┬─────── $f(b)$
│   ├── $h(b)$
│   └── $g(b)$
└─ᵃ┬── $f(\mathfrak{a})$
    ├── $g(\mathfrak{a})$
    └── $h(\mathfrak{a})$ (60)

This judgement replaces the mode of inference Barbara in the case in which the minor premise ($g(x)$) has a particular content.

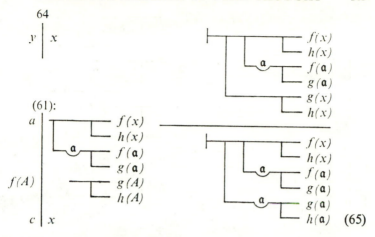

64

(61):

f(A)

(65)

Here a occurs in two scopes, but this does not indicate any particular connection between them. In one of these scopes, we could also write e instead of a. This judgement replaces the mode of inference Barbara for the case in which the minor premise

$$\begin{array}{c} g\,(a) \\ h\,(a) \end{array}$$

has a general content. The reader who has familiarized himself with the way in which derivations are made in the "conceptual notation" will be in a position to derive also the judgements which correspond to the other modes of inference. These may suffice as examples here:

65

(8):

(66)

58

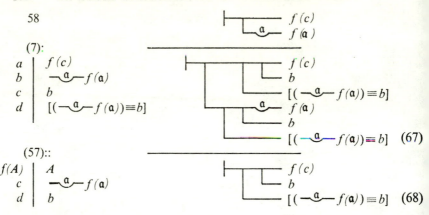

(7):

a	$f(c)$
b	$—\!\underset{a}{\frown}\!—f(\mathfrak{a})$
c	b
d	$[(—\!\underset{a}{\frown}\!—f(\mathfrak{a}))\equiv b]$

(57)::

$f(A)$	A
c	$—\!\underset{a}{\frown}\!—f(\mathfrak{a})$
d	b

III. SOME TOPICS FROM A GENERAL THEORY OF SEQUENCES

§23. The following derivations are meant to give a general idea of how to handle this "conceptual notation", even if they do not suffice, perhaps, to entirely reveal the advantage it possesses. This would only stand out clearly with more complicated propositions. Besides, we see in this example how pure thought {*reine Denken*} (regardless of any content given through the senses or even given *a priori* through an intuition) is able, all by itself, to produce from the content which arises from its own nature judgements which at first glance seem to be possible only on the grounds of some intuition. We can compare this to condensation by which we succeed in changing air, which appears to be nothing to the childlike mind, into a visible drop-forming fluid. The propositions about sequences developed in what follows far surpass in generality all similar propositions which can be derived from any intuition of sequences. Therefore, if one wishes to consider it more appropriate to take as a basis an intuitive idea of sequences, then he must not forget that the propositions so obtained, which might have somewhat the same wording as the ones given here, would not state nearly so much as these because they would have validity only in the domain of the particular intuition upon which they were founded.

§24.

$$\vdash \left(\left(\begin{array}{c} \rule{1.5cm}{0.4pt}\, \mathfrak{b} \rule{1cm}{0.4pt}\, \mathfrak{a} \rule{1cm}{0.4pt} \quad F(\mathfrak{a}) \\ f(\mathfrak{b}, \mathfrak{a}) \\ F(\mathfrak{b}) \end{array} \right) \equiv \begin{array}{c} \delta \\ | \\ \alpha \end{array} \left(\begin{array}{c} F(\alpha) \\ f(\delta, \alpha) \end{array} \right) \right) \qquad (69)$$

This sentence is different from those considered previously since symbols occur in it which have not been defined before; it itself gives the definition. It does not say, "The right side of the equation has the same content as the left side."; but, "They are to have the same content." This sentence is therefore not a judgement; and consequently, to use the Kantian expression, also *not a synthetic judgement*. I make this remark because Kant holds that all judgements of mathematics are synthetic. Now if (69) were a synthetic judgement, the propositions derived from it would be synthetic also. But we can do without the symbols introduced by this sentence, and thus the sentence itself as their definition: nothing follows from it which could not also be inferred without it. The only aim of such definitions is to bring about an extrinsic simplification by the establishment of an abbreviation. Besides, they serve to call special attention to a particular combination of symbols from the abundance of the possible ones and thereby obtain a firmer grasp [of it] for the imagination {*die Vorstellung*}.[1] Now, even if the simplification mentioned is hardly noticeable in the small number of judgements presented here, I have nevertheless adopted this formula to provide an example.

Although originally (69) is not a judgement, still it is readily converted into one; for once the meaning of the new symbols is specified, it remains fixed from then on; and therefore formula (69) holds also as a judgement, but as an analytic one, since we can only get out what was put into the new symbols [in the first place]. This dual role {*Doppelseitigkeit*} of the formula is indicated by the doubling of the judgement stroke. Thus, with respect to the derivations which follow, (69) can be treated as an ordinary judgement.

The lower-case Greek letters, used here for the first time, are like the German and italic letters in *representing no independent content*. With them, only identity and difference is to be noticed, so that we can arbitrarily put other lower-case Greek letters in the places of α and δ, provided the places which were previously occupied by the same letters are occupied again by the same letters and different letters are not replaced by the same letter. *But this identity or difference of Greek letters has importance only within the formula for which they have been especially introduced, as here for*

$$\delta \left\lvert\, \begin{matrix} F(\alpha) \\[4pt] f(\delta, \alpha). \end{matrix} \right.$$
$$\alpha$$

Their purpose is to enable us to unambiguously reconstruct the complete

---

[1 Bauer-Mengelberg renders this "our faculty of representation".]

at any time from the abbreviated form

$$\overset{\delta}{\underset{\alpha}{\big|}} \left(\begin{array}{l} F(\alpha) \\ f(\delta, \alpha). \end{array} \right.$$

For example,

$$\overset{\alpha}{\underset{\delta}{\big|}} \left(\begin{array}{l} F(\delta) \\ f(\delta, \alpha) \end{array} \right.$$

stands for the expression

while

$$\overset{\alpha}{\underset{\delta}{\big|}} \left(\begin{array}{l} F(\alpha) \\ f(\delta, \alpha) \end{array} \right.$$

makes no sense. We see that the unabbreviated expression, no matter how complicated the functions F and f may be, can always be re-established again with certainty apart from the arbitrary choice of German letters. [The formula]

$$\vdash\!\!\!\!\!\!\!\!\!\!\!\!\!\!\!\!\!\!\!- f(\Gamma, \Delta)$$

can be rendered, "Δ is a result of applying the procedure f to Γ.", or "Γ is the object of an application, with a result Δ, of the procedure f", or "Δ bears the f-relation to Γ.", or "Γ bears the converse of the f-relation to Δ." These expressions are to be taken as equivalent in meaning.

$$\overset{\delta}{\underset{\alpha}{\big|}} \left(\begin{array}{l} F(\alpha) \\ f(\delta, \alpha) \end{array} \right.$$

may be translated: "the circumstance that the property F is hereditary {*sich in der f-Reihe vererbt*} in the f-sequence". Perhaps the following example can make this expression acceptable: Let

$\Lambda(M, N)$ mean the circumstance that N is a child of M;

$\Sigma(P)$ mean the circumstance that P is a human being.

Then

$$\underset{\alpha}{\overset{\delta}{|}}\left(\begin{array}{l}\varSigma\,(\alpha)\\ \varLambda\,(\delta,\alpha)\end{array}\right. \qquad \text{or} \qquad \begin{array}{l}\varSigma\,(\mathfrak{a})\\ \varLambda\,(\mathfrak{b},\mathfrak{a})\\ \varSigma\,(\mathfrak{b})\end{array}$$

is the circumstance that each child of a human being is also a human being, or that the property being a human being is hereditary.

[Although this example was easy to put into words,] we can see, however, that it can become difficult and even impossible to give a rendering in words if very complicated functions occur in the places of F and f. Sentence (69) could be expressed in words this way:

   "*If from the proposition that* $\mathfrak{b}$ *has the property F, whatever* $\mathfrak{b}$ *may be, it can always be inferred that each result of an application of the procedure f to* $\mathfrak{b}$ *has the property F,*

then I say:

   '*The property F is hereditary in the f-sequence*'."

§25.

$$69 \quad \vdash \left(\left(\begin{array}{l}F(\mathfrak{a})\\ f(\mathfrak{b},\mathfrak{a})\\ F(\mathfrak{b})\end{array}\right) \equiv \underset{\alpha}{\overset{\delta}{|}}\left(\begin{array}{l}F(\alpha)\\ f(\delta,\alpha)\end{array}\right)\right.$$

(68): ——————————————————————————————

$$f(\Gamma)\ \begin{array}{c}\mathfrak{a}\\ \\ b\\ \\ c\end{array}\left|\begin{array}{l}\mathfrak{b}\\[2pt] \begin{array}{l}F(\mathfrak{a})\\ f(\Gamma,\mathfrak{a})\\ F(\Gamma)\end{array}\\[6pt] \underset{\alpha}{\overset{\delta}{|}}\left(\begin{array}{l}F(\alpha)\\ f(\delta,\alpha)\end{array}\right.\\[8pt] x\end{array}\right. \qquad \vdash\begin{array}{l}F(\mathfrak{a})\\ f(x,\mathfrak{a})\\ F(x)\\ \underset{\alpha}{\overset{\delta}{|}}\left(\begin{array}{l}F(\alpha)\\ f(\delta,\alpha)\end{array}\right.\end{array} \quad (70)$$

(19): ——————————————————————————————

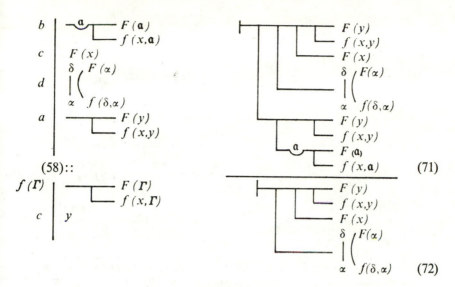

(71)

(72)

If the property F is hereditary in the f-sequence; and if x has the property F, and y is a result of an application of the procedure f to x: then y has the property F.

72

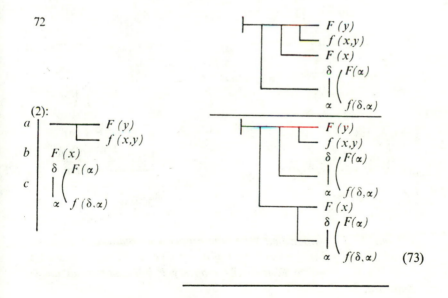

(73)

72

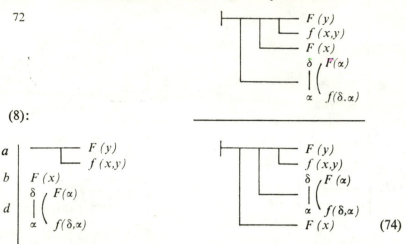

(8):

a

b

d

If x has a property F which is hereditary in the f-sequence, then every result of an application of the procedure f to x has the property F.

69

(52):

If from the proposition that ɒ has the property F, whatever ɒ may be, it can be inferred that every result of an application of the procedure f to ɒ has the property F, then the property F is hereditary in the f-sequence.

§26.

$$\vdash \left[\left[\begin{array}{c} \mathfrak{F} \\ \end{array} \right] \equiv \frac{\gamma}{\beta} f\left(x_\gamma, y_\beta\right) \right] \tag{76}$$

This is the definition of the symbol combination

$$\frac{\gamma}{\beta} f(x_\gamma, y_\beta)$$

which stands on the right. With regard to the doubling of the judgement stroke and to the Greek letters, I refer [the reader] to §24. It would not do to write simply

$$\overset{x}{\underset{y}{\sim}} f(x, y)$$

instead of the above expression because in a function of x and y written out in detail these letters could still occur also outside the argument places, in which case it then would not be discernible which places were to be considered argument places. The latter must therefore be marked as such. This is done here with the indices γ and β. We must choose different indices in view of the fact that both arguments might be the same. For this, we take Greek letters so that we will be sure to have a choice, so that for the case in which

$$\frac{\gamma}{\beta} f(x_\gamma, y_\beta)$$

includes within itself a similarly constructed expression, we will be able to mark the argument places of the included expression differently from the way we mark those of the including expression. *The identity and difference of the Greek letters here have significance only within the expression*

$$\frac{\gamma}{\beta} f(x_\gamma, y_\beta);$$

these same letters can occur outside [of this expression] without indicating any relation whatever to [the letters within the expression].

We translate $\quad\quad\quad\quad \overset{\gamma}{\underset{\beta}{\approx}} f(x_\gamma, y_\beta)$

by "y follows x in the f-sequence", a way of speaking which, to be sure, is possible only so long as the function f is determined. Accordingly, in words (76) can be expressed something like this:

> "*If from the two propositions, that every result of an application of the procedure f to x has the property F, and that the property F is hereditary in the f-sequence, it can be inferred, whatever F may be, that y has the property F;*

then I say:

> '*y follows x in the f-sequence*' *or* '*x precedes y in the f-sequence*'."*

§27.

---

* To make clearer the generality of the concept of ordering-in-a-sequence given in this way, I remind [the reader] of some possibilities. Among these are not only a sequence such as beads on a string exhibit, but also branching like a family tree, a merging of several branches, as well as ringlike self-linking {*ringartiges Insich-zurücklaufen*}. [Bauer-Mengelberg's translation of this last term.]

[² To prove 77, Frege cites 68; but he could not use 68 itself. He needs an analogous second-order principle (call it 68′) involving quantification over

Here, in accordance with §10, $F(y)$, $F(\mathfrak{a})$, $F(\alpha)$ are to be considered different functions of the argument F. (77) means:

> *If y follows x in the f-sequence; and if the property F is hereditary in the f-sequence; and if every result of an application of the procedure f to x has the property F; then y has the property F.*

77

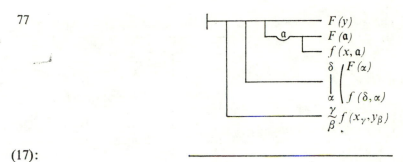

(17):

functions. In the later notation of F23 (ignoring the, for this purpose, irrelevant switch from '$\equiv$' to '$=$') it would look like this

68′

The substitutions (listed horizontally for convenience) would then be as follows:

These substitutions in 68′, and detachment of the definitionally true equivalence 76, yields 77 with flawless correctness.

The idea of treating $F(y)$ as a function of the function F is in no way contrary to Frege's later thought (see F23, p. 38, right column). To state his thought precisely, however, required the notational machinery (which he had not yet devised) to distinguish first- from second-level functions. With that available, the difficulty can be easily resolved. Van Heijenoort (in the Editor's Introduction to F7 (b)) is in error in supposing that any paradox can arise in the system. In the *Conceptual Notation* Frege never confuses first- and second-level functions, though he does not yet have separate terms for them. (See footnote 88 in **8** of the Editor's Introduction above.)]

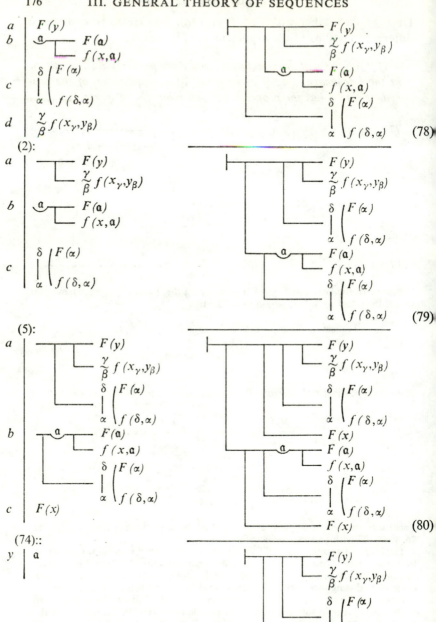

$$a \quad F(y)$$
$$b \quad \underset{}{\overset{a}{\frown}} \quad F(a)$$
$$\qquad\qquad f(x,a)$$
$$c \quad \overset{\delta}{\underset{\alpha}{|}} \begin{cases} F(\alpha) \\ f(\delta,\alpha) \end{cases}$$
$$d \quad \overset{\gamma}{\underset{\beta}{\sim}} f(x_\gamma,y_\beta)$$

(2):

$$a \quad \begin{array}{l} F(y) \\ \dfrac{\gamma}{\beta} f(x_\gamma,y_\beta) \end{array}$$
$$b \quad \underset{}{\overset{a}{\frown}} \begin{array}{l} F(a) \\ f(x,a) \end{array}$$
$$c \quad \overset{\delta}{\underset{\alpha}{|}} \begin{cases} F(\alpha) \\ f(\delta,\alpha) \end{cases}$$

(5):

$$a \quad \begin{array}{l} F(y) \\ \dfrac{\gamma}{\beta} f(x_\gamma,y_\beta) \\ \overset{\delta}{\underset{\alpha}{|}} \begin{cases} F(\alpha) \\ f(\delta,\alpha) \end{cases} \end{array}$$
$$b \quad \overset{a}{\frown} \begin{array}{l} F(a) \\ f(x,a) \\ \overset{\delta}{\underset{\alpha}{|}} \begin{cases} F(\alpha) \\ f(\delta,\alpha) \end{cases} \end{array}$$
$$c \quad F(x)$$

(74)::

$$y \quad | \quad a$$

(78)

(79)

(80)

(81)

Since in (74) y occurs only in

$$\text{---}\begin{array}{l} F(y) \\ f(x,y) \end{array}$$

in replacing the y by the German letter ɑ according to §11, the concavity can immediately precede this expression. We can translate (81):

If x has a property F which is hereditary in the f-sequence, and if y follows x in the f-sequence, then y has the property F. *

For example, let F be the property being a heap of beans; let the procedure f be the decreasing of a heap of beans by one bean, so that

$$f(a, b)$$

means the case that b contains all beans from the heap a except for one and nothing else but this. Then from our proposition we would obtain the result that a single bean or even no bean at all would be a heap of beans, if the property of being a heap [of beans] were hereditary in the f-sequence. However, this is not universally the case because there are certain z's for which, because of the indeterminateness of the concept "heap", $F(z)$ is not an assertible [or deniable] content.

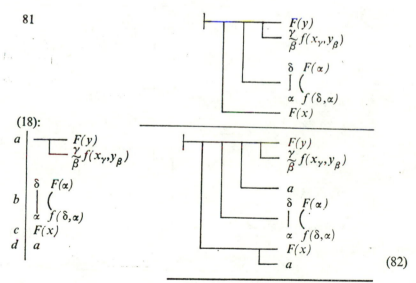

81

(18):

(82)

* Bernoullian induction is based upon this. [Jakob Bernoulli is considered one of the first to use mathematical induction. He employed it starting in 1686 in

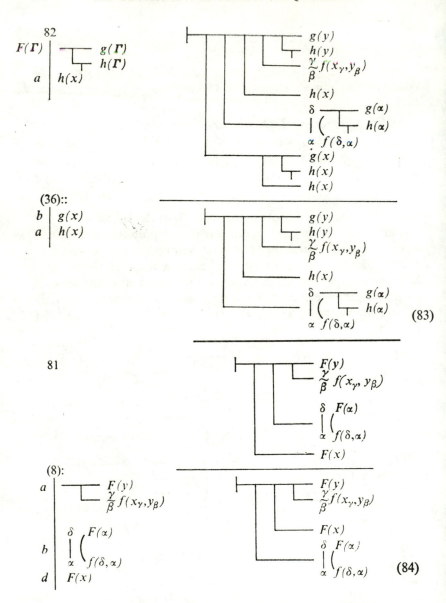

82

$F(\Gamma) \Big|$ $g(\Gamma)$
  $h(\Gamma)$
$a \Big| h(x)$

$g(y)$
$h(y)$
$\dfrac{\gamma}{\beta} f(x_\gamma, y_\beta)$

$h(x)$

$\delta \underline{\quad\quad} g(\alpha)$
$\Big| \Big(\quad\quad h(\alpha)$
$\alpha \; f(\delta, \alpha)$
$g(x)$
$h(x)$
$h(x)$

(36)::

$b \Big| g(x)$
$a \Big| h(x)$

$g(y)$
$h(y)$
$\dfrac{\gamma}{\beta} f(x_\gamma, y_\beta)$

$h(x)$

$\delta \underline{\quad\quad} g(\alpha)$
$\Big| \Big(\quad\quad h(\alpha)$
$\alpha \; f(\delta, \alpha)$

(83)

81

$F(y)$
$\dfrac{\gamma}{\beta} f(x_\gamma, y_\beta)$

$\delta \; F(\alpha)$
$\Big| \Big($
$\alpha \; f(\delta, \alpha)$

$F(x)$

(8):

$a \Big|$ $F(y)$
$ $ $\dfrac{\gamma}{\beta} f(x_\gamma, y_\beta)$

$b \Big| \delta \; {}^{\Big(} F(\alpha)$
$ \Big| $
$ \alpha \; {}_{f(\delta, \alpha)}$

$d \Big| F(x)$

$F(y)$
$\dfrac{\gamma}{\beta} f(x_\gamma, y_\beta)$

$F(x)$
$\delta \; F(\alpha)$
$\Big| \Big($
$\alpha \; f(\delta, \alpha)$

(84)

"Demonstratio rationum *etc.*", *Acta eruditorum*, pp. 360–1 (reprinted in his *Opera*, vol. 1, Geneva, 1744).]

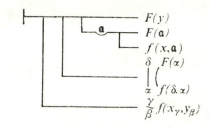

(12):

_____

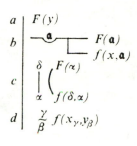

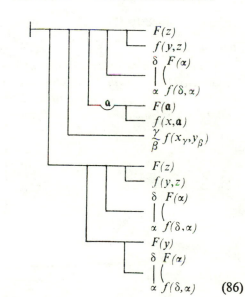

(19):

_____

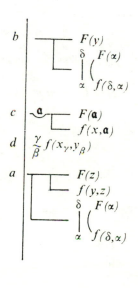

(73)::

_____

$$\begin{array}{c|c} y & z \\ x & y \end{array}$$

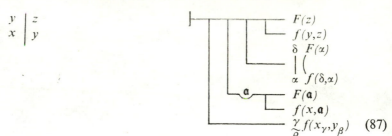

$$(87)$$

The derivation of this proposition in words will read something like:

(α) Let y follow x in the f-sequence;
(β) Let every result of an application of the procedure f to x have the property F;
(γ) Let the property F be hereditary in the f-sequence.

From these assumptions it follows according to (85) that

(δ) y has the property F.
(ϵ) Let z be a result of an application of the procedure f to y.

Then it follows from (γ), (δ), (ϵ) according to (73)[3] that

z has the property F.

Therefore:

If z is a result of an application of the procedure f to an object y, which follows x in the f-sequence; and if every result of an application of the procedure f to x has a property F which is hereditary in the f-sequence, then z has property F.

87

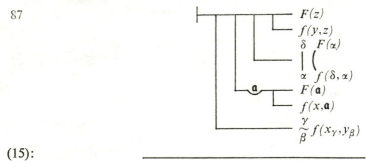

(15):   _____

---

[3] Frege's original text (1879) cites formula (72) here; but this is a typographical error. The minor premise actually used is (73).

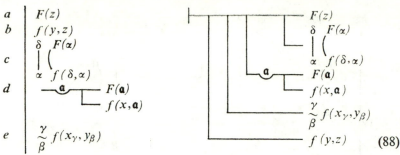

a $F(z)$
b $f(y,z)$
c
d
e $\underset{\beta}{\overset{\gamma}{\sim}} f(x_\gamma, y_\beta)$

(88)

§28.

76

$$\equiv \underset{\beta}{\overset{\gamma}{\sim}} f(x_\gamma, y_\beta)$$

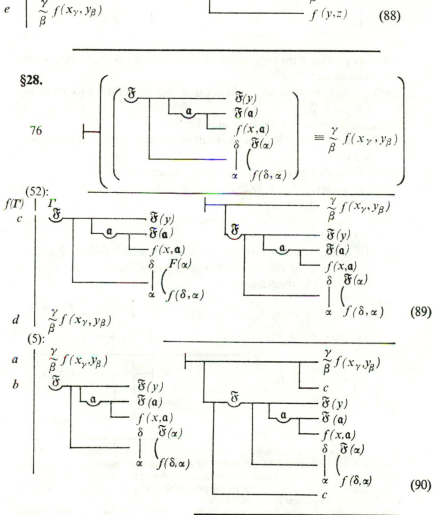

$f(\Gamma)$ (52): Γ
c

d $\underset{\beta}{\overset{\gamma}{\sim}} f(x_\gamma, y_\beta)$

(89)

(5):
a $\underset{\beta}{\overset{\gamma}{\sim}} f(x_\gamma, y_\beta)$
b

(90)

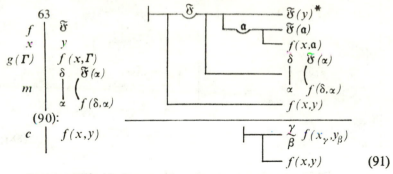

$$
\begin{array}{c|c}
63 & \\
f & \mathfrak{F} \\
x & y \\
g(\varGamma) & f(x,\varGamma) \\
 & \delta \quad \mathfrak{F}(\alpha) \\
m & \Big| \; \Big(\\
 & \alpha \quad f(\delta,\alpha) \\
(90): & \\
c & f(x,y)
\end{array}
$$

(91)

Let us give here the derivation of proposition (91) in words. From the proposition:

(α) "Every result of an application of the procedure f to x has the property $\mathfrak{F}$,"

it can be inferred, whatever $\mathfrak{F}$ may be, that

y has the property $\mathfrak{F}$ if y is a result of an application of the procedure f to x.[4]

Thus, it can also be inferred from proposition (α) and the proposition that the property $\mathfrak{F}$ is hereditary in the f-sequence, whatever $\mathfrak{F}$ may be, that

y has the property $\mathfrak{F}$ if y is a result of an application of the procedure f to x.[4]

Therefore, according to (90) the proposition which follows holds:

Every result of an application of a procedure f to an object x follows this x in the f-sequence.

91

(53):

$$
\begin{array}{c|c}
f(A) & \\
 & \\
d & x \\
c & z
\end{array}
$$

(92)

---

* With respect to the concavity with $\mathfrak{F}$ see §11. [Frege is referring here to his discussion of confinement of generality to a consequent. Note that the present application of such a procedure is second-order. Van Heijenoort (in the Editor's Introduction to F7(*b*)) is in error in supposing that any paradox can arise from the deductive procedure Frege uses here.]

[4 In place of the two occurrences of this clause, Frege had two occurrences

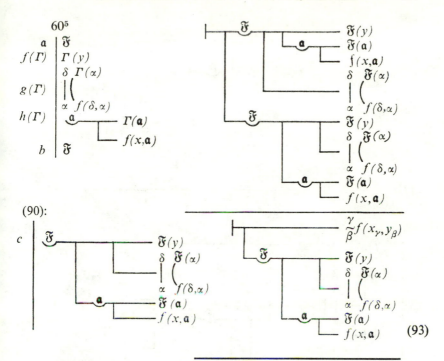

(93)

of the clause, "every result of an application of the procedure f to x has the property $\mathfrak{F}$"; but this makes the derivation in words unintelligible. On the assumption that the original was a typographical error, the appropriate changes are here included in the text.]

[5 Similar to the derivation of 77, that of 93 requires a principle (call it 60′) involving quantification over *functions*. The principle in question would be:

60′

$$
\begin{array}{l}
M_\beta\ f\ (\beta)\\
N_\beta\ f\ (\beta)\\
\Omega_\beta\ f\ (\beta)\\
M_\beta\ \mathfrak{f}\ (\beta)\\
N_\beta\ \mathfrak{f}\ (\beta)\\
\Omega_\beta\ \mathfrak{f}\ (\beta)
\end{array}
$$

The substitutions in this case would run as follows:

$\mathfrak{f}$	$M_\beta\ \Gamma(\beta)$	$N_\beta\ \Gamma(\beta)$	$\Omega_\beta\ \Gamma(\beta)$	f
$\mathfrak{F}$	$\Gamma(y)$	$\delta\ \Gamma(\alpha),\ \alpha\ f(\delta.\alpha)$	$\Gamma(a),\ f(x,a)$	$\mathfrak{F}$

(See above, §27, footnote 2.) Frege also uses a second-order confinement principle here.]

93
$y \mid z$

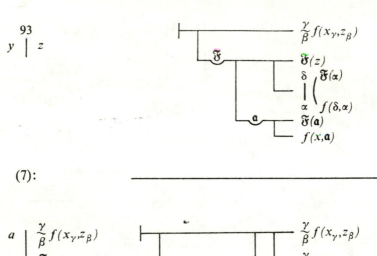

(7): ─────────────────────────────────────

$a \mid \dfrac{\gamma}{\beta} f(x_\gamma, z_\beta)$

$b \mid \mathfrak{F}$

$c \mid \dfrac{\gamma}{\beta} f(x_\gamma, y_\beta)$

$d \mid f(y,z)$

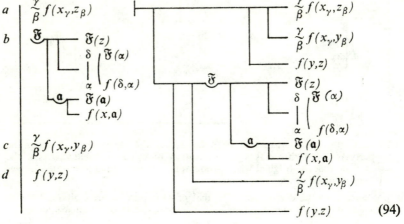

(94)

(88):: ─────────────────────────────────────

$F \mid \mathfrak{F}$

$\dfrac{\gamma}{\beta} f(x_\gamma, z_\beta)$

$\dfrac{\gamma}{\beta} f(x_\gamma, y_\beta)$

$f(y,z)$ (95)

(8): ─────────────────────────────────────

a | $\frac{\gamma}{\beta} f(x_\gamma, z_\beta)$

b | $\frac{\gamma}{\beta} f(x_\gamma, y_\beta)$

d | $f(y,z)$

$$\frac{\gamma}{\beta} f(x_\gamma, z_\beta)$$
$$f(y,z)$$
$$\frac{\gamma}{\beta} f(x_\gamma, y_\beta) \tag{96}$$

Every result of an application of the procedure f to an object which follows x in the f-sequence, follows x in the f-sequence.

96
z | $\mathfrak{a}$
y | $\mathfrak{d}$

$$\frac{\gamma}{\beta} f(x_\gamma, \mathfrak{a}_\beta)$$
$$f(\mathfrak{d}, \mathfrak{a})$$
$$\frac{\gamma}{\beta} f(x_\gamma, \mathfrak{d}_\beta)$$

(75):
$F(\Gamma)$ | $\frac{\gamma}{\beta} f(x_\gamma, \Gamma_\beta)$

$$\delta \left| \begin{array}{l} \frac{\gamma}{\beta} f(x_\gamma, \alpha_\beta) \\ f(\delta, \alpha) \end{array} \right. \tag{97}$$
α

The property of following x in the f-sequence is hereditary in the f-sequence.

97

$$\delta \left| \begin{array}{l} \frac{\gamma}{\beta} f(x_\gamma, \alpha_\beta) \\ f(\delta, \alpha) \end{array} \right.$$
α

(84):
$F(\Gamma)$ | $\frac{\gamma}{\beta} f(x_\gamma, \Gamma_\beta)$

x | y
y | z

$$\frac{\gamma}{\beta} f(x_\gamma, z_\beta)$$
$$\frac{\gamma}{\beta} f(y_\gamma, z_\beta)$$
$$\frac{\gamma}{\beta} f(x_\gamma, y_\beta) \tag{98}$$

If y follows x in the f-sequence, and if z follows y in the f-sequence; then z follows x in the f-sequence.

§29.

$$\vdash\left(\left(\begin{array}{c} \quad (z \equiv x) \\ \dfrac{\gamma}{\beta}\, f(x_\gamma, z_\beta) \end{array}\right) \equiv \dfrac{\gamma}{\widetilde{\beta}} f(x_\gamma, z_\beta)\right) \tag{99}$$

I refer [the reader] here to what has been said with respect to formulas (69) and (76) about the introduction of new symbols.

$$\frac{\gamma}{\widetilde{\beta}} f(x_\gamma, z_\beta)$$

may be translated: "z belongs to the f-sequence beginning with x", or "x belongs to the f-sequence ending with z." In words, then, (99) reads this way:

If z is identical with x or follows x in the f-sequence, then I say:

"z belongs to the f-sequence beginning with x"; or, "x belongs to the f-sequence ending with z."

99     $$\vdash\left(\left(\begin{array}{c} \quad (z \equiv x) \\ \dfrac{\gamma}{\beta} f(x_\gamma, z_\beta) \end{array}\right) \equiv \dfrac{\gamma}{\widetilde{\beta}} f(x_\gamma, z_\beta)\right)$$

(57): _____

$$\begin{array}{c|c} f(\Gamma) & \Gamma \\ c & \begin{array}{c} (z \equiv x) \\ \dfrac{\gamma}{\widetilde{\beta}} f(x_\gamma, z_\beta) \end{array} \\ d & \dfrac{\gamma}{\widetilde{\beta}} f(x_\gamma \cdot z_\beta) \end{array} \qquad \begin{array}{c} (z \equiv x) \\ \dfrac{\gamma}{\widetilde{\beta}} f(x_\gamma, z_\beta) \\ \dfrac{\gamma}{\widetilde{\beta}} f(x_\gamma, z_\beta) \end{array} \tag{100}$$

(48): _____

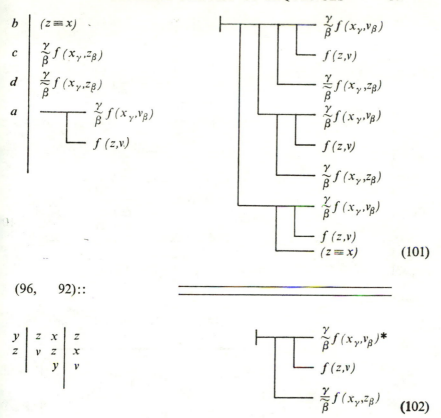

$$b \quad (z \equiv x)$$
$$c \quad \underset{\beta}{\overset{\gamma}{}} f(x_\gamma, z_\beta)$$
$$d \quad \underset{\beta}{\overset{\gamma}{\approx}} f(x_\gamma, z_\beta)$$
$$a \qquad \underset{\beta}{\overset{\gamma}{}} f(x_\gamma, v_\beta)$$
$$f(z,v)$$

$$\underset{\beta}{\overset{\gamma}{}} f(x_\gamma, v_\beta)$$
$$f(z,v)$$
$$\underset{\beta}{\overset{\gamma}{\approx}} f(x_\gamma, z_\beta)$$
$$\underset{\beta}{\overset{\gamma}{}} f(x_\gamma, v_\beta)$$
$$f(z,v)$$
$$\underset{\beta}{\overset{\gamma}{}} f(x_\gamma, z_\beta)$$
$$\underset{\beta}{\overset{\gamma}{}} f(x_\gamma, v_\beta)$$
$$f(z,v)$$
$$(z \equiv x) \tag{101}$$

(96, 92)::

y	z	x	z
z	v	z	x
		y	v

$$\underset{\beta}{\overset{\gamma}{}} f(x_\gamma, v_\beta)*$$
$$f(z,v)$$
$$\underset{\beta}{\overset{\gamma}{}} f(x_\gamma, z_\beta) \tag{102}$$

Let us give here the derivation of (102) in words.

If z is identical with x, then according to (92), every result of an application of the procedure f to z follows x in the f-sequence. If z follows x in the f-sequence, then according to (96), every result of an application of the procedure f to z follows x in the f-sequence.

From these two propositions it follows, according to (101):

If z belongs to the f-sequence beginning with x, then every result of an application of the procedure f to z follows x in the f-sequence.

* With regard to this last inference, see §6.

100

$$\begin{array}{l} (z \equiv x) \\ \dfrac{\gamma}{\beta}\, f(x_\gamma, z_\beta) \\ \dfrac{\gamma}{\overline{\overline{\beta}}}\, f(x_\gamma, z_\beta) \end{array}$$

(19):

b	$(z \equiv x)$
c	$\dfrac{\gamma}{\beta}\, f(x_\gamma, z_\beta)$
d	$\dfrac{\gamma}{\overline{\overline{\beta}}}\, f(x_\gamma, z_\beta)$
a	$(x \equiv z)$

$$\begin{array}{l} (x \equiv z) \\ \dfrac{\gamma}{\beta}\, f(x_\gamma, z_\beta) \\ \dfrac{\gamma}{\beta}\, f(x_\gamma, z_\beta) \\ (x \equiv z) \\ (z \equiv x) \end{array} \qquad (10$$

(55)::

d	x
c	z

$$\begin{array}{l} (x \equiv z) \\ \dfrac{\gamma}{\beta}\, f(x_\gamma, z_\beta) \\ \dfrac{\gamma}{\overline{\overline{\beta}}}\, f(x_\gamma, z_\beta) \end{array} \qquad (10$$

§30.

99

$$\left(\left(\begin{array}{l} (z \equiv x) \\ \dfrac{\gamma}{\beta}\, f(x_\gamma, z_\beta) \end{array} \right) \equiv \dfrac{\gamma}{\overline{\overline{\beta}}}\, f(x_\gamma, z_\beta) \right)$$

(52):

$f(\Gamma)$	Γ
c	$\begin{array}{l} (z \equiv x) \\ \dfrac{\gamma}{\beta}\, f(x_\gamma, z_\beta) \end{array}$
d	$\dfrac{\gamma}{\overline{\overline{\beta}}}\, f(x_\gamma, z_\beta)$

$$\begin{array}{l} \dfrac{\gamma}{\overline{\overline{\beta}}}\, f(x_\gamma, z_\beta) \\ (z \equiv x) \\ \dfrac{\gamma}{\beta}\, f(x_\gamma, z_\beta) \end{array} \qquad (10$$

(37):

a	$\dfrac{\gamma}{\overline{\overline{\beta}}}\, f(x_\gamma, z_\beta)$
b	$(z \equiv x)$
c	$\dfrac{\gamma}{\beta}\, f(x_\gamma, z_\beta)$

$$\begin{array}{l} \dfrac{\gamma}{\overline{\overline{\beta}}}\, f(x_\gamma, z_\beta) \\ \dfrac{\gamma}{\overline{\overline{\beta}}}\, f(x_\gamma, z_\beta) \end{array} \qquad (10$$

Whatever follows x in the f-sequence belongs to the f-sequence beginning with x.

106

x	z
z	v

$$\frac{\gamma}{\overset{\approx}{\beta}} f(z_\gamma, v_\beta)$$

$$\frac{\gamma}{\overset{\approx}{\beta}} f(z_\gamma, v_\beta)$$

(7):

a	$\dfrac{\gamma}{\overset{\approx}{\beta}} f(z_\gamma, v_\beta)$
b	$\dfrac{\gamma}{\beta} f(z_\gamma, v_\beta)$
c	$f(y,v)$
d	$\dfrac{\gamma}{\overset{\approx}{\beta}} f(z_\gamma, y_\beta)$

$$\frac{\gamma}{\overset{\approx}{\beta}} f(z_\gamma, v_\beta)$$

$$f(y,v)$$

$$\frac{\gamma}{\beta} f(z_\gamma, y_\beta)$$

$$\frac{\gamma}{\beta} f(z_\gamma, v_\beta)$$

$$f(y,v)$$

$$\frac{\gamma}{\overset{\approx}{\beta}} f(z_\gamma, y_\beta)$$ (107)

(102)::

x	z
z	y

$$\frac{\gamma}{\overset{\approx}{\beta}} f(z_\gamma, v_\beta)$$

$$f(y,v)$$

$$\frac{\gamma}{\overset{\approx}{\beta}} f(z_\gamma, y_\beta)$$ (108)

Let us give here the derivation of (108) in words.

If y belongs to the f-sequence beginning with z, then according to (102), every result of an application of the procedure f to y follows z in the f-sequence. Then according to (106), every result of an application of the procedure f to y belongs to the f-sequence beginning with z.

Therefore:

If y belongs to the f-sequence beginning with z, then every result of an application of the procedure f to y belongs to the f-sequence beginning with z.

$$108$$

$$
\begin{array}{c|c}
v & \mathfrak{a} \\
z & x \\
y & \mathfrak{d}
\end{array}
$$

(75):

$$F(\Gamma) \quad\bigg|\quad \frac{\gamma}{\beta} f(x_\gamma \Gamma_\beta)$$

$$
\vdash \!\!-\!\!\!\overset{\mathfrak{d}}{\underset{}{}}\!\!-\!\!\!\overset{\mathfrak{a}}{\underset{}{}}
\begin{cases}
\frac{\gamma}{\beta} f(x_\gamma, \mathfrak{a}_\beta) \\
f(\mathfrak{d}, \mathfrak{a}) \\
\frac{\gamma}{\beta} f(x_\gamma, \mathfrak{d}_\beta)
\end{cases}
$$

$$
\vdash \!\!-\!\! \overset{\delta}{\underset{\alpha}{|}} \left(\begin{array}{l} \frac{\gamma}{\beta} f(x_\gamma, \alpha_\beta) \\ f(\delta, \alpha) \end{array} \right. \tag{109}
$$

The property of belonging to the f-sequence beginning with x is hereditary in the f-sequence.

$$109$$

$$
\vdash \!\!-\!\! \overset{\delta}{\underset{\alpha}{|}} \left(\begin{array}{l} \frac{\gamma}{\beta} f(x_\gamma, \alpha_\beta) \\ f(\delta, \alpha) \end{array} \right.
$$

(78):

$$
\begin{array}{c|c}
F(\Gamma) & \frac{\gamma}{\beta} f(x_\gamma, \Gamma_\beta) \\
x & y \\
y & m
\end{array}
$$

$$
\vdash \begin{cases}
\frac{\gamma}{\beta} f(x_\gamma, m_\beta) \\
\frac{\gamma}{\beta} f(y_\gamma, m_\beta) \\
\!\!-\!\!\overset{\mathfrak{a}}{}\begin{cases}\frac{\gamma}{\beta} f(x_\gamma, \mathfrak{a}_\beta) \\ f(y, \mathfrak{a})\end{cases}
\end{cases} \tag{110}
$$

$$108$$

$$
\vdash \begin{cases}
\frac{\gamma}{\beta} f(z_\gamma, v_\beta) \\
f(y, v) \\
\frac{\gamma}{\beta} f(z_\gamma, y_\beta)
\end{cases}
$$

(25):

$$
\begin{array}{c|l}
a & \frac{\gamma}{\beta} f(z_\gamma, v_\beta) \\
c & f(y, v) \\
d & \frac{\gamma}{\beta} f(z_\gamma, y_\beta) \\
b & \!-\!\!\!\top\frac{\gamma}{\beta} f(v_\gamma, z_\beta)
\end{array}
$$

$$
\vdash \begin{cases}
\frac{\gamma}{\beta} f(z_\gamma, v_\beta) \\
\top \frac{\gamma}{\beta} f(v_\gamma, z_\beta) \\
f(y, v) \\
\frac{\gamma}{\beta} f(z_\gamma, y_\beta)
\end{cases} \tag{111}
$$

The following is the derivation of (111) in words:

> If y belongs to the f-sequence beginning with z, then according to (108), every result of an application of the procedure f to y belongs to the f-sequence beginning with z.

> Therefore, every result of an application of the procedure f to y belongs to the f-sequence beginning with z, or precedes z in the f-sequence.

Thus:

> *If y belongs to the f-sequence beginning with z, then every result of an application of the procedure f to y belongs to the f-sequence beginning with z, or precedes z in the f-sequence.*

105

$$\frac{\gamma}{\beta} f(x_\gamma, z_\beta)$$

$$(z \equiv x)$$

$$\frac{\gamma}{\beta} f(x_\gamma, z_\beta)$$

(11):

a $\frac{\gamma}{\beta} f(x_\gamma, z_\beta)$

b $(z \equiv x)$

c $\frac{\gamma}{\beta} f(x_\gamma, z_\beta)$

$$\frac{\gamma}{\beta} f(x_\gamma, z_\beta)$$

$$(z \equiv x) \qquad (112)$$

(7):

a $\frac{\gamma}{\beta} f(x_\gamma, z_\beta)$

b $(z \equiv x)$

c $\frac{\gamma}{\beta} f(z_\gamma, x_\beta)$

d $\frac{\gamma}{\beta} f(z_\gamma, x_\beta)$

$$\frac{\gamma}{\beta} f(x_\gamma, z_\beta)$$

$$\frac{\gamma}{\beta} f(z_\gamma, x_\beta)$$

$$\frac{\gamma}{\beta} f(z_\gamma, x_\beta)$$

$$(z \equiv x)$$

$$\frac{\gamma}{\beta} f(z_\gamma, x_\beta)$$

$$\frac{\gamma}{\beta} f(z_\gamma, x_\beta) \qquad (113)$$

(104)::

$$
\begin{array}{c|c}
x & z \\
z & x
\end{array}
$$

$$
\begin{array}{l}
\overset{\gamma}{\underset{\beta}{\cdot}}f(x_\gamma,z_\beta) \\[4pt]
\overset{\gamma}{\underset{\beta}{\cdot}}f(z_\gamma,x_\beta) \\[4pt]
\overset{\gamma}{\underset{\beta}{\cdot}}f(z_\gamma,x_\beta)
\end{array}
\qquad (114)
$$

The following is the derivation of this formula in words:

Let x belong to the f-sequence beginning with z.

Then, according to (104), z is identical with x; or else x follows z in the f-sequence.

If z is identical with x, then according to (112), z belongs to the f-sequence beginning with x.

From the last two propositions it follows that z belongs to the f-sequence beginning with x, or x follows z in the f-sequence.

Therefore:

If x belongs to the f-sequence beginning with z, then z belongs to the f-sequence beginning with x, or x follows z in the f-sequence.

§31.

$$
\Vdash\left(\left(\begin{array}{l}
\underset{e}{\quad}\underset{b}{\quad}\underset{a}{\quad}(a\equiv e) \\
f(b,a) \\
f(b,e)
\end{array}\right) \;\equiv\; \overset{\delta}{\underset{\epsilon}{I}}f(\delta,\epsilon)\right)^{*} \qquad (115)
$$

I translate $\quad\overset{\delta}{\underset{\epsilon}{I}}f(\delta,\epsilon)$

by "the circumstance that the procedure f is many-one {*eindeutig*}".[6] (115), then, can be rendered this way:

* See §24.
[6 Here I follow Furth in F50. Bauer–Mengelberg uses "single valued".]

If it can be inferred from the circumstance that ε is a result of an application of the procedure f to δ, whatever δ may be, that every result of an application of the procedure f to δ is identical with ε,

then I say:

"*f is a many-one procedure.*"

115

$$\vdash\!\left[\left[\underset{f(\mathfrak{d},\mathfrak{a})}{\overset{(\mathfrak{a}\equiv\mathfrak{e})}{\underset{f(\mathfrak{d},\mathfrak{e})}{\overbrace{\;\mathfrak{e}\;-\;\mathfrak{d}\;-\;\mathfrak{a}}}}}\right] \equiv \overset{\delta}{\underset{\epsilon}{\mathrm{I}}} f(\delta,\epsilon)\right]$$

(68):
$$f(\Gamma)\;\Big|\;\begin{array}{c}\overset{(\mathfrak{a}\equiv\Gamma)}{\underset{f(\mathfrak{d},\Gamma)}{\overbrace{\mathfrak{d}-\mathfrak{a}}}}\\[2mm] b\;\;\overset{\delta}{\underset{\epsilon}{\mathrm{I}}}f(\delta,\epsilon)\\ c\;\;x\\ a\;\;e\end{array}$$

$$\vdash\;\overset{(\mathfrak{a}\equiv x)}{\underset{f(\mathfrak{d},x)}{\overbrace{\mathfrak{d}-\mathfrak{a}}}}\;-\;\overset{\delta}{\underset{\epsilon}{\mathrm{I}}}f(\delta,\epsilon)$$ (116)

(9):
$$b\;\;\begin{array}{c}\overset{(\mathfrak{a}\equiv x)}{\underset{f(\mathfrak{d},x)}{\overbrace{\mathfrak{d}-\mathfrak{a}}}}\\ c\;\;\overset{\delta}{\underset{\epsilon}{\mathrm{I}}}f(\delta,\epsilon)\\ a\;\;\overset{(\mathfrak{a}\equiv x)}{\underset{f(y,x)}{\overbrace{\mathfrak{a}}}}\end{array}$$

$$\vdash\begin{array}{c}\overset{(\mathfrak{a}\equiv x)}{\underset{f(y,x)}{\overbrace{\mathfrak{a}}}}\;\overset{\delta}{\underset{\epsilon}{\mathrm{I}}}f(\delta,\epsilon)\\[2mm]\overset{(\mathfrak{a}\equiv x)}{\underset{f(y,x)}{\overbrace{\mathfrak{a}}}}\\[2mm]\overset{(\mathfrak{a}\equiv x)}{\underset{f(\mathfrak{d},x)}{\overbrace{\mathfrak{d}-\mathfrak{a}}}}\end{array}$$ (117)

(58)::
$$\begin{array}{c|c}a & \mathfrak{d}\\ f(\Gamma) & \overset{(\mathfrak{a}\equiv x)}{\underset{f(\Gamma,x)}{\overbrace{\mathfrak{a}}}}\\ c & y\end{array}$$

$$\vdash\begin{array}{c}\overset{(\mathfrak{a}\equiv x)}{\underset{f(y,x)}{\overbrace{\mathfrak{a}}}}\\ \overset{\delta}{\underset{\epsilon}{\mathrm{I}}}f(\delta,\epsilon)\end{array}$$ (118)

(19):

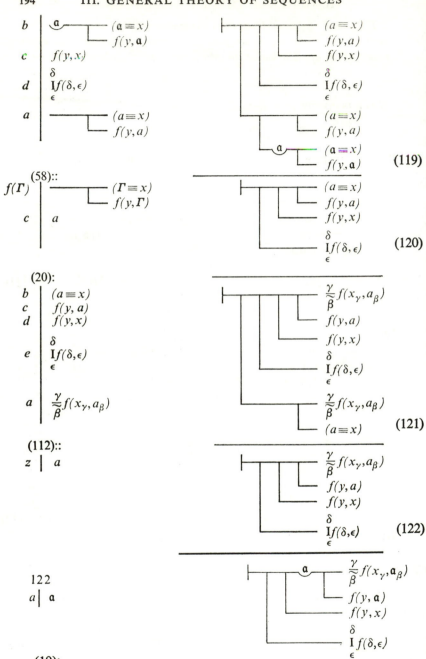

b $\mathfrak{a}$ $(\mathfrak{a} \equiv x)$
        $f(y, \mathfrak{a})$

c $f(y, x)$

d $\begin{matrix}\delta\\ \mathrm{I}f(\delta, \epsilon)\\ \epsilon\end{matrix}$

a $(a \equiv x)$
        $f(y, a)$

(119)

$f(\Gamma)$ (58)::
     $(\Gamma \equiv x)$
     $f(y, \Gamma)$

c a

(120)

(20):

b $(a \equiv x)$
c $f(y, a)$
d $f(y, x)$

e $\begin{matrix}\delta\\ \mathrm{I}f(\delta, \epsilon)\\ \epsilon\end{matrix}$

a $\dfrac{\gamma}{\beta} f(x_\gamma, a_\beta)$

(121)

(112)::

z a

(122)

122

a $\mathfrak{a}$

(19):

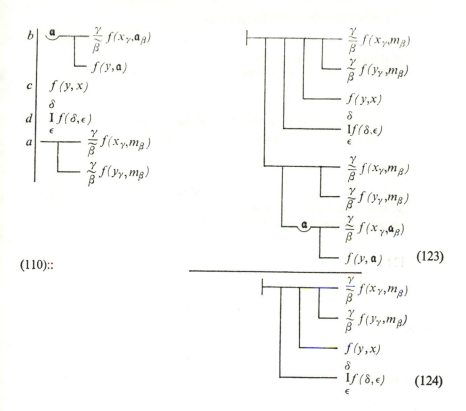

(110)::

(123)

(124)

Let us give here the derivation of formulas (122) and (124) in words.

Let x be a result of an application of the many-one procedure f to y.

Then, according to (120), every result of an application of the procedure f to y is identical with x.

Therefore, according to (112), every result of an application of the procedure f to y belongs to the f-sequence beginning with x.

Thus:

If x is a result of an application of the many-one procedure f to y, then every result of an application of the procedure f to y belongs to the f-sequence beginning with x. (Formula 122.)

Let m follow y in the f-sequence.

Then from (110) it follows that if every result of an application of the procedure f to y belongs to the f-sequence beginning with x, then m belongs to the f-sequence beginning with x.

This together with (122) shows that

if x is a result of an application of the many-one procedure f to y, m belongs to the f-sequence beginning with x.

Thus:

If x is a result of an application of the many-one procedure f to y, and if m follows y in the f-sequence, then m belongs to the f-sequence beginning with x. (Formula 124.)

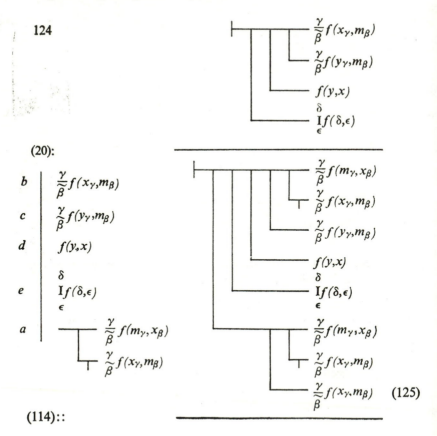

124

(20):

$$b \quad \frac{\gamma}{\beta} f(x_\gamma, m_\beta)$$

$$c \quad \frac{\gamma}{\beta} f(y_\gamma, m_\beta)$$

$$d \quad f(y, x)$$

$$e \quad \underset{\epsilon}{\overset{\delta}{I}} f(\delta, \epsilon)$$

$$a$$

(114)::

(125)

$$
\begin{array}{c|c}
x & m \\
z & x
\end{array}
$$

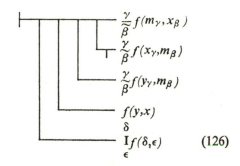

$$\underset{\beta}{\overset{\gamma}{\equiv}} f(m_\gamma, x_\beta)$$

$$\underset{\beta}{\overset{\gamma}{\sim}} f(x_\gamma, m_\beta)$$

$$\underset{\beta}{\overset{\gamma}{\sim}} f(y_\gamma, m_\beta)$$

$$f(y, x)$$

$$\underset{\epsilon}{\overset{\delta}{I}} f(\delta, \epsilon) \qquad (126)$$

The following is the derivation of this formula in words:

Let x be a result of an application of the many-one procedure f to y.

Let m follow y in the f-sequence.

Then, according to (124), m belongs to the f-sequence beginning with x.

Consequently, according to (114), x belongs to the f-sequence beginning with m; or m follows x in the f-sequence.

We can also express this:

x belongs to the f-sequence beginning with m, or precedes m in the f-sequence.

Therefore:

If m follows y in the f-sequence, and if the procedure f is many-one, then every result of an application of the procedure f to y belongs to the f-sequence beginning with m or precedes m in the f-sequence.

126

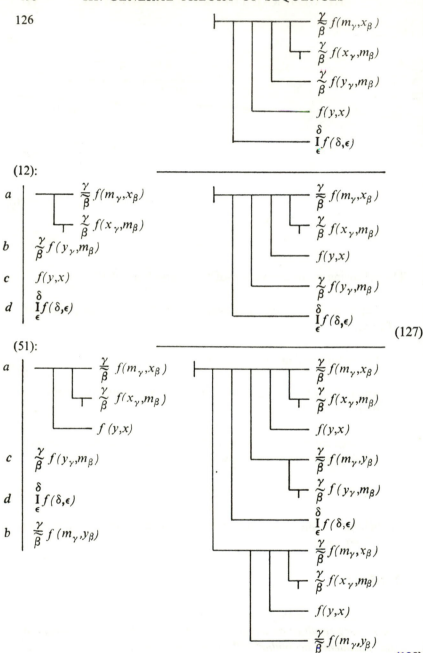

(12):

(51):

(111)::

(127)

(128)

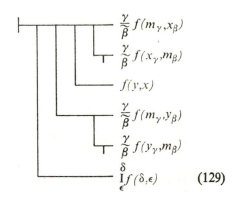

$$\begin{array}{l} \dfrac{\gamma}{\beta}\, f(m_\gamma , x_\beta) \\[4pt] \dfrac{\gamma}{\beta}\, f(x_\gamma , m_\beta) \\[4pt] f(y,x) \\[4pt] \dfrac{\gamma}{\beta}\, f(m_\gamma , y_\beta) \\[4pt] \dfrac{\gamma}{\beta}\, f(y_\gamma , m_\beta) \\[4pt] \underset{\epsilon}{\overset{\delta}{\mathrm{I}}}\, f(\delta , \epsilon) \end{array}$$ (129)

In words, (129) reads this way:

> *If the procedure f is many-one, and if y belongs to the f-sequence beginning with m, or precedes m in the f-sequence; then every result of an application of the procedure f to y belongs to the f-sequence beginning with m, or precedes m in the f-sequence.*

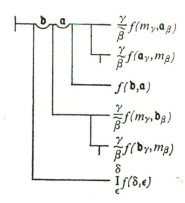

$$\begin{array}{l} \dfrac{\gamma}{\beta} f(m_\gamma , \mathfrak{a}_\beta) \\[4pt] \dfrac{\gamma}{\beta} f(\mathfrak{a}_\gamma , m_\beta) \\[4pt] f(\mathfrak{b},\mathfrak{a}) \\[4pt] \dfrac{\gamma}{\beta} f(m_\gamma , \mathfrak{b}_\beta) \\[4pt] \dfrac{\gamma}{\beta} f(\mathfrak{b}_\gamma , m_\beta) \\[4pt] \underset{\epsilon}{\overset{\delta}{\mathrm{I}}}\, f(\delta , \epsilon) \end{array}$$

(9):   ———————————————

(75)::

$$(130$$

$$(131$$

In words, (131) reads this way:

If the procedure f is many-one, then the property of belonging to the f-sequence beginning with m, or preceding m in the f-sequence is hereditary in the f-sequence.

131

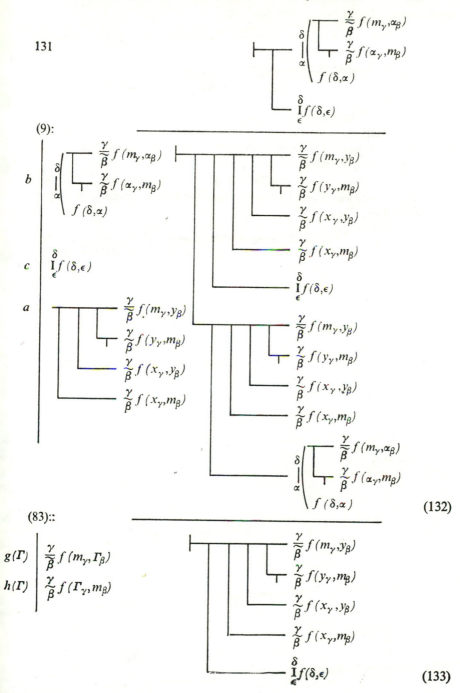

(9):

b

c

a

(83)::

$g(\Gamma)$

$h(\Gamma)$

(132)

(133)

In words, this proposition reads this way:

> *If the procedure f is many-one, and if m and y follow x in the f-sequence; then y belongs to the f-sequence beginning with m, or precedes m in the f-sequence.*

I provide here a table that shows where use is made of one formula in the derivation of another. It can be used to look up the ways in which a formula has been employed. We can also learn from it how frequently a formula has been used.

The formula whose number stands to the right of the [thin] line was derived with the help of the formula whose number stands to the left [of the thin line].[7]

[7 Instead of using dots, Frege repeated the numerals when a formula was used more than once. Dots are used here to make the table easier to read.]

1	3	.	62	.	21	47	48	.	75	100	101
.	5	.	66	.	71	.	49	70	71		103
.	11	.	74	.	86	48	101	71	72	101	102
.	24	.	84	.	103	49	50	72	73	102	108
.	26	.	96	.	119	50	51	.	74	103	104
.	27	9	10	.	123	51	128	73	87	104	114
.	36	.	11	20	121	52	53	74	81	105	106
2	3	.	19	.	125	.	57	75	97		112
.	4	.	21	21	44	.	75	.	109	106	107
.	39	.	37	.	47	.	89	.	131	107	108
.	73	.	56	22	23	.	105	76	77	108	109
.	79	.	61	23	48	53	55	.	89		111
3	4	.	117	24	25	.	92	77	78	109	110
4	5	.	130	.	63	54	55	.	85	110	124
5	6	.	132	25	111	55	56	78	79	111	129
.	7	10	30	26	27	.	104	.	110	112	113
.	9	11	112	27	42	56	57	79	80		122
.	12	12	13	28	29	57	68	80	81	113	114
.	14	.	15	.	33	.	100	81	82	114	126
.	16	.	16	29	30	58	59	.	84	115	116
.	18	.	24	30	59	.	60	82	83	116	117
.	22	.	35	31	32	.	61	83	133	117	118
.	25	.	49	32	33	.	62	84	98	118	119
.	29	.	60	33	34	.	67	85	86	119	120
.	34	.	85	.	46	.	72	86	87	120	121
.	45	.	127	34	35	.	118	87	88	121	122
.	80	13	14	.	36	.	120	88	95	122	123
.	90	14	15	35	40	59	—	89	90	123	124
6	7	15	88	36	37	60	93	90	91	124	125
7	32	16	17	.	38	61	65	.	93	125	126
.	67	.	18	.	83	62	63	91	92	126	127
.	94	.	22	37	106	.	64	92	102	127	128
.	107	17	50	38	39	63	91	93	94	128	129
.	113	.	78	39	40	64	65	94	95	129	130
8	9	18	19	40	43	65	66	95	96	130	131
.	10	.	20	41	42	66	—	96	97	131	132
.	12	.	23	42	43	67	68	.	102	132	133
.	17	.	51	43	44	68	70	97	98	133	—
.	26	.	64	44	45	.	77	98	100		
.	38	.	82	45	46	.	116	99	105		
.	53	19	20	46	47	69	70	.			

APPLICATIONS OF THE "CONCEPTUAL NOTATION"[1]

IN the following [essay] several examples are to be given of how arithmetical and geometric relations can be expressed with the help of my "conceptual notation".

It should be emphasized here that the symbols employed have not been invented *especially* for each particular case, but have such general meanings that they suffice for rendering very diverse relations.

Let $$AB \cong CD$$

denote the congruence of the two pairs of points AB and CD.

Then we can express the circumstance that the point D lies in the straight line determined by points B and C this way:

$$\mathfrak{A} \vdash\!\!\!\begin{array}{l} (D \equiv \mathfrak{A}) \\ (BD \cong B\mathfrak{A}) \\ (CD \cong C\mathfrak{A}) \end{array}$$

The affirmation of the content of this formula would mean: From the congruence of the pairs of points BD and $B\mathfrak{A}$ and from the congruence of the pairs of points CD and $C\mathfrak{A}$, whatever $\mathfrak{A}$ may be, it can be deduced that $\mathfrak{A}$ is the same point as D;

or,

We can find absolutely no point other than D which forms pairs of points with B and C that would be congruent with BD and CD respectively.

But this is the case when and only when D lies in the straight line determined by B and C.

In a similar way, we can express [the fact] that a point lies in the plane determined by three points.

By $$\frac{\gamma}{\beta} f(x_\gamma, y_\beta)$$

I signify that y belongs to the f-sequence beginning with x. According to the more general conception of function {*allgemeinerer Funktions-*

[1 This is F8, delivered before the *Jenaische Gesellschaft für Medicin und Naturwissenschaft* on 24 January 1879.]

begriff} that I took as a basis [for my "conceptual notation"], we can regard

$$u+1 = v$$

as a function of u and v and can therefore view it as a particular case of $f(u, v)$. Accordingly

$$\frac{\gamma}{\beta}\,(0_\gamma+1 = a_\beta)$$

means that a belongs to the sequence which begins with 0 and arises from a constant increase by 1, namely

$$0, 1, 2, 3, 4\dots\,.$$

Hence, a is a positive whole number.

$$\frac{\gamma}{\beta}\,(0_\gamma+1 = a_\beta)$$

is therefore the expression for the circumstance that a is a positive whole number. Similarly,

$$\frac{\gamma}{\beta}\,(0_\gamma+d = a_\beta)$$

means that a belongs to the sequence

$$0, d, 2d, 3d\dots$$

and thus is a multiple of d.

says that a is divisible by none of the numbers

$$2, 3, 4,\dots$$

except by itself. If we add further that a is a positive whole number, then we obtain in

$$\frac{\gamma}{\beta}(0_\gamma + \mathfrak{d} = a_\beta)$$

$$\frac{\gamma}{\beta}(2_\gamma + 1 = \mathfrak{d}_\beta)$$

$$(\mathfrak{d} \equiv a)$$

$$\frac{\gamma}{\beta}(0_\gamma + 1 = a_\beta)$$

the designation of the circumstance that a is a *prime number*.

It can now be demonstrated how the "conceptual notation" renders the theorem of number theory that each positive whole number can be represented as the sum of four squares.

The equation $\qquad 30 = a^2 + \mathfrak{d}^2 + e^2 + g^2$

does not say

(1) that a, $\mathfrak{d}$, e, g are to be whole numbers,
(2) that there are such numbers.

The first shortcoming is met by

$$(30 = a^2 + \mathfrak{d}^2 + e^2 + g^2)$$

$$\frac{\gamma}{\beta}(0_\gamma + 1 = a_\beta)$$

$$\frac{\gamma}{\beta}(0_\gamma + 1 = \mathfrak{d}_\beta)$$

$$\frac{\gamma}{\beta}(0_\gamma + 1 = e_\beta)$$

$$\frac{\gamma}{\beta}(0_\gamma + 1 = g_\beta)$$

for this denotes the circumstance that 30 is the sum of the squares of a, $\mathfrak{d}$, e, g, and that a, $\mathfrak{d}$, e, g are positive whole numbers.

We must still say that such whole numbers exist. If we omit the negation stroke in front of the whole, then we obtain in

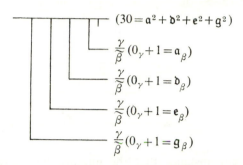

the denial of the circumstance that a, b, e, g are whole numbers which have 30 as the sum of their squares; that is, that at least one of a, b, e, g is not a whole number, or that the sum of their squares is not 30. Now, if we place generalizing symbols {*Allgemeinheitszeichen*} [universal quantifiers] for a, b, e, g before the whole:

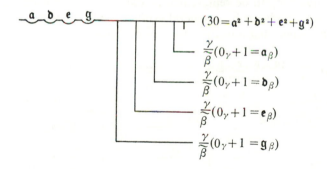

then, in this way, the sense of the formula will be generalized. It now signifies the circumstance that, whatever a, b, e, g may be, in case they are positive whole numbers, the sum of their squares cannot be 30; in other words, that there are not four positive whole numbers the sum of whose squares is 30. Now this is exactly the opposite of what we wish to express. Therefore, if we place the negation stroke before the whole, we then achieve our goal. Thus

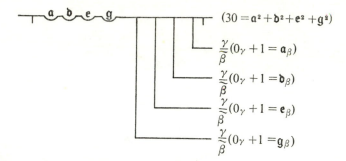

$(30 = a^2 + b^2 + e^2 + g^2)$

$\frac{\gamma}{\beta}(0_\gamma + 1 = a_\beta)$

$\frac{\gamma}{\beta}(0_\gamma + 1 = b_\beta)$

$\frac{\gamma}{\beta}(0_\gamma + 1 = e_\beta)$

$\frac{\gamma}{\beta}(0_\gamma + 1 = g_\beta)$

denotes the circumstance that the number 30 is "representable" {*darstellbar*} as the sum of four squares. Possibility, which lies in the ending "able" {*bar*} of the word "representable", is thus expressed by two denials, which do not simply cancel each other out because one does not follow immediately after the other. The first denial is generalized; and through this we obtain the generality of denial, that is, impossibility. Thereupon, the denial of impossibility yields possibility.

Now, if we wish to express the proposition that each positive whole number can be represented as the sum of four squares, then 30 must be replaced by a general symbol, say a; and the condition must be added that a is a positive whole number:

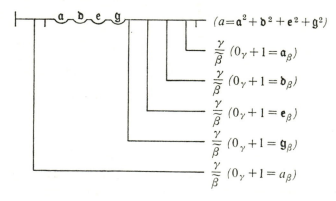

$(a = a^2 + b^2 + e^2 + g^2)$

$\frac{\gamma}{\beta}(0_\gamma + 1 = a_\beta)$

$\frac{\gamma}{\beta}(0_\gamma + 1 = b_\beta)$

$\frac{\gamma}{\beta}(0_\gamma + 1 = e_\beta)$

$\frac{\gamma}{\beta}(0_\gamma + 1 = g_\beta)$

$\frac{\gamma}{\beta}(0_\gamma + 1 = a_\beta)$

The judgement stroke before the whole presents this theorem as an assertion.

APPENDIX I

REVIEWS OF THE *CONCEPTUAL NOTATION* BY FREGE'S CONTEMPORARIES

A. Review of Frege's *Conceptual Notation* by R. Hoppe, *Archiv der Mathematik und Physik*, 1st ser. 63 (1879), Litterarischer Bericht CCLII, pp. 44–5.

The author wishes to rescue mathematical logic from the deficiency of [ordinary] language by replacing concepts and their relations with symbols. The deficiency is especially evident in this: in [ordinary] language the essentially important elements are intermingled with those which serve only [correct] sentence construction—logically unimportant distinctions required by grammar conceal and disguise the essential ones.

[In the present work], thought contents {*Gedankeninhalte*} are symbolized by a letter apiece. The mode in which the thought content is related [to others]—the affirmation and denial, the conditional, the definitive assertion (as opposed to the mere presentation of the thought), and so on—is symbolized by means of strokes. Function-letters serve to indicate substitutivity and to designate argument places that permit substitution.

If we wish to evaluate this undertaking, the peculiar fact is that the execution gives a more favourable impression than the original plan. The title mentions a "pure thought", and the Preface admits pure logic "which, disregarding the particular state of things, is based solely upon the laws on which all knowledge rests". From this it appears at first that the author considers the symbol arrangements he presents valid for the domain of ideas of all of life {*das Gedankenbereich des ganzen Lebens*} and wishes to use the mathematical modes of thought even for these. However, this mistake, inherited from formal logic, remains completely outside the [author's] work and has no influence on it. The author does not proceed with preconceived ideas, but sets to work with the most cautious observation; he does not begin with forms that are empty of content, but even restricts his actual goal to specific regions of mathematics, so that the objective therefore always remains mathematical.

Now we doubt that anything has been gained by the invented formula language itself. To us, the critique of mathematical logic to which the author directed his work seems to be much more valuable. He has learned from this [effort] and in turn taught [others]. During his work it first became clear to him that in a judgement of mathematics the distinction of subject and attribute is useless; for, as he himself explains, when he first started working he held the opposite view. Even though this observation seems obvious, it appears to have been unnoticed by all logicians up to now. Hauber, for example, whose merits in mathematical logic are praised by Günther in his article T. LVI p. 26, nevertheless commits the error of distinguishing subject and predicate. The author characterizes this mistake more generally by pointing out that logic up to now has adhered too closely to [ordinary] language and grammar, a criticism which is supported to a strong degree so far as it characterizes the biased dependence upon language in the thinking of most logicians. The author reveals by his treatment of his subject-matter that he is one of the few for whom thought holds sway over the word.

The critique [of mathematical logic] appears not only in the fundamental views {*Grundsätze*} developed in the beginning, but is also evident in the entire exposition. We shall forgo the particulars. On the whole, the book, as suggestive and pioneering, is worth while.

H.

B. Review of the *Conceptual Notation* by K. Lasswitz, *Jenaer Literaturzeitung*, 6 (1879), pp. 248–9.

It is a long-known complaint that [ordinary] language is a most inadequate [means of] expression of thought; and thus the wish (which already is evident in Leibniz' attempt at a pasigraphy) that thinking be freed from these chains of language asserts itself again and again. But obviously, we need for this purpose an awareness of the proper functioning of the instruments of reasoning {*die eigenthumliche Functionirung des Denkapparates*} which far surpasses the formal logic of old.

Now English logicians, first Boole and then Jevons building upon him, have derived from the language of algebra the purely logical operations holding for concepts in general and have based a conceptual calculus {*Begriffsrechnung*} upon them. In Germany, the works of R. Grassmann and E. Schröder are in this field. The result of these investigations was namely the apprehension of a judgement as an equation with the help of the quantification {*Quantificirung*} of concepts, and the apprehension of deduction as a [sort of] substitution. Certainly, a onesidedness which causes great doubt is present here, since the real nature and formation of concepts in their relation to deducing and judging (which may not be separated from the content) are insufficiently considered.

It is thus gratifying to encounter in the present work an attempt to attack this problem in a different way. The title of the work, to be sure, gives cause for scepticism at first, but a closer examination of the book soon dispels this. When the author calls his "conceptual notation" "a formula language modelled upon that of arithmetic", this refers more to the fundamental ideas of the book, and not to that artificial similarity with algebra which is attained through the inadmissible apprehension of a concept as the sum of its characteristic marks {*Merkmale*}.[1] Nevertheless, it would have been desirable for the author to have gone into more detail about his position regarding these (above mentioned) efforts. Furthermore, calling the "conceptual notation" "a formula language of pure thought" could obviously frighten off those, like the reviewer, who cannot believe in the existence of a pure thought which would be possible without a definite content. It must be said, therefore, that [the apparent difficulty] here is only a matter of a partially unfortunate choice of expression. The author delineates his task so clearly that no doubt can persist about the justification of his project. There are obviously certain groups of concepts whose contents have such a general nature that they can be treated in a way similar to that of general concepts of mathematics. Now the project of [developing] a formula language arising from an investigation into the general concept of sequence (therefore from a mathematical inquiry) should be based only upon such concepts. The author intends that his "conceptual notation" be applied at first only in arithmetic; then perhaps in mechanics and physics; and finally in general wherever a special value must be placed upon the validity of the method of proof {*Beweisführung*}.

The author very aptly explains the relation of the "conceptual notation" to [ordinary] language with a comparison of the microscope and the eye: "The latter, because of the range of its applicability and because of the ease with which it can adapt to the most varied circumstances, has a great superiority over the microscope. Of course, viewed as an optical instrument it reveals many imperfections, which usually remain unnoticed only because of its intimate connection with mental life. But as soon as scientific purposes place strong requirements upon sharpness of resolution, the eye proves to be inadequate. On the other hand, the microscope is perfectly suited for such purposes; but, for this very reason it is useless for all others. Similarly, this "conceptual notation" is devised for particular scientific purposes; and therefore one may not condemn it because it is useless for other purposes."

These general observations should have been considered in more detail to induce those who are discouraged by the difficulty of getting the author's train of thought (and wish to excuse their rejection by [citing] the usual sterility of such efforts) not to shun the toil of reading [the book]. For, also, those who plan at first to make use of the "conceptual notation" itself find in a few pages a series of very penetrating and significant remarks about logical and epistemological concepts. Thus, [for example], the apprehension

[1 For Frege's account of characteristic marks, see F14, §53.]

of the judgement as a unified whole which is independent of the linguistic distinction of subject and predicate is a conclusion which confirms anew the epistemological results already obtained in some other way.

There are interesting investigations [in this book] concerning conditionality, negation (with respect to concepts like "or", "and", and so on) and especially equality of content and the concept of function. We cannot go into details here of the specific form and construction of the "conceptual notation" itself; we can merely draw attention to the applications of it in Chapter III, "Some Topics from a General Theory of Sequences".

This book is small, but carefully thought through. It is obviously the result of long, toilsome work and is highly recommended to all those interested as a valuable contribution to the theory of thinking.

Gotha   K. LASSWITZ

C. Review of Frege's *Conceptual Notation* by C. Th. Michaëlis, *Zeitschrift für Völkerpsychologie und Sprachwissenschaft*, 12 (1880), pp. 232–40.

In Germany, the union of philosophy and mathematics is not new. The Leibnizian–Wolfian philosophy clearly shows in its method and its principles the influence of mathematics. Kant compared the methods of philosophy and mathematics in one of his earliest works and then borrowed sections and ideas from it for his principal work. He owes the best part of his philosophical conceptions to the contemplation of mathematics. In our century, the union of these two sciences is most prominent in Herbart's mathematical psychology and the philosophical speculations about the foundations of mathematics and n-dimensional space. Last year brought us a new, related creation: a "conceptual notation", a "formula language of pure thought modelled upon the formula language of arithmetic", which reveals in form and in name its double origin, and which makes a strange and chilling impression with its long and short, vertical and horizontal strokes; with its concavities and snaky lines; its double colon and function symbols; its German, Greek, and italic large and small letters.

Efforts to assist philosophy with mathematics and *vice versa* have not been equally successful [in the past]; and it would [thus] be understandable if, at first, the reviewer were to approach with a certain mistrust a publication based upon an old idea, but executed in a completely original fashion. The history of philosophy justifies such misgivings. The union between mathematical and philosophical modes of thought and definition is surely not to be excluded {*nicht zu perhorresciren*}; but experience certainly shows that when an effort is made to join the two there is the impending danger that one of the two sciences will suffer from the relationship and, untrue to its proper task, will adopt a false direction.

After a repeated study of Frege's book, however, we can say from the beginning that the diligence, the acuteness and the consistency with which he has elaborated his system deserves admiration. We hope that the author's efforts may have thorough study and wider circulation among the intellectuals; and we also do not doubt that his work will find application within the limits which he himself indicates and will contribute to the improvement or assurance of scientific method. He does not claim to have spoken new truths or advanced quantitative science.

According to remarks in the Preface and also in Part III of his book, Frege happened to invent his "conceptual notation" or "formula language of pure thought" through investigations into judgements of arithmetic and the authority of the laws of pure thought in the domain of arithmetic, and especially through the effort to reduce the concept of "sequence" to that of "logical ordering". The inadequacy of [ordinary] language stood in the way of the strong demand for a "gapless" chain of deduction. The "conceptual notation" is supposed to eliminate this difficulty. It is to render the thought purely; or if this demand is an unattainable ideal for an external means of expression [that is, external to the mind], it should [nevertheless] yield the best possible rendering and limit the discrepancies to the unavoidable and harmless. It should guarantee the validity of a chain of deduction and reveal the structure of that chain to the inquiring eye.

The "conceptual notation" has only a limited scope. Just as the microscope does not make the eye dispensable, and is itself the more dispensable of the two in ordinary life, so the "conceptual notation" does not make [ordinary] language and usual scientific description superfluous. It was devised merely for particular scientific purposes. "If it fulfils these aims to some degree", then it has accomplished what it was meant to do. Through it, the Leibnizian idea of a *calculus philosophicus*—which in its generality is a gigantic [task], but has already been realized for separate realms through the arithmetic, geometric, and chemical modes of notation— should be fulfilled in a new domain, that of logical deduction. This "conceptual notation" is to find application in mathematical and physical inquiries and also contribute to the advancement of logic and the modification of certain logical theories. Thus, its scope, according to its creator, is confined to definite, not very extensive boundaries. To apply this notation, special symbols must be added according to the particular scientific domain under consideration. In general, however, a few symbols suffice to exhibit, derive and solve problems of logical deduction.

In the first part of his work, Frege discusses the meaning of the basic symbols of the "conceptual notation"; then in the second part he expresses by means of the notation some judgements of pure thought; and [finally], in the third part, he develops some propositions of a general theory of ordering-in-a-sequence. Only the first part is introductory; the second part demonstrates the employment of the invented symbolism within logic; and the third part leads over into the realm of mathematics. A discussion of the latter (as well as Frege's postscript[1] in the *Sitzungsberichte der Jenaischen Gesellschaft für Medicin und Naturwissenschaft* of January 1879) is best reserved for a review in a mathematical journal. We can go into it here only in so far as it sheds light upon the range of applicability {*Leistungsfähigkeit*} of the new "conceptual notation".

Frege uses two kinds of symbols for his "conceptual notation": letters to express a general, not fully determinate concept which is replaceable [by a determinate concept or name] in each particular case; and unequivocal, determinate, invariable symbols for logical operations. Mathematics also makes this distinction, at least to some degree; and it has the great advantage, above all, of making immediately clear to the eye the structure of a very complicated formula. The mathematical expression, so written, exhibits the constituent elements and their union, the parts by themselves and their combined structure.

The Fregean notation has seven unequivocal, determinate symbols that render only one sense [each]—certainly a relatively small number. Let us see what it accomplishes with them:

The first two symbols are (1) the short vertical *judgement stroke*, and (2) the thin horizontal stroke of the complex of ideas {*Vorstellungsverbindung*}, the *content stroke*, which can be used by itself or also attached to the middle of the right side of the judgement stroke and can be of various lengths according to requirements. The judgement, however, must change its form in order to be expressed by the symbols. The usual distinction of subject and predicate is dropped. The Greek letter situated to the right of the content stroke is considered to be the whole, unified conceptual content {*begrifflicher Inhalt*} of the judgement, and we must mentally add "is a fact" to this each time to complete the thought. The sentence, "Archimedes perished at the conquest of Syracuse," would be rendered in this form: "The violent death of Archimedes at the conquest of Syracuse is a fact." Also, Frege does not have the classification of judgements as given by School-logic [universal, particular, singular], interpreting this [classification] as merely an analysis of the conceptual content of judgements [and not of judgements themselves]. He also limits himself to one single Aristotelian mode of inference [*modus ponens*].[2]

The most important symbol, and the one which gives the whole notation its basic external charater, is (3) the *conditional stroke*, a thin vertical line attached to the content stroke to the right of the judgement stroke and

[1 This is F8, which is included in English translation in the present volume, pp. 204–8.]

[2 Frege claims to use only *modus ponens*, though he also uses substitution, confinement of quantifiers to a consequent, and several other rules of inference. In §6 of his book Frege seems aware that he uses these other rules. Apparently, Michaëlis fails to see that Frege uses them, or fails to realize that they are modes of inference, or both.]

drawn downward. It can vary in length according to need; and a new content stroke with its own particular letters can be attached to the right of its lower end. If several conditional strokes belong to one judgement stroke, then all of the content strokes attached to these are just long enough so that they all end [on the right-hand side] at the same imaginary vertical line.

(4) The fourth basic symbol is that of *negation*, which consists of a small vertical stroke attached to the underside of the content stroke. (In fact, in the printing of the book, an inverted [numeral] one was used; but this does not appear to be the author's intention. In any case, the inverted numeral is not displeasing to the eye.) When the negation symbol is attached to the content stroke, this means that the attached content finds no instantiation.

The last three symbols are (5) that of *equality of content*, (6) *function symbols*, and (7) that of *generality*. The symbol for equality of content, one used also in mathematics, consists of three short, parallel, horizontal lines placed between two letters which are supposed to denote the same conceptual content. The form of the function symbols is the same as the usual one of mathematics. It differs in sense [however] from the mathematical one since it signifies, not the whole of the dependent expression of magnitude, but, unlike the argument, only the invariant part of the expression. Also, the logical function symbol allows interchange {*Vertauschung*} of argument and function.

The symbol for generality consists of a semicircular concavity in the content stroke. It opens upwards, and written in it is a letter borrowed from an argument of the function standing to the right. If the concavity follows directly after the judgement stroke (and the generality thus covers the content of the whole judgement), then by omitting the concavity [and the accompanying German letter], the German letter [in the complex of symbols following the content stroke] is replaced by an italic letter.

The judgement and content stroke with a function $\Phi(A)$, which contains only the one argument A, written to the right of it means: "A has the property Φ." On the other hand, if a function $\Psi(A, B)$ contains two arguments, A and B, then its meaning is: "B stands in the Ψ relation to A." or "B is the result of an application of the procedure Ψ on A." A judgement containing the symbol for generality means: "The function is the case, whatever we take its argument to be."

There is a large number of combinations of the simple symbols. Some of these have already been mentioned. The content stroke accompanies all other symbols; the judgement stroke also is seldom lacking, and [it *is* missing] only where a mere complex of ideas {*blosse Vorstellungsverbindung*}, and not a judgement, is under consideration. If two judgements A and B are connected by the conditional stroke, this means that if B is affirmed, then A cannot be denied. Thus, it excludes one of the four possible combinations of A and B: the possibility that A is denied, while B is affirmed is excluded, leaving the three equal possibilities: (1) A and B are both affirmed, (2) both are denied, and (3) A is affirmed, B is denied.

The possible combinations of the conditional stroke and the negation symbol are these: the latter can occur to the right or to the left of the former or in both places; and it can occur on the upper or lower content stroke or on both. Through these various possibilities, a whole series of judgement relations and conceptual relations can be expressed, but we shall not enumerate them here. By piling up combinations of strokes, chains of [logical] connections can be symbolized in many different ways. Through the combination of symbols for conditionality, negation, and generality the relations of subalternate, contrary, subcontrary, and contradictory judgements can be rendered, and so on.

Now, in the second part of the book, with the help of his "conceptual notation", by using one single Aristotelian mode of inference,[3] Frege develops 68 propositions, whose derivation from each other is meant to show that they are independent of experience and discoverable purely logically from the relations of pure thought. These [68 logical propositions] imply 65 propositions from a general theory of sequences which are presented in the third part. Frege himself designates 9 of the 68 logical propositions (or 8, if we use an improvement mentioned in the Preface) as the most important. We cite these propositions as examples of statements expressible [in Frege's system]:

(1) If a proposition a holds, then it holds also in case an arbitrary proposition b holds.

(2) If a proposition a follows from two propositions b and c; and if one of these, b, again follows from the other, c; then the proposition a follows from this latter c alone.

(3) If a proposition follows from two conditions, then the order in which [the conditions] occur is indifferent.

(4) If a proposition a follows from b, then the non-occurrence of b can be deduced from the non-occurrence of a.

(5) The denial of denial is affirmation.

(6) The affirmation of a denies the denial of a.

Both propositions [(5) and (6)] can be combined by the expression, "The denial of denial has the same meaning as affirmation".

(7) We can replace c everywhere by d, if $c = d$.[4]

(8) The content of c is equal to the content of c.

Finally, the content of the ninth proposition is really nothing more than the definition of a symbol.

[3 See footnote 2 of the present review.]

[4 It is clear here that Michaëlis does not understand that Frege's symbol for identity of content is not the same as the identity sign of mathematics.]

This brief description of Frege's symbols and propositions is sufficient to give at least an idea of his intentions and the scope of his notation. It is obvious that the content of the propositions expressed [above] is very meagre and that a somewhat richer {*mannigfaltiger*} content can be obtained only by replacing the general symbols with more particular ones; but the Fregean notation is not able to produce this transition or can do so only to a limited extent. To be able to express the various possible relations between conditional connections [which is about all Frege can do] is certainly not worthless; but whether straightforward logic would gain considerably if it were to improve its tools and expand in this direction may justly be doubted. For his purposes, Frege has to pass over many things in formal logic and detract even more from its [already meagre] content. Who does not agree that the usual classification of judgements is an artificial one, which categorizes, not the judgement itself, but only the content; and who does not know that the Aristotelian classification of modes of inference is pretty superfluous? And it is remarkable that Frege expresses these thoughts without at least mentioning the well-known authorities who made those objections long ago!

I do not doubt, however, that, with the exception of the unsatisfactory classification [of judgements], the [Aristotelian] job is complete. One must not only criticize, one must contribute constructively. If [, on the one hand,] De Morgan discovered the general character of the copula in transitivity and commutativity, then, on the other hand, we must now analyse the properties of the copula and use an idea which was pointed out by Kant, but incorrectly worked out. A new, correct classification of judgements, which at the same time makes possible the correct classification of concepts and modes of inference, would be an advancement of logic which should not be rejected. The content of logic which has been much too meagre up to now, should not be decreased, but increased.

Also, I cannot completely agree with the comments which Frege makes about the relations which the fundamental concepts of mathematics have to each other. I cannot agree that the concept of ordering-in-a-sequence can be reduced to that of logical ordering, let alone that the concept of number can be advanced by investigations into ordering-in-a-sequence. On the contrary, the concept of ordering-in-a-sequence is a secondary one, dependent upon the concept of time; while the concept of number is a primary mathematical one—indeed, the simplest, most general concept of all. The concept of logical ordering {*logische Folge*}, however, seems to me to be more closely correlated with the concept of causality than the concept of ordering-in-a-sequence {*Reihenfolge*}. With the latter, it [the concept of logical ordering] has only the name in common.[5] These thoughts

[5 The two corresponding German words share the part "*folge*", just as the English words share the part "ordering".]

of Frege, however, are so briefly considered and so little worked out, that a detailed polemic is impossible.

It is also regrettable that Frege takes no notice at all of the previously existing works on the same subject. I mean the investigations of Boole, Jevons, Schröder, MacColl, and others who—partly seeking to solve exactly the same problems as Frege, and partly wishing to establish a logical calculus—necessarily occupied themselves with the establishment of formulas and symbols for logical operations. So far as MacColl is concerned, what sufficiently proves the kinship of Frege's investigations and his (mentioned in the *Educational Times* under the title "Symbolic Language") is that with the help of his symbols, [MacColl] succeeds in easily solving some problems from integral and probability calculus.

Perhaps the utilization of these previous works, which are simple, adaptable, and partly correct, would not be without value to the author. His work [however] remains obviously so much more original and certainly does not lack importance.

Berlin   C. Th. Michaëlis

D. Review of Frege's *Conceptual Notation* by E. Schröder, *Zeitschrift für Mathematik und Physik*, 25 (1880), pp. 81–94.[1]

This very unusual book—obviously the original work of an ambitious thinker with a purely scientific turn of mind—pursues a course to which the reviewer is naturally highly sympathetic, since he himself has made similar investigations. The present work promises to advance toward Leibniz's ideal of a universal language, which is still very far from its realization despite the great importance laid upon it by that brilliant philosopher!

The fact that a *completed* universal language, characteristic, or general conceptual notation {*allgemeine Begriffschrift*} does not exist even today justifies my trying to say from the beginning what is to be understood by it. I almost want to say, "it is a risk to state [what a completed universal language would be like]"; for, as history teaches, in the further pursuit of such ideals, we often find ourselves led to modify the original ones very significantly; especially once we have succeeded in advancing substantially toward [our goal]. Perhaps one begins by considering the most important point unimportant or overlooking it; one is compelled to leave matters

[1 This translation was made independently of the one by V. H. Dudman which appears in *The Southern Journal of Philosophy*, 7 (1969), pp. 139–50; and then the two were compared. Wherever Dudman's interpretation or wording seemed better, it was adopted and duly noted. Wherever important differences of interpretation remained, they were also noted to give the reader the benefit of both views.]

which are impossible to know, or to make compromises with reality—not to mention the fact that new aims, which emerge as desirable along the way, may perhaps turn out to be achievable in unexpected ways.

I believe I do not depart from the historical interpretation by formulating the problem in the following way (*mutatis mutandis* for the various basic fields of knowledge):[2] *to construct all complex concepts by means of a few simple, completely determinate and clearly classified operations from the fewest possible fundamental concepts {Grundbegriffen} (categories) with clearly delimited extensions.*

In considering an ideal, it is not improper to refer to an analogue which has already been used. Thus, I wish to add a comparison already employed by Leibniz (if I remember rightly): compare, say, how composite numbers arise from prime numbers through multiplication—or also, if you will, how in a similar way the natural numbers are constructed {*zusammengesetzt*} in general from the first eleven [*sic*] such numbers through the relations of multiplication and addition to form the decimal system. Incidentally, in recent times several other works have been published which concern themselves with listing the fundamental concepts {*Kategorien*}. Nevertheless, such schematizations may be granted only a minor value so long as the proof (which I find lacking in them) is omitted that, in fact, through the combination of the fundamental concepts which those works lay down, all the remaining concepts follow—thus also so long as the investigation lacks [an account of] which combining operations come into question and by which laws the combinations are governed.

Even if, in spite of all earlier attempts and also the latest one now under discussion, the idea of a universal language has not yet been realized in a nearly satisfactory sense; it is still the case that the impossibility of the undertaking has not come to light. On the contrary, there is always hope, though remote, that by making existing scientific technical language {*wissenschaftliche Kunstsprache*} precise, or by developing a special such language, we may gain a firm foundation by means of which it would someday become possible to emerge from the confusion of philosophical controversies, terminologies, and systems whose conflict or disagreement is to be mainly attributed (as indeed can be generally seen) to the lack of definiteness of the basic concepts. The blame must be placed almost entirely upon the imperfections of the language in which we are forced to argue from the outset.

Given the sense [of 'conceptual notation'] which I sought to indicate in the above remarks, it must be said that Frege's title, *Conceptual Notation*, promises too much—more precisely, that the title does not correspond at all to the content [of the book]. Instead of leaning toward a universal characteristic, the present work (perhaps unknown to the author himself)

[2 Dudman's turn of phrase.]

definitely leans toward Leibniz's "*calculus ratiocinator*". In the latter
direction, the present little book makes an advance which I should consider
very creditable, if a large part of what it attempts had not already been
accomplished by someone else, and indeed (as I shall prove) in a doubtlessly
more adequate fashion.

The book is clearly and refreshingly written and also rich in perceptive
comments. The examples are pertinent; and I read with genuine pleasure
nearly all the *secondary discussions* which accompany Frege's theory; for
example, the excellently written Preface. On the other hand, I can pass no
such unqualified judgement upon the major content—the formula notation
itself. Nevertheless, anyone interested in the methodology of thinking will
derive much stimulation by working through the book; and I state explicitly
that it merits a recommendation for closer study, in spite of the numerous
and in part serious criticisms which now I shall also objectively put forward.

First of all, I consider it a shortcoming that the book is presented in too
isolated a manner and not only seeks no serious connection with achievements that have been made in essentially similar directions (namely those
of Boole), but even disregards them entirely. The only comment that the
author makes which is remotely concerned with [Boole's achievements][3]
is the statement on page iv of the Preface, which reads, "I have strictly
avoided those efforts to establish an artificial similarity (between the arithmetical and logical formula languages)[4] through the interpretation of the
concept as the sum of its characteristic marks {*Merkmale*}." This comment
even by itself lends a certain probability to the supposition—which gains
confirmation in other ways— that the author has an erroneous low opinion
of "those efforts" simply because he lacks knowledge of them.

It may be mentioned here that the book has been reviewed by someone
else—Kurt Lasswitz, *Jenaer Literaturzeitung* (1879), No. 18, pp. 248 f.
To be sure, I can agree with this very kindly written review on many points,
while nevertheless allowing myself at the same time to cast a disapproving
glance at it. I must criticize its particular opinions of Boole's orientation;
it carries the above-mentioned erroneous conception even further than the
author.

Of course the Boolean theory is "onesided", just as almost every
investigation within a special scientific field naturally is. It fails, by far,
to achieve everything that one could wish and will still require further
development in various ways. On the other hand, so long as proof of the
contrary has not been specifically furnished, Boolean theory "is based"
neither upon an "inadmissible apprehension of the concept", nor above all
upon "doubtful" presuppositions (see my argument below).

[3 Schröder assumes that the quoted passage refers to the work of Boole. To
the present editor it seems more likely that it refers to the work of Leibniz, which
Frege knew well. See the present volume, p. 105.]
[4 Schröder's parenthetical insertion.]

However, the comment (which I shall prove below) that might contribute most effectively to the correction of opinions is that the Fregean "conceptual notation" does not differ so essentially from Boole's formula language as the Jena reviewer (perhaps also the author) takes for granted. With the exception of what is said on pages 15–22 about "function" and "generality" and up to the supplement beginning on page 55 [Part III of Frege's book], the book is devoted to the establishment of a formula language, which essentially coincides with Boole's mode of presenting *judgements* and Boole's calculus of judgements, and which certainly in no way achieves more.

With regard to its major content, the "conceptual notation" could be considered actually a *transcription* of the Boolean formula language. With regard to its form, though, the former is different beyond recognition—and not to its advantage. As I have said already it was without doubt developed completely independently—all too independently!

If the author's notation does have an advantage over the Boolean one, which eluded me, it certainly also has a disadvantage. I think that to anyone who is familiar with both, [the author's notation] must above all give the impression of hiding—to be sure not intentionally, but certainly "artificially"—the many beautiful, real, and genuine analogies which the logical formula language naturally bears with regard to the mathematical one.

In the subtitle, "A Formula Language Modelled Upon that of Arithmetic", I find the very point in which the book corresponds least to its advertised program,[5] but in which a much more complete correspondence could be attained—precisely by means of the neglected emulation of previous works. If, to the impartial eye, the "modelling" appears to consist of nothing more than using *letters* in both cases, then it seems to me this does not sufficiently justify the epithet used.

Now in order to prove my above assertions and be able to critically examine the formula language itself, I cannot help presupposing as known the basic concepts of logical calculus. Concerning the literature of this discipline, which I have described elsewhere, an extensive appendix is to be found at the end [of the present review]. Instead of merely referring to my book (6),[6] in view of the doubts expressed by the other side, I want to explain here the few things which are essential for understanding what follows.

As a propaedeutic for the logical calculus, one can introduce the calculus of identity of *domains of a manifold* {*Calcul der Identität von Gebieten einer Mannigfaltigkeit*}. This is a purely mathematical discipline whose theorems {*Sätze*} clearly must be granted complete certainty and correctness. Then, a mere change in the interpretation or meaning of the symbols

[5 Dudman's turn of phrase.]
[6 Numerals in parentheses refer to the book list at the end of this review.]

leads from this first calculus to the present logical one, which corresponds entirely to the first so far as the [calculating] technique is concerned.

Let there be a manifold of elements—for example, the [elements] of the points of an arbitrarily bounded or even unbounded plane. Letters, such as $a, b, c,...$, are to represent arbitrary domains which belong entirely to this manifold, thus—for our example—to speak generally, any parts of the plane. These domains are to be considered equal only when they are identical.

Relations of size should be entirely disregarded. (The mathematician is so used to associating letters with the idea of the number representing a quantity that for a beginner in our calculus a conscious effort is necessary to free himself from this habit, even though it is not given to him by nature, but laboriously instilled in school. Hence, a stands for the planar region itself, but not the number representing its size.)

The entire domain of the given manifold is symbolized by 1; while the "negation" of a by means of a_1 symbolizes the domain which is the complement of a in the manifold. 0 stands for a supposed domain of the manifold if it happens that [the supposed domain] has absolutely no element in common [with the manifold] and hence actually does not exist as a domain of the latter.

Now, if by $a.b$ (or ab) is understood that domain which the domains a and b have in common, thus [that domain] in which [a and b] intersect each other; and if by $a+b$ [is understood] that domain in which [a and b] are added together; then it is evident that the operations, thus explained, of "logical" multiplication and addition are just as commutative and associative as the arithmetical operations with the same name, which the following formulas express:

$$ab = ba, \quad a(bc) = (ab)c, \quad a+b = b+a, \quad a+(b+c) = (a+b)+c.$$

Because of this, the parentheses can be omitted in products or sums composed of several simple operation terms. Moreover, it is evident that the two operations stand in distributive relation to each other, but not just in one direction (as in arithmetic), but reciprocally. Thus, as it is expressed in formulas:

$$a.(b+c) = (a.b)+(a.c) \quad \text{and} \quad a+(b.c) = (a+b).(a+c).$$

The first to make the latter observation, which I had also made independently, was the American C. S. Peirce (see (4), vol. I).

Obviously, a sum can equal 0 only when each one of its terms equals 0; a product can equal 1 only if each factor also equals 1. Similarly, the little theorems {*Sätze*} expressed in the formulas,

$$a+ab = a, \quad a(a+b) = a, \quad aa = a, \quad a+a = a,$$

which have no analogue in arithmetic, hold as immediately obvious.

Of special note is the first of these according to which terms of a sum which are "contained" {*enthielt*} (included {*mitinbegriffen*}) in other terms (as *ab* is included in *a*) may be omitted {*unterdrückt*} at any time.

Once one has convinced oneself—say by thinking about regions of planes—of the validity of the formulas

$$a.1 = a, \quad a+0 = a, \quad a.0 = 0, \quad a+1 = 1$$

(only the first three of which hold in arithmetic),* and then the theorems concerned with negation,

$$a.a_1 = 0, \quad a+a_1 = 1, \quad (a_1)_1 = a, \quad (a.b)_1 = a_1+b_1, \quad (a+b)_1 = a_1.b_1$$

(the latter two of which were partly expressed by Boole and Jevons (1), and first completely expressed by Robert Grassmann), one has acquired everything necessary to understand what follows and indeed many beautiful applications of the logical calculus (such as (8)).

Now, the preceding propaedeutic discipline is converted into the proper logical calculus—more precisely, into the first part of it—or the *calculus of concepts* (where the extension {*Umfang*} of the concept is kept in mind) if one takes *a*, *b*, ... as referring to "classes" {*Classen*} of those individuals which fall under the concepts to be investigated, hence which constitute their extension. Then, in this way, 1 will stand for the manifold of all the objects of thought which fall within the sphere of any of the concepts related to the domain under investigation (if necessary Boole's entire "*universe of discourse*" or "*of thought*"). Logical multiplication, then, corresponds to the so-called "determination" of one concept by another,† [logical] addition corresponds to collective union [of sets].

Now, there certainly is a onesidedness in completely disregarding the "*content*" [i.e. intension] of the concept. Also, it should not be claimed that the above [described] calculus has to replace all of logic together with its eventual future development. Nevertheless, it does allow the greatest part of formal logic to date to appear in a new and wonderfully clear light.

That onesidedness, however, is motivated—indeed, justified for the immediate aim—by the fact that many concepts with undoubtedly definite

* The choice of the symbol ∞ instead of 1, to which Wundt (9) is partial, would deprive us also of the first of the three mentioned formulas;[7] though in this way the fourth, less familiar, formula would then conform to arithmetic. Moreover, this symbol [i.e. ∞] would be just as unsuitable for all finite manifolds as the symbol 1, to which he objected, would be for the infinite ones. Over and above this, the applications of the present discipline to the calculus of probabilities undoubtedly urges retention of the [symbol 1].

† Wundt (9) has recently opposed this claim—a point which I intend to consider on another occasion.

[7 Dudman incorrectly has "would deprive us of the first three of these formulas".]

extension have no existing content [intension] at all. So it is for most concepts which arose through negation; for example, as H. Lotze‡ wittily remarks, for the human mind it remains an ever unfulfillable task to abstract the common characteristics from everything which is not a man—thus from triangle, melancholy, and sulphuric acid—to combine them into the concept "non-man".

Now Frege's "conceptual notation" actually has almost nothing in common with that portion of the logical calculus just characterized; that is, with the Boolean calculus of concepts; but it certainly does have something in common with the second part, the Boolean calculus of judgements.§ The following simple consideration brings us to this [second part of the logical calculus]: the calculus of domains {*Calcul mit Gebieten*} is also applicable to the domain of intervals on a straight line; it is just as applicable to periods of time, if again these are not thought of as measured, but simply taken as manifolds (classes) of the (individual) moments contained in them or also as arbitrary time segments.

Every investigation proceeds from certain presuppositions which are constantly taken as fulfilled throughout the entire course of the investigation. Now, in order to leave eternity out of the question here as far as possible, let 1 stand for the time segment during which the presuppositions of an investigation to be conducted are satisfied. Then let a, b, c,... be considered *judgements* {*Urtheile*} (propositions {*Aussagen*}, assertions {*Behauptungen*}—English equivalent "*statements*") (8), and at the same time, *as soon as one constructs formulas or calculates* (a small change of meaning taking place), *the time segments during which these given propositions are true*. Thereupon, it is obvious from what has been said that one will be in a position to represent—through formulas or equations obeying the laws of the logical calculus—simultaneous holding and mutual exclusion, even one-directional implication (conditional) {*das einseitige Zurfolgehaben* (*Bedingen*)} of the most diverse propositions. The applications which follow will illustrate this sufficiently; and we can now proceed to the main part of Frege's book, which culminates with the section "Representation and Derivation of Some Judgements of Pure Thought". To this end, I must first introduce and explain some of the simplest of the author's schemata.

Frege signifies by ├───── a that a holds; which, according to the above, is to be represented in Boolean notation by $a = 1$ or $a_1 = 0$. Frege signifies by ├──┬── b that b does not hold;[8] that is, that $b_1 = 1$ or $b = 0$. (It is obvious that the latter [of Boole's] ways of writing it could also be

‡ *Logik*, Leipzig, 1874.
§ The title is incorrect in this respect as well, and actually should have been replaced by "Judgemental Notation" {*Urtheilsschrift*}.
[8 Dudman is missing the negation stroke here.]

introduced purely conventionally in order to represent, respectively, the truth or falsehood of a proposition—without at all introducing, as Boole does, the intervening time segments; MacColl, among others, does it this way.)

With the first of the schemata,

Frege represents the proposition: When {*wann*} b holds, then a also holds (if not actually necessarily, then at least in fact); that is, in the notation of the logical calculus, $a_1 b = 0$ or also $a + b_1 = 1$—two equations, the first of which asserts that the case in which b holds but at the same time a does not hold does not occur; the second emphasizes that the cases in which a holds or b does not hold are the only possible ones. Also, one equation would be derivable from the other through negation (more precisely, duality {*Opposition*}), since $(a_1 b)_1 = a + b_1$ and $0_1 = 1$.

With the second schema, the author represents the proposition: When {*wann*} b and c both hold, then a holds also; that is $a_1 bc = 0$ or $a + b_1 + c_1 = 1$.

With the third schema, which is of fundamental importance for the book, the author unfortunately makes a mistake (p. 7—however, it is the only one which I noticed in the whole book): he gives two explanations which do not correspond with each other; and only the second one, which is correct, is in accordance with all further applications made or intended. In addition, the wording of the assertion represented by the schema is misleading because of the synonymity of the conjuctions "if" {*wenn*} and "when" {*wann*} ("as soon as" {*sobald*}, **"in** case" {*falls*}, "always, when" {*immer dann, wenn*}, etc.) which, though often interchangeable, here yield an essentially different sense. For this reason, it is perhaps instructive to dwell on the point for a moment. The schema is supposed to link the assertion $\vdash\!\!\!-\!\!\!-$ a (that is, that a holds) to the antecedent $\vdash\!\!\!\sqsupset$ b (or,

$b_1 c = 0$), which is thought of as represented in the manner of the first schema. Hence, it says: a holds as soon as b holds when c holds. More precisely: if we assume that the antecedent of the sentence is fulfilled, then the possibility of $b_1 c$ (that is, c holds, but b does not) is ruled out; then only the possibilities remain which can be summarized in several ways in

$$(b_1 c)_1 = b + c_1 = bc_1 + bc + b_1 c_1 = bc + c_1.$$

Now, for all these possibilities which still remain, a should hold. Consequently, this is expressed by the equation

$$a_1(b_1 c)_1 = 0,$$

Q

in other words $a_1(b+c_1) = 0,$

or also $a+b_1\,c = 1.$

(The mentioned mistake of the author is only that, basically, he omits the negation of $b_1\,c$ in the first equation. Thus, $a_1\,b_1\,c = 0$ is assigned as the *first* interpretation of his schema, since according to the [assigned] wording, the schema "denies the case in which c is affirmed, but b and a are denied".)*

Now, if we were to take as the meaning of the [third] schema the proposition:

> "If b is dependent upon c, then a holds.",

which fairly accurately corresponds to the author's second interpretation (which, properly understood, is correct); then it would seem inconceivable to common sense that this sentence is fully synonymous with the following two taken together:

> "If b holds, a holds." and

> "If c does not hold, a holds."

And, yet, this is the case, since in fact the equation

$$a_1(b+c_1) = 0$$

can be divided into the two equations

$$a_1\,b = 0 \quad \text{and} \quad a_1\,c_1 = 0.$$

The difficulty arises because, from the wording of the sentence—not only from the use of the grammatical particle "if" instead of "whenever", but also from the designation of the relation as a conditional (as Frege puts it "a necessary consequence")—the reader will tend to make the following interpretation: either b is always dependent (as it were, causally) upon c, and then a surely holds; or else, this is not always the case, and then the proposition is empty {*inhaltlos*}—gives us no information at all about whether a holds or does not hold. This latter is not at all what is intended; on the contrary, even if the conditional of b and c does not come true at times, the schema is to state—assert—something for these times; namely that a holds. The conditional wording,† therefore, misleads one into the

---

* I employ different letters here, since it seems to me that the author's frequent, utterly unnecessary, change in the choice of letters only detracts from the perspicuity and rather offends good taste.

† For reasons of brevity, I shall have to adopt this wording myself hereafter.

unintended interpretation of the antecedent as holding universally—into an imputation of "generality"—about which, by the way, the author later (p. 19) makes some very pertinent remarks.

Now, in order to represent, for example, the disjunctive "or"— namely, to state that *a holds or b holds, but not both*—the author has to use the schema

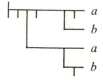

$$a$$
$$b$$
$$a$$
$$b$$

which definitely appears clumsy compared to the Boolean mode of writing:

$$ab_1 + a_1\, b = 1$$

or also

$$ab + a_1\, b_1 = 0.$$

From the section "Representation . . . of Some Judgments of Pure Thought" I cite an example as an illustration:

Nr. 2

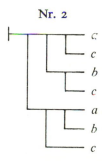

$$c$$
$$c$$
$$b$$
$$c$$
$$a$$
$$b$$
$$c$$

This should be read: if *a* is dependent upon *b* and *c*, and *b* is dependent upon *c*, and *c* holds, then *a* holds. In the Boolean fashion, this would be expressed: if $a_1\, bc = 0$ and $b_1\, c = 0$, then it is also the case that $a_1\, c = 0$. Here is the proof:

$$a_1\, c = a_1(b + b_1)c = a_1\, bc + a_1\, b_1\, c = 0 + a_1 .0 = 0.$$

Of course, we can also write it all in a *single* formula; namely, as you like:

$$a + c_1 + b_1\, c + a_1\, bc = 1$$

or also

$$a_1\, c(b + c_1)(a + b_1 + c_1) = 0.$$

The latter form is the easiest to verify as an identity (by cross-multiplication), since in this way factors keep coming together which, as negations of each other, mutually cancel and yield the product 0. Also, from the latter form, one can easily derive (going from right to left) the interpretation desired by the author, by taking it as a guideline that if, in one of the products equal to 0—A, B, C ... $= 0$—some of the factors—... C, B ... are considered equal to 1 (that is, are taken as true), then (the product of) the remaining factor(s) A vanishes (that is, A_1 must be true).

Let no one conceive it an advantage of the Fregean notation that it employs only one mode of connection of its judgement (or better, inference) links,[9] while Boole's calculus, except for negation (to be sure, also abundantly used by the author), needs two kinds ($+$ and $\times$) of linking operations; for it can be shown that the latter [that is, Boole's calculus] can get by with just one—and indeed in four ways. Written with only multiplication, the latter formula, for example, runs as follows:

$$a_1 c(b_1 c)_1(a_1 bc)_1 = 0;$$

and the dual would also yield a formula with only addition. On the other hand, since an equation is itself an assertion, nothing prevents our allowing an equation to occur as a logical factor, etc.; thus writing

$$a_1 c(b_1 c = 0)(a_1 bc = 0) = 0,$$

to which there is again a dual.

The author also uses identities as inference links. Perhaps Robert Grassmann was the first to introduce formulas as operation links; yet, it seems to me, [he did it] in an illicit way, not conforming to the principles of his own calculus, always linking them by means of the plus sign instead of the multiplication sign.

Besides, it has no great value; it verges upon pedantry to actually express the theorems with one single connective each time they occur. One can be justly satisfied to have recognized once and for all the theoretical possibility of doing it.

We list here a few further "judgements of pure thought", with the numbers given them by the author, in a form of notation modelled upon the Leibnizian–Boolean calculus:

(1) $a_1 ba = 0$, (5) $a_1 c(b+c_1)(a+b_1) = 0$,

(7) $a_1 cd(b+c_1+d_1)(a+b_1) = 0$, (11) $a_1 b(a+b_1 c) = 0$,

(12) $a_1 cbd(a+b_1+c_1+d_1) = 0$, (21) $a_1(b+c_1)(c+d_1)(a+b_1 d) = 0$,

(24) $a_1 bc(a+c_1) = 0$, (27) $a_1 a = 0$, (28) $ba_1(a+b_1) = 0$,

(33) $b_1 a_1(a+b) = 0$, (46) $a_1(a+c_1)(a+c) = 0$,

(51) $a_1(b+c)d(a+b_1)(a+c_1+d_1) = 0$, etc.

[9 Dudman's turn of phrase.]

All of the "judgements etc." which the author compiled and derived on pages 25 to 50 could easily be rendered in the above manner on *half* a printed page; and would, at the same time, immediately show themselves as evident (through mental cross-multiplication); namely, by leading to identity (27). In fact, the author's formula language not only indulges in the Japanese practice of writing vertically, but also restricts him to only *one* row per page, or at most, if we count the column added as explanation, two rows! This monstrous waste of space which, from a typographical point of view (as is evident here), is inherent in the Fregean "conceptual notation", should definitely decide the issue in favour of the Boolean school—if, indeed, there is still a question of choice.

In other respects, the numerous "judgements, etc." presented by the author seem to be logical identities (from which I sought above to pick out only the most interesting) which, for the most part, offer nothing especially interesting. Also to be criticized with regard to the arrangement and choice of theorems is the really enormous lack of systematization (which, to be sure, is acknowledged in the title of the section).

In addition, numerous *repetitions* also occur—statements differ only with regard to the order in which the factors appear or only in that an element is replaced by its double negation. After the commutativity of the former or the substitutivity of the latter is recognized and exhibited in the simplest possible schema, it seems hardly worth also expressing it again and again in complicated examples. Finally, expendable premises (that is superfluous ones contained in others) of judgements or deductions—and thus some of these deductions themselves—should have been suppressed; see Nos. (3), (4), (32), (45).

The author's method of deduction consists essentially, either directly or indirectly, of enumerating and summarizing which cases remain if one eliminates from all imaginable ones those excluded by the premises.

The preceding criticisms do not concern the clarity and readability of the book, which in other sections offers something of more value; and anyone who cares to do so will *easily* be able to translate into the better notation in accordance with the examples given above.

There is a defect in Boole's theory, perceived by many and recently very effectively illustrated by Wundt (9) against Jevons, in the fact that particular judgements are only inadequately expressed in it (strictly speaking, not at all). The indeterminate factor v, which Boole uses, for example, in the first part of the logical calculus in the form $va = vb$ to express the sentence "Some a's are b's.", does not fulfil his purpose because, through the hypothesis $v = ab$, this equation always comes out an identity, even when no a is a b. Now in the section concerning "generality", Frege correctly lays down stipulations that permit him to express such judgements precisely. I shall not follow him slavishly here; but on the contrary, show that one may not perchance find a justification here for his other deviations from Boole's notation, and the analogous modification or extension can easily be achieved in Boolean notation as well. The author achieves this essentially by introducing Gothic letters as symbols for generality and establishing a notation for negating this generality—for which I shall use a stroke above [the symbol in question]. The equation $f(\mathfrak{a}) = 1$ asserts: all $\mathfrak{a}$'s have the property f. Then $\{f(\mathfrak{a})\}_1$, or more briefly $f_1(\mathfrak{a}) = 1$, will assert: all $\mathfrak{a}$'s have the property not-f; that is, all $\mathfrak{a}$'s lack the property f. On the other hand, $f(\overline{\mathfrak{a}}) = 1$ will assert: not all $\mathfrak{a}$'s have the property f, or: some $\mathfrak{a}$'s do not have the property f. The equation $P(\mathfrak{a})M(\mathfrak{a}) = 0$ asserts (also in agreement with Frege): no M is a P. Then, the equation

$$P(\overline{\mathfrak{a}})M(\overline{\mathfrak{a}}) = 0$$

will deny that the previous equation would be true for *every* meaning one could assign to $\mathfrak{a}$; hence, expressing that there is at least one $\mathfrak{a}$ for which [the first equation] would be false, or [in other words] that some M's are P's, etc.

By the way, one can adopt various methods to accomplish the same thing; for example (the basic idea of Cayley), through a sign such as $\neq$ for "not equal", in which case $va = vb$ together with $va \neq 0$ (or, even shorter, $ab \neq 0$) would say that some a's are also b's. Peirce (4, I) corrected the mentioned deficiency in another way.[10]

The explanation which the author gives for the concept of (logical) "function" is very broad and entirely original. It is much broader than all previous explanations and to me seems to be not without justification. With regard to this, however, because of limited space, I wish to refer [the reader] to the book itself and merely mention that through the kindness of the publisher I have received an offprint from the *Sitzungsberichte der Jenaischen Gesellschaft für Medizin und Naturwissenschaft* (1879, the session of 10 January) in which the author presents two applications of his "conceptual notation"—one regarding the expression of a geometrical relation (that three points lie on a straight line), the other regarding a number-theoretical theorem—which are indeed appropriate to elucidate the way in which he intends to apply his "notation"—though less appropriate to indicate its value.

The "appendix" [Ch. III] of the *Conceptual Notation* concerns "Some Topics from a General Theory of Sequences" and appears very abstruse— the schemata are ornate with symbols! Here it would be desirable that if new symbols do have to be introduced for certain complicated relations which are expressible in the existing system, simpler ones should be chosen (even at the expense, temporarily, of complete expression {*Ausdrucksfülle*}). Three such relations occur, which concern [1] the following of one element after another in a certain "sequence", which is left very indeterminate; [2]

[10 Dudman left out the reference to Peirce.]

the "inheritance" of a property in the same [kind of "sequence"] by one element from the previous element; and [3] the "many-one-ness of a (not further characterized) procedure". The "sequence" is characterized only by the fact that a certain kind of advancement (which is otherwise left general) from one element to another is possible—I want to say, perhaps, that a particular procedure of deduction leads from one element to another. Of course, the deductive paths here can eventually also intersect, branch off, and run together again; and the author is proud of the great generality that is given in this way to the concept of *sequence*. It seems to me, however, that there is absolutely nothing of value in such a generalization; on the contrary, in my opinion, if the graphic ordering[11] of elements along a straight line is immaterial, unfounded, or inadmissible, then instead of "sequence", one should use simply the designation "set" {*Menge*}, "system" {*System*}, or "manifold" {*Mannigfaltigkeit*}.

According to the author, he undertook the entire work with the intention of obtaining complete clarity with regard to the logical nature of *arithmetical* judgements, and above all to test "how far one could get in arithmetic by means of logical deductions alone". If I have properly understood what the author wishes to do, then this point would also be, in large measure, already settled—namely, through the perceptive investigations of Hermann Grassmann. However, given the considerable extent of the literature related to this effort, it seems in any case not unjustified to wish that the author had taken better account of already existing efforts. May my comments, however, have the over-all effect of encouraging the author to further his research, rather than discouraging him.

In conclusion, I believe I shall earn the thanks of all those interested in the more recent analytical development of logic (and at the same time fulfil an obligation to the works that were unknown to me when I wrote my book) (6), if I give below a list of the relevant works of which I am now aware, though they cannot be found in the Bibliography of (6).

(1) William Stanley Jevons: *Pure Logic, or the Logic of Quality Apart from Quantity, with Remarks on Boole's System and on the Relation of Logic and Mathematics.* London and New York, 1864. 87 pp.

(2) ——: *The Substitution of Similars, the True Principle of Reasoning, Derived from a Modification of Aristotle's Dictum.* London, 1869. 86 pp.

(3) ——: *The Principles of Science, a Treatise on Logic and Scientific Method*—a very significant work, whose 3rd edition,[12] London, 1879, 786 pp., is now before me.

[11] Dudman's turn of phrase.]
[12] {*dessen 3. Aufl.*} Dudman renders this "whose three volumes".]

(4) Charles S. Peirce: (Three papers on logic, read before the American Academy of Arts and Sciences) I. "On an Improvement in Boole's Calculus of Logic", pp. 250–61. II. "On the Natural Classification of Arguments", pp. 261–87. III. "On a New List of Categories", pp. 287–98. *Proceedings of the American Academy of Arts and Sciences* (1867). Article I anticipates various results at which the present reviewer arrived in (6).

(5) ——: *Description of a Notation for the Logic of Relatives Resulting from an Amplification of the Conceptions of Boole's Calculus of Logic*, extracted from the *Memoirs of the American Academy*, vol. IX. Cambridge, 1870. iv+62 pp.

(6) Ernst Schröder: *Der Operationskreis des Logikkalkuls*. Leipzig: Teubner, 1877. 37 pp.

(7) J. Delboeuf: *Logique algorithmique*. Liège and Bruxelles, 1877. 99 pp.

(8) Hugh MacColl: "The Calculus of Equivalent Statements and Integration Limits", *Proceedings of the London Mathematical Society*, vol. IX (1877–78), pp. 9–20, 177–86. The first part gives an interesting application of the logical calculus to the (purely mechanical) solution of problems: to determine the new limits, if with repeated integrations between variable limits the sequence of integration is modified as desired. The second part is spoiled by the fact that the author introduces symmetrical symbols (: and –) to express the asymmetrical relations of subordination and non-subordination, as a result of which he certainly gets himself confused.

(9) Wilhelm Wundt: *Logik, eine Untersuchung der Principien der Erkenntniss und der Methoden wissenschaftlicher Forschung*, vol. I: *Erkenntnisslehre*. Stuttgart, 1880. 585 pp.—The work devotes 52 pages to the logical calculus. Even if some details in it may be criticized, we should welcome the fact that professional philosophers are beginning to concern themselves with the *mathematical reform of logic*, which certainly deserves consideration.

Karlsruhe   ERNST SCHRÖDER

E. Review of Frege's *Conceptual Notation*[1] by P. Tannery, *Revue Philosophique*, 8 (1879), pp. 108–9.

The author attempts to establish a system of symbolic notation applicable to all types of judgement, to all modes of reasoning. His small book

[1 The present review appeared originally in French. Tannery gives the following French translation of the title of Frege's book: *Représentation écrite des concepts, système de formules construit pour la pensée pure d'après celui de l'algèbre*. In a footnote, he reports that a literal translation (into French) of the title would be nearly unintelligible.]

contains little more than an explanation of the symbols which he believes he must adopt and the combinations which he forms with them. They differ essentially from those of algebra: the two algorithms have nothing in common but their use of letters. On the other hand, the logical point of view is most unique.

In such circumstances, we should have a right to demand complete clarity or a great simplification of formulas or important results. But much to the contrary, the explanations are insufficient, the notations are excessively complex; and as far as applications are concerned, they remain only promises.

Dr. Frege has very few illusions about the greeting which the present work will probably receive. To defend it, he compares ordinary language to the human eye and his "conceptual notation" to the microscope, a valuable instrument, but one too difficult to use outside of the special studies for which it was meant. The author intends to apply his invention at first to arithmetic. With it, he plans to illuminate the concepts of number, magnitude, and so on. We strongly advise him, if it attains his goal, to *project* a given image with his microscope; that is, to translate his arguments into ordinary language.

It will suffice for the moment to indicate the salient point of his system as far as logic is concerned. The [author] abolishes the concepts of *subject* and *predicate* and replaces them by others which he calls *function* and *argument*. Thus, 'the circumstance that carbon-dioxide is heavier than hydrogen' and 'the circumstance that carbon-dioxide is heavier than oxygen' can be considered indifferently either as the same function with different arguments (hydrogen, oxygen) or as different functions with the same argument (carbon-dioxide). We cannot deny that this conception does not seem to be very fruitful.

If we wish an example of the notation, this is how the four kinds of propositions usually considered in logic are rendered:

(a)	All X is P.	$P(\mathfrak{a})$ / $X(\mathfrak{a})$
(e)	No X is P.	$P(\mathfrak{a})$ / $X(\mathfrak{a})$
(i)	Some X is P.	$P(\mathfrak{a})$ / $X(\mathfrak{a})$
(o)	Some X is not P.	$P(\mathfrak{a})$ / $X(\mathfrak{a})$

The first symbol-combination can be analysed this way:
The vertical stroke on the left indicates that a judgement is affirmed.

$\vdash\!\!\!-\!\!\!-\ P\ (\alpha)$ would be a singular proposition; namely, "the function P holds for the argument α."

$-\!\!\!-\!\!\!^{\alpha}\!\!\!-\!\!\!-\ P\,(\alpha)$, by itself, denotes the proposition—posed only hypothetically without judging its truth—that the function P holds whatever the argument (α) might be.

Attaching the vertical stroke in the middle with the horizontal stroke on the lower end establishes a conditional relation between the functions $X(\alpha)$ and $P(\alpha)$. This relation is that we cannot simultaneously affirm the former and deny the latter.

Thus, we can translate [the first symbol-combination] this way: "If an individual (α) has property X, it also has property P"; or, in other words: "All X is P."

In the other formulas, the little vertical strokes are the signs for negation.

PAUL TANNERY

F. Review of Frege's *Conceptual Notation* by John Venn, *Mind*, 5 (1880), p. 297.

Dr. Frege's work seems to be a somewhat novel kind of Symbolic Logic, dealing much more in diagrammatic or geometric forms than Boole's. A certain arrangement of horizontal and vertical lines connected with letters or symbols expresses the truth or falsity of propositions involving those letters or symbols; the latter by themselves standing for terms or combinations of terms.

Symbolic systems are, I know, very difficult to judge by those unfamiliar with them; they will almost necessarily appear cumbrous and inconvenient to those who have been accustomed to make use of some different system. But, making all due allowance for these considerations, it does not seem to me that Dr. Frege's scheme can for a moment compare with that of Boole. I should suppose, from his making no reference whatever to the latter, that he has not seen it, nor any of the modifications of it with which we are familiar here. Certainly the merits which he claims as novel for his own method are common to every symbolic method. For instance, he complains that logicians have not duly employed distinct sets of symbols for terms and for operations, and he makes use of letters and of lines for this purpose: in which there would seem no novelty surely to any one who had met with such expressions as $x(y+z) = xy+xz$ as significant of logical operations. Similarly, he calls attention to the fact that, on his scheme, the distinction, so important in grammar and on the predication-view of ordinary logic, between subject and predicate loses all its significance, that hypothetical and disjunctive propositions become equivalent to categorical, and so on; all these being points which must have forced themselves upon the attention of those who have studied this development of Logic. I have not made myself sufficiently familiar with Dr. Frege's system to attempt to work out problems by help of it, but I must confess that it seems to me cumbrous and inconvenient.

[J. V.]

APPENDIX II

EVALUATIONS OF FREGE'S *CONCEPTUAL NOTATION* BY PRESENT-DAY SCHOLARS

A. [From W. V. Quine, Preface to J. T. Clark, *Conventional Logic and Modern Logic* (Woodstock, Maryland: Woodstock College Press, 1952), pp. v–vii.]

Logic is only now emerging from a renaissance such as was undergone by physics centuries ago. Pinpointed, the logical renaissance might be identified with the publication of Frege's *Begriffsschrift* in 1879—a book which is no older today than was Copernicus's *De revolutionibus* in the heyday of Galileo. Insufficiently removed to command a proper perspective, we tend to overlook the continuities and to exaggerate the disparities between the old logic and the new. . . .

But if it is deplorable to exaggerate the cleavage between the old and the new logic, it would be yet more deplorable to underestimate the novelty and importance of the new. 1879 did indeed usher in a renaissance, bringing quantification theory and therewith the most powerful and most characteristic instrument of modern logic. Logical and semantical problems with which Aquinas and others had grappled admit of simpler and clearer treatment in light of quantification theory; and with the aid of quantification theory modern logicians have been able to illuminate the mechanism of deduction in general, and the foundations of mathematics in particular, to a degree hitherto undreamed of.

B. [From Wm. Kneale and Martha Kneale, *The Development of Logic* (London: Oxford University Press, 1962), pp. 510–11.]

Frege's *Begriffsschrift* is the first really comprehensive system of formal logic. Aristotle was interested chiefly in certain common varieties of general propositions. He did indeed formulate the principles of non-contradiction and excluded middle, which belong to a part of logic more fundamental than his theory of the syllogism; but he failed to recognize the need for a systematic account of primary logic. Such an account was supplied, at least in part, by Chrysippus; but neither he nor the medieval logicians who wrote about *consequentiae* succeeded in showing clearly the relation between primary and general logic. Leibniz and Boole, recognizing a parallelism between primary and certain propositions of general logic about attributes or classes, worked out in abstract fashion a calculus that seemed to cover both; but neither of these enlarged the traditional conception of logic to include the theory of relations. Working on some suggestions of DeMorgan, Peirce explored this new field, and shortly after the publication of the *Begriffsschrift* he even produced independently a doctrine of functions with a notation adequate for expressing all the principles formulated by Frege; but he never reduced his thoughts to a system or set out a number of basic principles like those given in the last section. Frege's work, on the other hand, contains all the essentials of modern logic, and it is not unfair either to his predecessors or to his successors to say that 1879 is the most important date in the history of the subject.

C. [From I. M. Bochenski, *A History of Formal Logic*, trans. I. Thomas (Notre Dame, Indiana: University of Notre Dame Press, 1962), p. 268.]

Among all these logicians, Gottlob Frege holds a unique place. His *Begriffsschrift* can only be compared with one other work in the whole history of logic, the *Prior Analytics* of Aristotle. The two cannot quite be put on a level, for Aristotle was the very founder of logic, while Frege could as a result only develop it. But there is a great likeness between these two gifted works. The *Begriffsschrift*, like the *Prior Analytics*, contains a long series of quite new insights, e.g. Frege formulates for the first time the sharp distinction between variables and constants, the concepts of logical function, of a many-place function, of the quantifier; he has a notably more accurate understanding of the Aristotelian theory of an axiomatic system, distinguishes clearly between laws and rules, and introduces an equally sharp distinction between language and meta-language, though without using those terms; he is the author of the theory of description; without having discovered, indeed, the notion of a value, he is the first to have elaborated it systematically. And that is far from being all.

At the same time, and just like Aristotle, he presents nearly all these new ideas and intuitions in an exemplarily clear and systematic way. Already in the *Begriffsschrift* we have a long series of mathematico-logical theorems derived from a few axioms 'without interruption' (*lückenlos*), as Frege says, for the first time in history. Various other mathematical logicians at the same time, or even earlier, expounded similar ideas and theories, but none of them had the gift of presenting all at once so many, often quite original, innovations in so perfect a form.

It is a remarkable fact that this logician of them all had to wait twenty years before he was at all noticed, and another twenty before his full strictness of procedure was resumed by Łukasiewicz. In this last respect, everything published between 1879 and 1921 fell below the standard of Frege, and it is seldom attained even today. The fate of Frege's work was in part determined by his symbolism. It is not true that it is particularly difficult to read, as the reader can assure himself from the examples given below; but it is certainly too original, and contrary to the age-old habits of mankind, to be acceptable.

D. [From M. Dummett, Review of G. Boole, *Studies in Logic and Probability*, ed. R. Rhees, *Journal of Symbolic Logic*, 24 (1959), pp. 203–9.]

Feys regards Boole as *the* originator of modern logic: it seems to the reviewer, on the contrary, that if (say) the development of logic had stopped short with Schröder, there would have been no clear sense in which contemporary logic would be superior to that of, for example, the Scholastics. Feys starts with a contrast between the logical work of Leibniz and of Boole, which seems to the reviewer to overstress the superiority of Boole's achievement: the most important difference was surely that Boole published and Leibniz did not.

There can be no doubt that Boole deserves great credit for what he achieved, in the sense that in those historical circumstances what he did must have been very difficult to do. If, however, we ask after the historical significance, and in particular, the present interest in Boole's writings, a different answer must be given. Boole cannot correctly be called "the father of modern logic". *The* discoveries which separate modern logic from its precursors are of course the use of quantifiers (or, more generally, of operators which bind variables and can be nested) and a concept of a formal system, both due to Frege and neither present even in embryo in the work of Boole. Boole has indeed a great historical importance both for abstract algebra and for logic. As had Leibniz two centuries earlier, he devised a general theory of classes under Boolean operations, a theory which of course contained the traditional theory of the syllogism. This move gained its importance for logic rather from the novelty of *any* extension of logical theory than from the magnitude of the extension itself; and anyone unacquainted with Boole's works will receive an unpleasant surprise when he discovers how ill-constructed his theory actually was and how confused his explanations of it.

A FREGE BIBLIOGRAPHY, 1873-1966

Compiled by Terrell Ward Bynum *and* Aline W. Bynum

THE compilers have attempted to provide a Bibliography that is easy to use and of value to everyone—from those casually interested in Frege to scholars engaged in detailed Frege research. An effort has been made to include every secondary source, no matter in what language it happens to be published, and to list all reprints and translations, so that the reader may conduct his Frege investigations with the editions that he can obtain most easily, and, wherever possible, in the language in which he reads most freely. Sufficient cross-references are included to enable the reader quickly to find reviews of Frege's works, or to follow the chains of argument and reply in the secondary literature.

This Bibliography is divided into three parts. The first part lists (chronologically) all the published works of Frege, from his doctoral dissertation of 1873 to his recently released scientific *Nachlass*. It is intended to include all translations and republications of Frege's works. It does not list, however, the unpublished scientific letters which are collected in Münster, Germany, at the *Institut für mathematische Logik und Grundlagenforschung*.

The second part lists (alphabetically) published secondary sources primarily or extensively concerned with Frege. It is meant to be a complete list of such works from 1879 to 1966 (a few entries from 1967 and 1968 have also been included); and the compilers would sincerely appreciate any suggested additions or corrections.

The third part lists (alphabetically) additional sources which, although not primarily or extensively concerned with Frege, include material of value for Frege research. Each entry in this section is followed by an alphabetical list of the Frege topics handled in the corresponding work. This section of the bibliography is not meant to be complete, though, again, the compilers would gratefully receive suggested additions or corrections.

Each entry has been assigned a serial number for easy reference. The numbers of the works of Frege all begin with the letter 'F'; while the secondary-source numbers start with 'S', and the additional-source numbers begin with 'A'.

ABBREVIATIONS

A	*Analysis*
AR	*Archiv der Mathematik und Physik*
DLZ	*Deutsche Literarzeitung*
E	*Erkenntnis*

JDMV	Jahresberichte der Deutschen Mathematiker-Vereinigung
JLZ	Jenaer Literaturzeitung
JZN	Jenaische Zeitschrift für Naturwissenschaft
JP	Journal of Philosophy
JSL	Journal of Symbolic Logic
M	Mind
MO	The Monist
PQ	Philosophical Quarterly
PR	Philosophical Review
PAS	Proceedings of the Aristotelian Society
PAS, SV	Proceedings of the Aristotelian Society, Supplementary Volume
RM	Review of Metaphysics
S	Synthese
T	Theoria
ZPPK	Zeitschrift für Philosophie und philosophische Kritik

THE WORKS OF FREGE

F1. *Über eine geometrische Darstellung der imaginären Gebilde in der Ebene* (Jena: A. Neuenhann, 1873). Doctoral Dissertation, Göttingen. Reprinted in F′52.

F2. *Rechnungsmethoden, die sich auf eine Erweiterung des Grössenbegriffes gründen* (Jena: F. Fromann, 1874). [*Habilitationsschrift*, Jena.] Reprinted in F′52.

F3. Review of H. Seeger, *Die Elemente der Arithmetik, für den Schulunterricht bearbeitet*, *JLZ* 1 (1874), p. 722. Reprinted in F′52.

F4. Review of A. von Gall and E. Winter, *Die analytische Geometrie des Punktes und der Geraden und ihre Anwendung auf Aufgaben*, *JLZ* 4 (1877), pp. 133–4. Reprinted in F′52.

F5. Review of J. Thomae, *Sammlung von Formeln, welche bei Anwendung der elliptischen und Rosenhain'schen Funktionen gebraucht werden*, *JLZ* 4 (1877), p. 472. Reprinted in F′52.

F6. "Über eine Weise, die Gestalt eines Dreiecks als komplexe Grösse aufzufassen", *Sitzungsberichte der Jenaischen Gesellschaft für Medicin und Naturwissenschaft*, in *JZN* 12 (1878). Reprinted in F′52.

F7. *Begriffsschrift, eine der arithmetischen nachgebildete Formelsprache des reinen Denkens* (Halle: L. Nebert, 1879). Reprinted in F′49. [See: F8, F11, F12, F27, S1, S89, S141, S184, S203, S246, S257, S278, S291. Reviews: S135, S176, S205, S256, S283, S292.]

Translations:
- (a) English translation by P. Geach of part of Chapter 1 in F'47.
- (b) English translation by S. Bauer-Mengelberg of the entire book in *Source Book in Mathematical Logic*, ed. J. van Heijenoort (Cambridge, Massachusetts: Harvard University Press, 1967); also in *Frege and Gödel*, ed. J. van Heijenoort (Cambridge, Massachusetts: Harvard University Press, 1970).
- (c) English translation by T. W. Bynum in F'53.

F8.   "Anwendungen der Begriffsschrift", *Sitzungsberichte der Jenaischen Gesellschaft für Medicin und Naturwissenschaft, JZN* 13 (1879), pp. 29–33. Reprinted in F'49. [See: F7, S89.]
Translation:
English translation by T. W. Bynum in F'53.

F9.   Review of R. Hoppe, *Lehrbuch der analytischen Geometrie I, DLZ* 1 (1880), pp. 210–11. Reprinted in F'52. [See: S134.]

F10.   "Über den Briefwechsel Leibnizens und Huygens mit Papin", *Sitzungsberichte der Jenaischen Gesellschaft für Medicin und Naturwissenschaft, JZN* 15 (1881), pp. 29–32. Reprinted in F'49.

F11.   "Über die wissenschaftliche Berechtigung einer Begriffsschrift", *ZPPK* 81 (1882), pp. 48–56. Reprinted in F'48 and F'49. [See: F7, S89, S217.]
Translations:
- (a) English translation by J. Bartlett in *M* 73 (1964), pp. 155–60.
- (b) English translation by T. W. Bynum in F'53.

F12.   "Über den Zweck der Begriffsschrift", *Sitzungsberichte der Jenaischen Gesellschaft für Medicin und Naturwissenschaft, JZN* 16 (1882–3), pp. 1–10. Reprinted in F'49. [See: F7, S89, S256.]
Translations:
- (a) English translation by V. H. Dudman, in *Australasian Journal of Philosophy* 46 (1968), pp. 89–97.
- (b) English translation by T. W. Bynum in F'53.

F13.   "Geometrie der Punktpaare in der Ebene", *Sitzungsberichte der Jenaischen Gesellschaft für Medicin und Naturwissenschaft, JZN* 17 (1884), pp. 98–102. Reprinted in F'52.

F14.   *Die Grundlagen der Arithmetik. Eine logisch-mathematische Untersuchung über den Begriff der Zahl* (Breslau: W. Koebner, 1884). [See: S139, S161, S215. Reviews: S60 (and F17, S306), S138, S177.]

Reprints:
(a) Reprinted in 1934 by M. and H. Marcus, in Breslau. [Review: S250.]
(b) §§6, 62–5, 68 reprinted in O. Becker, *Grundlagen der Mathematik in geschichtlicher Entwicklung* (Freiburg i. B. and Munich: K. Alber, 1954).
(c) Entire book reprinted in 1961 by G. Olms in Hildesheim.

Translations:
(a) Entire book translated into Italian by L. Geymonat in F'46. [See: S107. Reviews: S72, S223, S260, S271.]
(b) Entire book translated into English by J. Austin, *The Foundations of Arithmetic* (Oxford: Blackwell and Mott, 1950, 1953). Reprinted in 1960 by Harper and Brothers, New York. [Reviews: S19, S20, S30, S52, S76, S106, S127, S166, S200, S201, S209, S228, S275.]
(c) §§6, 62–5, 68 translated into Spanish by A. Moreno in "Crítica de Frege a una demostración de Leibniz y definición del concepto de número con medios-lógico-puro", *Sapientia* 16 (1961), pp. 140–44.
(d) §§55–91, 106–9 translated into English by M. Mahoney in *Philosophy of Mathematics: Selected Readings*, ed. P. Benacerraf and H. Putnam (Englewood Cliffs, New Jersey: Prentice-Hall, 1964), pp. 85–112.
(e) Pp. v–vii and §§21–7 of Austin's translation ((b) above) included in W. E. Kennick and M. Lazerowitz, ed., *Metaphysics: Readings and Reappraisals* (Englewood Cliffs, New Jersey: Prentice-Hall, 1966), pp. 67–74.

F15. Review of H. Cohen, *Das Prinzip der Infinitesimal-Methode und seine Geschichte*, *ZPPK* 87 (1885), pp. 324–9. Reprinted in F'52.

F16. "Über formale Theorien der Arithmetik", *Sitzungsberichte der Jenaischen Gesellschaft für Medicin und Naturwissenschaft*, *JZN* 19 (1885–6), pp. 94–104. Reprinted in F'52. [See: S161.]

F17. "Erwiderung [auf Cantors Rezension der *Grundlagen der Arithmetik*]", *DLZ* 6 (1885), p. 1030. Reprinted in F'52. [See: F14, S60, S306.]

F18. "Über das Trägheitsgesetz", *ZPPK* 98 (1891), pp. 145–61. Reprinted in F'52. [See: S173.]

Translations:
(a) Italian translation by L. Geymonat of part in F'46.
(b) English translation by Rose Rand in S 13 (1961), pp. 350–63.

F19.   *Funktion und Begriff* (Jena: H. Pohle, 1891). Reprinted in F′48
        and F′52. [See S141, S217. Reviews: S136, S255.]
        Translation:
        English translation by P. Geach in F′47.

F20.   "Über Sinn und Bedeutung", *ZPPK* 100 (1892), pp. 25-50.
        Reprinted in F′48 and F′52. [See: S25, S156, S180, S217, S230,
        S236, S237, S238, S263, S284, S303.]

        Translations:
        (*a*) Italian translation by L. Geymonat in F′46.
        (*b*) English translation by M. Black in *PR* 57 (1948), pp. 207-30.
              Reprinted in F′47. [Review: S73.]
        (*c*) English translation by H. Feigl in *Readings in Philosophical
              Analysis*, ed. H. Feigl and W. Sellars (New York: Appleton-
              Century-Crofts, 1949), pp. 85-102. [Review: S53.] Reprinted
              in *Meaning and Knowledge*, ed. E. Nagel and R. Brandt
              (New York: Harcourt, Brace and World, 1965), pp. 69-78.

F21.   Review of G. Cantor, *Zur Lehre vom Transfiniten*, *ZPPK* 100
        (1892), pp. 269-72. Reprinted in F′52. [See: F17.]

F22.   "Über Begriff und Gegenstand", *Vierteljahrsschrift für wissen-
        schaftliche Philosophie*, 16 (1892), pp. 192-205. Reprinted in F′48
        and F′52. [See: F14, S160, S161, S217. Reviews: S9, S112.]

        Translations:
        (*a*) Italian translation by L. Geymonat in F′46.
        (*b*) English translation by P. Geach, revised by M. Black, in
              M 60 (1951), pp. 168-80. Reprinted in F′47.

F23.   *Grundgesetze der Arithmetik, Begriffsschriftlich abgeleitet*, Band I
        (Jena: H. Pohle, 1893). Reprinted, together with Volume II, in
        1962 by G. Olms, Hildesheim. [See: F28, S151, S171, S210, S219,
        S248, S257, S284, S297. Reviews: S137, S220.]

        Translations:
        (*a*) English translation by P. Jourdain and J. Stachelroth of
              part of the Preface, the entire Introduction, and §§1-7 in
              MO 25 (1915), pp. 481-98; 26 (1916), pp. 182-99; 27 (1917),
              pp. 114-27. Reprinted in F′47. [See: S151.]
        (*b*) Italian translation by L. Geymonat of part of the Preface in
              F′46.
        (*c*) English translation by M. Furth of the Preface, Introduction,
              and §§1-52 in F′50. [See: S 99. Reviews: S123, S266, S281.]

F24.   Review of E. Husserl, *Philosophie der Arithmetik*, *ZPPK* 103 (1894), pp. 313–32. Reprinted in F'52. [See: S139, A136.]

Translation:
        English translation by P. Geach of some parts in F'47.

F25.   "Kritische Beleuchtung einiger Punkte in E. Schröders Vorlesungen über die Algebra der Logik", *Archiv für systematische Philosophie*, 1 (1895), pp. 433–56. Reprinted in F'51 and F'52.

Translation:
        English translation by P. Geach in F'47.

F26.   "Le nombre entier", *Revue de métaphysique et de morale*, 3 (1895), pp. 73–8. Reprinted in F'52.

Translation:
        German translation by M. Held and K. Held in F'52.

F27.   "Über die Begriffsschrift des Herrn Peano und meine eigene", *Berichte über die Verhandlungen der Königlich Sächsischen Gesellschaft der Wissenschaften zu Leipzig: Mathematisch-Physische Klasse*, 48 (1896), pp. 361–78. Reprinted in F'52. [See: F7, F8, F11, F12, F23, F28, S219, S220.]

F28.   "Lettera del sig. G. Frege all'editore [A letter from Frege to G. Peano dated "Jena, 29 September 1896"]", *Rivista di Matematica* (*Revue de mathématiques*), 6 (1896–9), pp. 53–9. [See: S219.]

Reprints:
        (*a*) Reprinted in G. Peano, *Opere scelte* (Rome: 1958), pp. 288–294.
        (*b*) Reprinted in F'52.

F29.   *Über die Zahlen des Herrn H. Schubert* (Jena: H. Pohle, 1899). Reprinted in F'51 and F'52.

F30.   *Grundgesetze der Arithmetik, Begriffsschriftlich abgeleitet II* (Jena: H. Pohle, 1903). Reprinted, together with Volume I, in 1962 by G. Olms, Hildesheim. [See: F23, S102, S171, S210, S229, S234, S240, S267, S270.]

Translations:
        (*a*) English translation of §§ 86–137 ["Frege Against the Formalists"] by M. Black in *PR* 59 (1950), pp. 332–45; 60 (1951), pp. 77–93, 202–20. Reprinted in F'47. [See: F16, S50.]

(b) English translation by P. Geach of §§56–67, 139–44, 146–7 ["Frege on Definitions"] in F'47. Reprinted in *Classics in Logic, Readings in Epistemology, Theory of Knowledge and Dialectics*, ed. Runes (New York: Philosophical Library, 1962), pp. 329–42.

(c) English translation by P. Geach of the Appendix in F'47.

(d) English translation by M. Furth of the Appendix in F'50. [See: S99.]

F31.   "Über die Grundlagen der Geometrie", *JDMV* 12 (1903), pp. 319–24. Reprinted in F'52. [See: F32.]
Translation:
English translation by M. Szabo in *PR* 69 (1960), pp. 3–9.

F32.   "Über die Grundlagen der Geometrie, II", *JDMV* 12 (1903), pp. 368–75. Reprinted in F'52. [See: F31.]
Translation:
English translation by M. Szabo in *PR* 69 (1960), pp. 9–17.

F33.   "Was ist eine Funktion?", in *Festschrift* Ludwig Boltzmann *gewidmet zum sechzigsten Geburtstage, 20. Februar 1904* (Leipzig: A. Barth, 1904), pp. 656–66. Reprinted in F'48 and F'52. [See: S217.]
Translation:
English translation by P. Geach in F'47.

F34.   "Über die Grundlagen der Geometrie, I, II, III", *JDMV* 15 (1906), pp. 293–309, 377–403, 423–30. Reprinted in F'52.
Note. These articles are not to be confused with F31, F32 above, which are entirely different.

F35.   "Antwort auf die Ferienplauderei des Herrn Thomae", *JDMV* 15 (1906), pp. 586–90. Reprinted in F'52. [See: F36, F37, S285, S286, S287.]

F36.   "Die Unmöglichkeit der Thomaeschen formalen Arithmetik aufs neue nachgewiesen", *JDMV* 17 (1908), pp. 52–5. Reprinted in F'52. [See: F35, F37, S285, S286, S287.]

F37.   "Schlußbemerkung", *JDMV* 17 (1908), p. 56. Reprinted in F'52. [See: F35, F36, S285, S286, S287.]

F38.   "Remarks on P. Jourdain, 'The Development of the Theories of Mathematical Logic and the Principles of Mathematics' [Printed as footnotes to this article]", *Quarterly Journal of Pure and Applied Mathematics*, 43 (1912), pp. 237–69. The remarks are translated into English by P. Jourdain. Reprinted in F'52. [See: S149.]

F39.   "Der Gedanke: Eine logische Untersuchung", *Beiträge zur Philosophie des deutschen Idealismus*, 1 (1918), pp. 58–77. Reprinted in F′51 and F′52. [See: F40, F41, F45, S218.]

Translation:
English translation by A. Quinton and M. Quinton in *M* 65 (1956), pp. 289–311; also included in P. F. Strawson, ed., *Philosophical Logic* (Oxford: Oxford University Press, 1967), pp. 17–38. [Reviews: S34, S83, S96.]

F40.   "Die Verneinung: Eine logische Untersuchung", *Beiträge zur Philosophie des deutschen Idealismus*, 1 (1918), pp. 143–57. Reprinted in F′51 and F′52. [See: F39, F41, F45, S218.]

Translation:
English translation by P. Geach in F′47.

F41.   "Logische Untersuchungen; Dritter Teil: Gedankengefüge", *Beiträge zur Philosophie des deutschen Idealismus*, 3 (1923), pp. 36–51. Reprinted in F′51 and F′52. [See: F39, F40, F45, S218.]

Translation:
English translation by R. Stoothoff in *M* 72 (1963), pp. 1–17.

F42.   "Ein unbekannter Brief von Gottlob Frege über Hilberts erste Vorlesung über die Grundlagen der Geometrie [Aus dem Nachlaß von Heinrich Liebmann herausgegeben von Max Steck]", *Sitzungsberichte der Heidelberger Akademie der Wissenschaften: Mathematisch-naturwissenschaftliche Klasse, Jahrgang 1940* (Heidelberg, 1940). Reprinted in F′52. [See F43, S42, S43, S132, S274. Review: S38.]

Translation:
Dutch translation by M. G. Beumer in *Simon Stevin* 25 (1946–47), pp. 146–9.

F43.   "Unbekannte Briefe Freges über die Grundlagen der Geometrie und Antwortbrief Hilberts an Frege [Aus dem Nachlaß von Heinrich Liebmann herausgegeben und mit Anmerkungen versehen von Max Steck]", *Sitzungsberichte der Heidelberger Akademie der Wissenschaften: Mathematisch-naturwissenschaftliche Klasse, Jahrgang 1941* (Heidelberg, 1941). Reprinted in F′52. [See: F42, S132, S274.]

F44.   "A Letter to Bertrand Russell on Russell's Paradox [Dated "Jena, 22 June 1902"]", translated into English by B. Woodward, in *Source Book in Mathematical Logic*, ed. J. van Heijenoort (Cambridge, Massachusetts: Harvard University Press, 1967). [See: F30, S102, S229, S234, S240, S241, S270.]

F45.   *Nachgelaßene Schriften*, ed. H. Hermes, F. Kambartel, and F. Kaulbach (Hamburg: Felix Meiner Verlag, 1970). [See: S175, S253.]

Collections of Frege's Works

F'46.   *Aritmetica e logica*, trans. and ed. L. Geymonat (Turin: Giulio Einaudi, 1948). [See: S107. Reviews: S72, S223, S260, S271.] Contains Italian translations of: F14, part of F18, F20, F22, part of the Preface of F23.

F'47.   *Translations from the Philosophical Writings of Gottlob Frege*, trans. and ed. P. Geach and M. Black (Oxford: Blackwell, 1952, 1960). [See S50, S73, S102, S151, S229, S234. Reviews: S3, S31, S57, S75, S84, S111, S118, S126, S182, S189, S252, S290.] Contains English translations of: part of Chapter 1 of F7; F19; F20; F22; part of the Preface, the entire Introduction, and §§1-7 of F23; part of F24; F25; §§56-67, 86-137, 139-44, 146-7, and the Appendix of F30; F33; F40.

F'48.   *Funktion, Begriff, Bedeutung: Fünf logische Studien*, ed. G. Patzig (Göttingen: Vandenhoeck and Ruprecht, 1962). [See: S217.] Contains reprints of: F11, F19, F20, F22, F33.

F'49.   *Begriffsschrift und andere Aufsätze*, ed. I. Angelelli (Hildesheim: G. Olms, 1964). [See S141, S246. Review: S197.] Contains reprints of: F7, F8, F10, F11, F12.

F'50.   *The Basic Laws of Arithmetic: Exposition of the System*, trans. and ed. M. Furth (Los Angeles: University of California Press, 1964). [See: S99, S102. Reviews: S123, S266, S281.] Contains English translations of: the Preface, Introduction, and §§1-52 of F23; the Appendix to F30.

F'51.   *Logische Untersuchungen*, ed. G. Patzig (Göttingen: Vandenhoeck and Ruprecht, 1966). [See: S 218.] Contains reprints of: F25, F29, F39, F40, F41.

F'52.   *Kleine Schriften*, ed. I. Angelelli (Darmstadt: Wissenschaftliche Buchgesellschaft, 1967). [See: S140, S142, S248.] Contains reprints of: F1, F2, F3, F4, F5, F6, F9, F13, F15, F16, F17, F18, F19, F20, F21, F22, F24, F25, F26 (includes a German translation of this), F27, F28, F29, F31, F32, F33, F34, F35, F36, F37, F38, F39, F40, F41, F42, F43.

F'53.   *Conceptual Notation and Related Articles*, trans. and ed. T. W. Bynum (Oxford: Clarendon Press, 1972). [See: S59.] Contains English translations of F7, F8, F11, F12, S135, S176, S205, S256, S283; and a reprint of S292.

SECONDARY SOURCES

S1.   Abbe, E., "*Gutachten* Concerning Frege's Promotion to *Außeror-dentlicher Professor*", in *Ernst Abbes akademische Tätigkeit an der Universität Jena — Jenaer Reden und Schriften*, ed. F. Stier (Jena, 1955), Heft 3, Bestand C, Number 612, pp. 26-8. [See: S278.]

S2.   Akesson, E., "Frege, Gottlob", in *Svensk Uppslagsbok* (Malmö: Norden AB, 1949), vol. 10, pp. 529-30.

S3.   Albertson, J. S., Review of *Translations from the Philosophical Writings of Gottlob Frege*, ed. and trans. P. Geach and M. Black, in *The Modern Schoolman* 30 (1953), pp. 179-80.

S4.   Angelelli, I., Introduction to B. V. Birjukov, *Two Soviet Studies on Frege* (Dordrecht, Holland: D. Reidel, 1964), pp. vii-xxi.

S5.   —— *Studies on Gottlob Frege and Traditional Philosophy* (Dordrecht, Holland: D. Reidel, 1967).

S6.   —— "Textkritische Bemerkungen", in G. Frege, *Begriffsschrift und andere Aufsätze* (Hildesheim: G. Olms, 1964), pp. 122-4.

S7.   —— Review of F. Rivetti Barbo, "Il senso e il significato di Frege", *JSL* 32 (1967), pp. 106-7.

S8.   —— Review of H. D. Sluga, "Frege und die Typentheorie", *JSL* 32 (1967), pp. 107-8.

S9.   Anonymous, Review of Frege's "Über Begriff und Gegenstand" *Philosophisches Jahrbuch*, 6 (1893), p. 196.

S10. —— "Frege, Frederico Luis Gottlob", in *Enciclopédia Brasileira Mérito* (Rio de Janeiro: Mérito, 1964), vol. 9, p. 372.

S11. —— "Frege, Friedrich Ludwig Gottlob", *Encyclopedia International*, 1st edn. (New York: Grolier, 1964), vol. 7, p. 363.

S12. —— "Frege, Gottlob", in *Algemene Winkler Prim Encyclopedie*, 7th edn. (Amsterdam: Elsevier, 1957), vol. 4, p. 211.

S13. —— "Frege, Gottlob", in *Chambers' Biographical Dictionary*, new edn. (New York: St. Martin's Press, 1962), p. 497.

S14. —— "Frege, Gottlob", in *Dictionar Enciclopedic Romîn* (Bucharest: Editura Politice, 1964), vol. 2, p. 463.

S15. —— "Frege, Gottlob", in *Der grosse Brockhaus*, 16th edn. (Wiesbaden: F. A Brockhaus, 1954), vol. 4, p. 268.

S16.   —— "Frege, Gottlob", in *Meyers neues Lexikon* (Leipzig: VEB Bibliographisches Institut, 1962), vol. 3, p. 409.

S17.   —— "Frege, Gottlob", in *Wielka Encyklopedia Powszechna PWN* (Warsaw: Państwowe Wydawnictwo Naukowe, 1964), vol. 4, p. 18.

S18.   —— "Frege, Teófilo", in *Enciclopedia Universal Ilustradca, Europeo-Americana* (Barcelona: Hijos de J. Espasa, 1924), vol. 24, pp. 1176–7.

S19.   —— Review of Frege's *Foundations of Arithmetic*, trans. J. Austin, *Philosophic Abstracts*, 13 (1951), pp. 7–8. [See: F14.]

S20.   —— Review of Frege's *Foundations of Arithmetic*, trans. J. Austin, *Thomist*, 14 (1951), pp. 296–7. [See: F14.]

S21.   Anscombe, G. E. M., *An Introduction to Wittgenstein's Tractatus* (New York: Hutchinson University Library, 1959, 1963). Reprinted—New York: Harper and Row, 1965. [See: S279.]

S22.   Anscombe, G. E. M. and P. Geach, "Gottlob Frege", in *Three Philosophers* (Oxford: Blackwell, 1961), pp. 129–62. [Reviews: S159, S282, S305.]

S23.   Arms, R. A., "The Notion of Number and the Notion of Class" (Philadelphia, 1917). Doctoral Dissertation, University of Pennsylvania.

S24.   Avey, A. E., "Gottlob Frege", *Handbook in the History of Philosophy* (New York: Barnes and Noble, 1954, 1961), p. 217.

S25.   Bachmann, F., *Untersuchungen zur Grundlegung der Arithmetik mit besonderer Beziehung auf Dedekind, Frege und Russell* (Münster, 1934). Doctoral Dissertation.

S26.   Baker, A. J., "Presupposition and Types of Clause", *M* 65 (1956), pp. 368–78. [See: F20.]

S27.   Bartlett, J., "Funktion und Gegenstand: Eine Untersuchung in der Logik von Gottlob Frege" (Munich, 1961). Doctoral Dissertation.

S28.   —— "On Questioning the Validity of Frege's Concept of Function" (Abstract of comments on R. Wells, "Is Frege's Concept of Function Valid"), *JP* 61 (1964), p. 203. [See: S301.]

S29.   Beard, R. W., "On the Church-Frege Analysis of Belief Sentences", *Logique et analyse*, 9 (1966), pp. 252–62.

S30.   Bedau, H., Review of Frege's *Foundations of Arithmetic*, trans.
        J. Austin, *Philosophical Forum*, 11 (1953), pp. 42–3. [See: F14.]

S31.   —— Review of *Translations from the Philosophical Writings of
        Gottlob Frege*, ed. and trans. P. Geach and M. Black, *Philosophical
        Forum*, 11 (1953), p. 43. [See: F'47.]

S32.   Bennett, D. W., "The Natural Numbers from Frege to Hilbert"
        (New York, 1961). Doctoral Dissertation, Columbia University.

S33.   Bennett, J., Review of M. Black, *Problems of Analysis*, *PQ* 6 (1956),
        pp. 90–1. [See: S49.]

S34.   —— Review of Frege's "The Thought: A Logical Inquiry", trans.
        A. M. Quinton and M. Quinton, *JSL* 22 (1957), p. 393. [See: F39.]

S35.   Bergmann, G., "Alternative ontologiche: una risposta alla Dr.
        R. Egidi", *Giornale critico della filosofia italiana*, 42 (1963), pp.
        377–406. [See: S91.]

S36.   —— "Frege's Hidden Nominalism", *PR* 67 (1958), pp. 437–59.
        Reprinted in G Bergmann, *Meaning and Existence* (Madison:
        University of Wisconsin Press, 1960). [See: S37, S61, S116, S144,
        S300, A122.]

S37.   —— "Sameness, Meaning, and Identity". *Proceedings of the 12th
        International Congress of Philosophy*, 4 (1960), pp. 19–27. [See:
        S36.]

S38.   Bernays, P., Review of "Ein unbekannter Brief von Gottlob Frege
        über Hilberts erste Vorlesung über die Grundlagen der Geome-
        trie", ed. M. Steck, *JSL* 7 (1942), pp. 92–3. [See: F42.]

S39.   Beth, E. W., "Gottlob Frege", in *Geschiedenis der logica* (The
        Hague: Servire, 1950), pp. 68–72.

S40.   —— "Het logicisme", in *Inleiding tot de wijsbegeerte der wiskunde*
        (Nijmegen and Utrecht: Dekker and van de Vegt, 1940), pp. 93–
        111.

S41.   —— "Logicism", in *The Foundations of Mathematics* (Amsterdam:
        North Holland, 1959), pp. 353–64.

S42.   —— "Nachschrift", in B. G. Beumer, "En historische bijzonder-
        heid uit het leven van G. Frege", *Simon Stevin*, 25 (1946–7), pp.
        150–1. [See: F42 S43, S56. Review: S55.]

S43.   Beumer, M. G., "En historische bijzonderheid uit het leven van
       G. Frege", *Simon Stevin*, 25 (1946–7), pp. 146–9. [See: F42,
       S42, S55. Review: S56.]

S44.   Bierich, M., *Freges Lehre von dem Sinn und der Bedeutung der
       Urteile und Russells Kritik an dieser Lehre* (Hamburg, 1951).
       Doctoral Dissertation. [See: F20, A140.]

S45.   Birjukov, B. V., "О работах Г. Фреге по философским вопросам
       математики" ["On the Work of Frege Concerning Philosophical
       Problems of Mathematics"], Философские вопросы в естество-
       знании [*Philosophical Problems in Natural Science*] (Moscow,
       1959). English translation in S47. [See: S280, S296.]

S46.   —— "Теория смысла Готлоба Фреге" ["Gottlob Frege's Theory
       of Sense"], Применение логики в науке и технике [*Applications
       of Logic in Science and Technology*] (Moscow, 1960). English trans-
       lation in S47. [See: F20, S280, S296.]

S47.   —— *Two Soviet Studies on Frege*, trans. and ed. I. Angelelli
       (Dordrecht, Holland: D. Reidel, 1964). English translations of
       S45 and S46. [Reviews: S280, S296.]

S48.   Black, M., *A Companion to Wittgenstein's 'Tractatus'* (Ithaca:
       Cornell University Press, 1964).

S49.   —— "Frege on Functions", in *Problems of Analysis* (Ithaca:
       Cornell University Press, 1954), pp. 229–54, 297–8. [See: S33, S80,
       S162. Reviews: S70, S199.]

S50.   —— "Introductory Note to Frege Against the Formalists", *PR*
       59 (1950), pp. 77–8. [See: F30.]

S51.   —— "Presupposition and Implication", in *A Way to the Philosophy
       of Science*, ed. S. Uyeda (Tokyo: Waseda University Press, 1958).
       Reprinted in M. Black, *Models and Metaphors* (Ithaca: Cornell
       University Press, 1962), pp. 48–63.

S52.   —— Review of Frege's *Foundations of Arithmetic*, trans. J. Austin,
       JSL 16 (1951), p. 67. [See: F14.]

S53.   —— Review of Frege's "On Sense and Nominatum", trans. H.
       Feigl, *JSL* 14 (1949), p. 185. [See: F20.]

S54.   Bocheński, I. M., *A History of Formal Logic*, trans. I. Thomas
       (Notre Dame, Indiana: University of Notre Dame Press, 1962).
       English translation of I. M. Bocheński, *Formale Logik* (Freiburg
       i. B. and Munich: Karl Alber, 1956). [Review: A22.]

252 A FREGE BIBLIOGRAPHY, 1873–1966

S55. Borgers, A., Review of E. W. Beth, "Nachschrift" to M. Beumer "En historische bijzonderheid uit het leven van Gottlob Frege", *JSL* 14 (1949), pp. 138–9. [See: F42, S42, S43, S56.]

S56. —— Review of M. Beumer, "En historische bijzonderheid uit het leven van Gottlob Frege", *JSL* 14 (1949), p. 138. [See F42, S42, S43, S55.]

S57. Bures, C. E., Review of *Translations from the Philosophical Writings of Gottlob Frege*, trans. and ed. P. Geach and M. Black, *The Personalist*, 35 (1954), p. 168. [See: F'47.]

S58. Burkamp, W., [§§72–77; 81–86], in *Begriff und Beziehung: Studien zur Grundlegung der Logik* (Leipzig: Meiner, 1927).

S59. Bynum, T. W., "On the Life and Work of Gottlob Frege" and "Editor's Introduction" in Frege's *Conceptual Notation and Related Articles* trans. and ed. T. W. Bynum (Oxford: Clarendon Press, 1972), pp. 1–54, 55–80. [See: F'53.]

S60. Cantor G., Review of Frege's *Grundlagen der Arithmetik*, *DLZ* 6 (1885), pp. 728–9. Reprinted in G. Cantor, *Gesammelte Abhandlungen* (Hildesheim: Olms, 1962). [See: F14, S306.]

S61. Caton, C. E., "An Apparent Difficulty in Frege's Ontology", *PR* 71 (1962), pp. 462–75. [See: S36, S144, S163. Review: S168.]

S62. —— Review of J. Walker, *A Study of Frege*, British Journal for Philosophy of Science, 16 (1966), pp. 396–7. [See: S295.]

S63. Christensen, N. E., "Three Different Occurrences of One and the Same 'Expression' " and "Frege's View of Meaning", in *On the Nature of Meanings* (Copenhagen: Munksgaard, 1961), pp. 59–68, 131–40. [See: F20.]

S64. —— "What Sort of Things are Meanings", *Proceedings of the 12th International Congress of Philosophy*, 4 (1960), pp. 69–76.

S65. Church, A., Abstract of: A. Church, "On Sense and Denotation", *JSL* 7 (1942), p. 47. [See: F20.]

S66. —— "Abstraction", "Arithmetic, Foundations of", "Assertion", "Cardinal Number", "Descriptions", "Frege, Gottlob", "Logic, Symbolic", "Logistic", "Mathematics", "Paradoxes, Logical", "Propositional Function", "Recursion, Proof by", in *Dictionary of Philosophy*, ed. D. D. Runes (New York: Philosophical Library, 1942).

S67. —— "A Formulation of the Logic of Sense and Denotation", in *Structure, Method and Meaning*, ed. Henle, Kallen, and Langer (New York: Liberal Arts Press, 1951), pp. 3–24. Abstract of this article in *JSL* 11 (1946), p. 31. [See: F20. Review: A168.]

S68. —— "Logic, History of: Gottlob Frege", in *Encyclopaedia Britannica* (Chicago, London, Toronto: Benton, 1960), vol. 14, p. 330.

S69. —— "The Need for Abstract Entities in Semantic Analysis", *Proceedings of the American Academy of Arts and Sciences*, 80 (1951), pp. 100–12. [See: S194.]

S70. —— Review of M. Black, "Frege on Functions", *JSL* 21 (1956), pp. 201–2. [See: S49.]

S71. —— Review of R. Carnap, *Introduction to Semantics*, *PR* 52 (1943), pp. 298–304. [See: S302.]

S72. —— Review of Frege's *Aritmetica e logica*, trans. and ed. L. Geymonat, *JSL* 13 (1948), p. 153. [See: F'46.]

S73. —— Review of Frege's "On Sense and Nominatum", trans. H. Feigl, *JSL* 13 (1948), pp. 152–3. [See: F20.]

S74. —— Review of H. R. Smart, "Frege's Logic", *JSL* 10 (1945), pp. 101–3. [See: S268.]

S75. —— Review of *Translations from the Philosophical Writings of Gottlob Frege*, trans. and ed. P. Geach and M. Black, *JSL* 18 (1953), pp. 92–3. [See: F'47, S229.]

S76. Coffey, B., Review of Frege's *Foundations of Arithmetic*, trans. J. Austin, *The Modern Schoolman*, 29 (1952), p. 157. [See: F14.]

S77. Dubislav, W., "Bemerkungen zur Definitionslehre", *E* 3 (1932–3), pp. 201–3.

S78. —— "Die Definitionen als Substitutionsregeln über Zeichen: Die Fregesche Theorie", in *Die Definition* [Beihefte der *Erkenntnis*] (Leipzig: Felix Meiner, 1931), pp. 30–68. [See: S113.]

S79. Dummett, M. "Frege, Gottlob", in P. Edwards, ed., *The Encyclopedia of Philosophy* (New York: Macmillan, 1967), vol. 3, pp. 225–37.

S80. —— "Frege on Functions: A Reply", *PR* 64 (1955), pp. 96–107. [See: S49, S82, S116, S162, S187, S188.]

S81. —— "Nominalism", *PR* 65 (1956), pp. 491–505. [See: A122.]

S82.   Dummett, M. "Note: Frege on Functions", *PR* 65 (1956), pp. 229-30. [See: S80, S187, S188.]

S83.   —— Review of Frege's "The Thought: A Logical Inquiry", trans. A. M. Quinton and M. Quinton, *M* 66 (1957), p. 548. [See: F39.]

S84.   —— Review of *Translations from the Philosophical Writings of Gottlob Frege*, trans. P. Geach and M. Black, *M* 63 (1954), pp. 102–5. [See: F'47.]

S85.   —— Review of F. Waismann, *Introduction to Mathematical Thinking*, *M* 62 (1953), pp. 535–45. [See: A164.]

S86.   Dürr, K., [§3 of] "Der Begriff der Funktion in der symbolischen Logik", *S* 7 (1948-9), pp. 420–2.

S87.   Egidi, R., "Aspetti della crisi interna del logicismo", in *Logica e analisi* (Archivio di filosofia, 1966), pp. 109–19.

S88.   —— "La consistenza filosofica della logica di Frege", *Giornale critico della filosofia italiana*, 41 (1962), pp. 194–208. [See: S35.]

S89.   —— "Matematica, logica e filosofia nell'opera di G. Frege; I: L'ideografia e i quattro scritti sulla ideografia", *Physis*, 4 (1962), pp. 5–32. [See: F7, F8, F11, F12.]

S90.   —— "Matematica, logica e filosofia nell'opera di Frege; II: La revisione della filosofia kantiana dell'aritmetica", *Physis*, 5 (1963), pp. 129–44.

S91.   —— *Ontologia e conoscenza matematica: un saggio su Gottlob Frege* (Florence: Sansoni, 1963). [See: S35. Review: S105.]

S92.   —— Review of G. Frege, *Funktion, Begriff, Bedeutung*, ed. G. Patzig, and of G. Frege, *Logische Untersuchungen*, ed. G. Patzig, *Giornale critico della filosofia italiana*, 46 (1967), pp. 596–8. [See: F'48, F'51.]

S93.   Ferrater Mora, J., "Frege, Gottlob", in *Diccionario de filosofia* (Buenos Aires: Editorial Sudamericana, 1965), vol. 1, p. 725.

S94.   —— Review of W. Kneale, "Gottlob Frege and Mathematical Logic", *JSL* 25 (1960), p. 261. [See: S165.]

S95.   Fisk, M., "A Paradox in Frege's Semantics", *Philosophical Studies*, 14 (1963), pp. 56–63.

S96.   Folch, V. R., Review [in Spanish] of Frege's "The Thought: A Logical Inquiry", trans. A. M. Quinton and M. Quinton, *Pensamiento*, 13 (1957), p. 379. [See: F39.]

S97.   Føllesdal, D., *Husserl und Frege: Ein Beitrag zur Beleuchtung der Entstehung der phänomenologischen Philosophie* (Oslo: Kommisjon Hos. H. Aschehong, 1958).

S98.   Fricke, W., "5. Kapitel, Gottlob Frege" in "Die Mathematik in Jena unter den Auswirkungen des Neuhumanismus und des Intellektualismus, 1824–1901". An unpublished manuscript to be found in the University Archives of Jena University.

S99.   Furth, M., Editor's Introduction to Frege's *The Basic Laws of Arithmetic, Exposition of the System*, trans. and ed. M. Furth (Berkeley and Los Angeles: University of California Press, 1964), pp. v–lvii. [See: F'50.]

S100.   ——— "On Concept and Object: Frege and a Problem of Universals" (Los Angeles, 1964). Doctoral Dissertation.

S101.   Geach, P., "Class and Concept", *PR* 64 (1955), pp. 561–70. [See S116, S188.]

S102.   ——— "On Frege's Way Out", *M* 65 (1956), pp. 408–9. [See: F30, F'47, F'50, S31, S229, S234, S252.]

S103.   ——— "Quine on Classes and Properties", *PR* 62 (1953), pp. 409–12. [See: A124.]

S104.   ——— "Russell on Meaning and Denoting", *A* 19 (1959), pp. 69–72. [See: S146.]

S105.   ——— Review of R. Egidi, *Ontologia e conoscenza matematica: un saggio su Gottlob Frege, JP* 62 (1965), pp. 276–7. [See: S91.]

S106.   ——— Review of Frege's *Foundations of Arithmetic*, trans. J. Austin, *PR* 60 (1951), pp. 535–44. [See: F14.]

S107.   Geymonat, L., [Preface and Notes to] Frege's *Aritmetica e logica*, trans. L. Geymonat (Turin: Giulio Einaudi, 1948). [See: F'46.]

S108.   Goodstein, R., "The Axiomatic Method", *PAS, SV* 36 (1962), pp. 145–54. Reprinted in R. Goodstein, *Essays in the Philosophy of Mathematics* (Leicester, England: Leicester University Press, 1965), pp. 116–25.

S109.   ——— "The Definition of Number", *Mathematical Gazette*, 41 (1957). Reprinted in R. Goodstein, *Essays in the Philosophy of Mathematics* (Leicester, England: Leicester University Press, 1965), pp. 68–78.

S110. Goodstein, R., "The Frege–Russell Definition", in *Mathematical Logic* (Leicester, England: Leicester University Press, 1957), pp. 2–10.

S111. —— Review of *Translations from the Philosophical Writings of Gottlob Frege*, trans. and ed. P. Geach and M. Black, *Mathematical Gazette*, 37 (1953), pp. 141–3. [See: F′47.]

S112. Grandgeorge, L., Review of Frege's "Über Begriff und Gegenstand", *Revue philosophique*, 34 (1892), p. 447. [See: F22.]

S113. Grelling, L., Bemerkungen zu Dubislavs "Die Definitionen", *E* 3 (1932–3), pp. 189–200. [See: S78.]

S114. Greniewski, H., Review of A. Korcik, "Gottlob Frege jako twórca pierwszego systemu aksjomatycznego współczesnej logiki zdań", *JSL* 14 (1950), p. 265. [See: S169.]

S115. Griffin, J., *Wittgenstein's Logical Atomism* (Oxford: Clarendon Press, 1964).

S116. Grossmann, R., "Frege's Ontology", *PR* 70 (1961), pp. 23–40. [See: S36, S80, S101, S163, S187, S300.]

S117. Grünbaum, A., "Some Recent Writings in the Philosophy of Mathematics", *RM* 5 (1951), pp. 281–92.

S118. Hänsel, L., Review of *Translations from the Philosophical Writings of Gottlob Frege*, trans. and ed. P. Geach and M. Black, *Wiener Zeitschrift für Philosophie, Psychologie, Pädagogik*, 4 (1953), pp. 205–6. [See: F′47.]

S119. Harris, N. G. E., "Geach and Frege's Assertion Sign", *A* 27 (1967), pp. 186–9.

S120. Hawkins, B., "Note on a Doctrine of Frege and Wittgenstein", *M* 75 (1966), pp. 583–5.

S121. van Heijenoort, J., Introductory Remarks to *Begriffsschrift*, in *From Frege to Gödel*, ed. J. van Heijenoort (Cambridge, Mass.: Harvard University Press, 1967), pp. 1–5.

S122. —— "Logic as Calculus and Logic as Language", *S* 17 (1967), pp. 324–30.

S123. —— Review of Frege's *The Basic Laws of Arithmetic, Exposition of the System*, trans. and ed. M. Furth, *JP* 63 (1966), p. 28. [See: F23, S99.]

S124. Heintz, J., "Subjects and Predicables" (Duke University, 1965). Doctoral Dissertation.

S125.   Henderson, G., "Intensional Entities and Ontology", *PAS* 58 (1957–8), pp. 269–88.

S126.   —— Review of *Translations from the Philosophical Writings of Gottlob Frege*, trans. and ed. P. Geach and M. Black, *PQ* 4 (1954), pp. 183–4. [See: F'47.]

S127.   Henkin, L., Review of Frege's *Foundations of Arithmetic*, trans. J. Austin, The *Personalist*, 33 (1952), p. 86. [See: F14.]

S128.   Hermes, H., "Frege, Friedrich Ludwig *Gottlob*", in *Neue Deutsche Biographie* (Berlin: Duncker und Humbolt, 1960), vol. 5, pp. 390–2.

S129.   Hermes, H. and H. Scholz, "Ein neuer Vollständigkeitsbeweis für das reduzierte fregesche Axiomensystem des Aussagenkalküls", *Deutsche Mathematik*, 1 (1936), pp. 733–72. Reprinted in *Forschungen zur Logik und zur Grundlegung der exakten Wissenschaften* (Leipzig: S. Hirzel, 1937).

S130.   —— "Mathematische Logik: Algebra und Zahlentheorie", in *Enzyklopädie der mathematischen Wissenschaften* (Leipzig: 1952).

S131.   Heyting, A., "Formal Logic and Mathematics", *S* 6 (1947–8), pp. 275–82. [Review: A20.]

S132.   Hilbert, D., [Antwortbriefe Hilberts an Frege über die Grundlagen der Geometrie] (Aus dem Nachlaß von H. Liebmann herausgegeben und mit Anmerkungen versehen von M. Steck), in *Sitzungsberichte der Heidelberger Akademie der Wissenschaften: Mathematisch-naturwissenschaftliche Klasse, Jahrgang 1940* (Heidelberg, 1940). [See: F42, F43, S42, S43, S55, S56, S274.]

S133.   Hoering, W., "Frege und die Schaltalgebra", *Archiv für mathematische Logik und Grundlagenforschung*, 3 (1957), pp. 125–6.

S134.   Hoppe, R., [Reply to Frege's review of his *Lehrbuch der analytischen Geometrie*], *AR* 1st Ser. 66 (1882), Litterarischer Bericht CCLXI, pp. 1–2. [See: F9.]

S135.   —— Review of Frege's *Begriffsschrift*, *AR*, 1st Ser. 63 (1879), Litterarischer Bericht CCLII, pp. 44–5. [See: F7, F'53, S59.]

S136.   —— Review of Frege's *Funktion und Begriff*, *AR*, 2nd Ser. 10 (1893), Litterarischer Bericht XXXIX, p. 27. [See: F19.]

S137.   —— Review of Frege's *Grundgesetze der Arithmetik I*, *AR*, 2nd Ser. 13 (1895), Litterarischer Bericht XLIX, p. 8. [See: F23.]

S138. Hoppe, R., Review of Frege's *Grundlagen der Arithmetik*, *AR*, 2nd Ser. 2 (1885), Litterarischer Bericht VII, pp. 28–35. [See: F14.]

S139. Husserl, E., "Freges Versuch", in *Philosophie der Arithmetik* (Leipzig: A. Kröner, 1891), pp. 129–34. [See: F14, F24, S213.]

S140. ——— "E. Husserls Anmerkungen [zu Freges Veröffentlichungen]", in Frege's *Kleine Schriften*, ed. I. Angelelli (Darmstadt: Wissenschaftliche Buchgesellschaft, 1967), pp. 423–4. [See: F'52.]

S141. ——— "Husserls Anmerkungen zur *Begriffsschrift*", in Frege's *Begriffsschrift und andere Aufsätze*, ed. I. Angelelli (Hildesheim: Olms, 1964), pp. 117–21. [See: F7.]

S142. ——— "Randbemerkungen Husserls zu G. Frege: *Funktion und Begriff*", in Frege's *Kleine Schriften*, ed. I. Angelelli (Hildesheim: Wissenschaftliche Buchgesellschaft, 1967), pp. 425–6. [See: F'52.]

S143. Jackson, H., "Frege on Sense-Functions", *A* 23 (1962–3), pp. 84–7.

S144. ——— "Frege's Ontology", *PR* 69 (1960), pp. 394–5. [See: S36, S61, S163.]

S145. ——— "Note on an Argument of Church", *T* 30 (1964), pp. 197–205.

S146. Jager, R., "Russell's Denoting Complex", *A* 20 (1960), pp. 53–62. [See: S104, S241, S258, A140.]

S147. Jones, E. E. C., "Mr. Russell's Objections to Frege's Analysis of Propositions", *M* 19 (1910), pp. 379–86. [See: A140.]

S148. Jørgensen, J., "Chapter 5, Development of Formal Logic in Recent Times.—Logistics", in *A Treatise of Formal Logic* (Copenhagen: Levin and Munksgaard; London: Humphrey Milford, 1931), pp. 147–75.

S149. Jourdain, P. E. B., "The Development of the Theories of Mathematical Logic and the Principles of Mathematics", *Quarterly Journal of Pure and Applied Mathematics*, 43 (1911–12), pp. 219–314. [See: F38, S256.]

S150. ——— "The Function of Symbolism in Mathematical Logic", *Scientia*, 21 (1917), pp. 1–12. French translation: "La fonction du symbolisme dans la logique mathématique", trans. E. Philippi, *Scientia*, 21 (1917), Supplément, pp. 3–15.

S151. ——— "Introductory Note to Frege's *Fundamental Laws of Arithmetic*", trans. P. Jourdain, *MO* 25 (1915), pp. 481–4. [See: F23.]

S152.   —— "Reply to J. J. Maxwell's Note", *M* 21 (1912), pp. 470–1. [See: S198, A112.]

S153.   Kalish, D., "Mr. Pap on Logic, Existence and Descriptions", *A* 15 (1955), pp. 61–5.

S154.   Kamiński, S., "Fregego logika zdań", *Roczniki filozoficzne*, 5 (1957–8), pp. 31–64. English Abstract: "Frege's Logic of Propositions", p. 226. [Review: S185.]

S155.   Kattsoff, L., "Chapter 4, Frege and Russell—Definition of Number", in *A Philosophy of Mathematics* (Ames, Iowa: The Iowa State College Press, 1948), pp. 24–47.

S156.   Kauppi, R., "Über Sinn, Bedeutung und Wahrheitswert der Sätze", *Acta Academiae Paedagogicae Jyväkyläensis*, 17 (1959), pp. 205–13. [See: F20.]

S157.   Keene, G. B., "Analytic Statements and Mathematical Truth", *A* 16 (1955–6), pp. 86–90.

S158.   Keferstein, H., "Über den Begriff der Zahl", *Mitteilungen der Mathematischen Gesellschaft in Hamburg*, 2 (1890), pp. 119–25.

S159.   Kenny, A., Review of Anscombe and Geach, *Three Philosophers*, *M* 74 (1965), pp. 92–105. [See: S22.]

S160.   Kerry, B., "Der von Frege versuchte Nachweis", in *System einer Theorie des Grenzbegriffs: Ein Beitrag zur Erkenntnistheorie* (Leipzig and Vienna: 1886), pp. 39–44. [See: F22.]

S161.   —— "Über Anschauung und ihre psychische Verarbeitung", *Vierteljahresschrift für wissenschaftliche Philosophie*, 11 (1887), pp. 249–307. [See: F7, F14, F16.]

S162.   Khatchadourian, H., "Frege on Concepts", *T* 22 (1956), pp. 85–100. [See: S49, S80.]

S163.   Klemke, E. D., "Professor Bergmann and Frege's 'Hidden Nominalism' ", *PR* 68 (1959), pp. 507–14. [See: S36, S61, S116, S144.]

S164.   Kneale, W. C., "Frege, Gottlob", in *Encyclopaedia Britannica* (Chicago, London, Toronto: Benton, 1960), vol. 9, p. 750.

S165.   —— "Gottlob Frege and Mathematical Logic", in *The Revolution in Philosophy*, ed. A. J. Ayer *et al.* (London: Macmillan; New York: St. Martin's Press, 1956), pp. 26–40. [Review: S94.]

S166. Kneale, W. C., Review of Frege's *Foundations of Arithmetic*, trans. J. Austin, *M* 59 (1950), pp. 395–7. [See: F14.]

S167. Kneale, W. C. and M. Kneale, *The Development of Logic* (London: Oxford University Press, 1962). [Review: A22.]

S168. Kokoszyńska, M., "Ze studiów nad Fregem" ["Studies in Frege's Philosophy", review of C. E. Caton, "An Apparent Difficulty in Frege's Ontology"], *Studia filozoficzne*, 1 (1964), pp. 196–7. [See: S61.]

S169. Korcik, A., "Gottlob Frege jako twórca pierwszego systemu aksjomatycznego współczesnej logiki zdań" ["Gottlob Frege, the Author of the First Axiomatic System of the Contemporary Logic of Propositions"], *Roczniki filozoficzne*, 1 (1948), pp. 138–64. French abstract included: "Gottlob Frege, auteur du premier système axiomatique de la logique contemporaine des propositions". [Review: S114.]

S169a. Korselt, A., "Über die Grundlagen der Geometrie", *JDMV* 12 (1903), pp. 402 ff. [See: F34.]

S170. Krenz, E. *Der Zahlbegriff bei Frege* (Vienna, 1942). Doctoral Dissertation.

S171. von Kutschera, F., "5.2. Freges Beweis der semantischen Vollständigkeit des Systems der *Grundgesetze*", in *Die Antinomien der Logik* (Freiburg and Munich: Karl Alber, 1964), pp. 69–72. [See: F23, F30.]

S172. —— "Das Verhältnis der modernen zur traditionellen Logik", *Philosophisches Jahrbuch*, 71 (1964), pp. 219–29.

S173. Lange, L., "Das Inertialsystem vor dem Forum der Naturforschung", *Philosophische Studien*, [*Festschrift, Wilhelm Wundt zum siebzigsten Geburtstage*], 20 (1902), pp. 1–71. [See: F18.]

S174. Langer, S. K., Review of Scholz, H., "Die klassische deutsche Philosophie und die neue Logik", *JSL* 2 (1937), p. 57. [See: A143.]

S175. —— Review of Scholz and Bachmann, "Der wissenschaftliche Nachlaß von Gottlob Frege", *JSL* 2 (1937), pp. 56–7. [See: S253.]

S176. Lasswitz, K., Review of Frege's *Begriffsschrift*, *JLZ* 6 (1879), pp. 248–9. [See: F7, F'53, S59.]

S177. —— Review of Frege's *Grundlagen der Arithmetik*, *ZPPK* 89 (1886), Supplement, pp. 143–8. [See: F14.]

S178.   Levison, A. B., "Frege on Proof", *Philosophy and Phenomeno-logical Research*, 22 (1961), pp. 40–9. [See: A172.]

S179.   Lewy, C., Review of R. Carnap, *Meaning and Necessity*, M 58 (1949), pp. 228–38. [See: A36.]

S180.   Linke, P., "Gottlob Frege als Philosoph", *Zeitschrift für philo-sophische Forschung*, 1 (1946), pp. 75–99.

S181.   Linsky, L., "Hesperus and Phosphorus", *PR* 68 (1959), pp. 515–18. [See: F20, A36, A121]

S182.   —— Review of *Translations from the Philosophical Writings of Gottlob Frege*, trans. and ed. P. Geach and M. Black, *Philosophy of Science*, 20 (1953), pp. 342–3. [See: F'47.]

S183.   Łukasiewicz, J., "I. 1. Trends in Mathematical Logic", in *Elements of Mathematical Logic*, trans. O. Wojtasiewicz (New York: Mac-millan, 1963), pp. 1–9. Translation of the original Polish: *Elementy logiki matematycznej* (Warsaw: Państwowe Wydawnictwo, 1958).

S184.   —— "Zur Geschichte der Aussagenlogik", *E* 5 (1935), pp. 111–31. German translation of the original: "Z historii logiki zdań", *Przeglad filozoficzny*, 37 (1934), pp. 369–77. English translation: "On the History of the Logic of Propositions", *Polish Logic, 1920–1939*, ed. S. McCall (Oxford: Clarendon Press, 1967). [See: F7.]

S185.   Luschei, E. C., Review of S. Kamiński, "Fregego logika zdań", *JSL* 27 (1962), pp. 222–3. [See: S154.]

S186.   Mangione, C., "Attualità dell'opera di Gottlob Frege alla luce di recenti studi di logica matematica", *Atti del Convegno Nazionale Logica* (Torino, 1961), pp. 167–76.

S187.   Marshall, W., "Frege's Theory of Functions and Objects", *PR* 62 (1953), pp. 374–90. [See: S80, S82, S116, S188.]

S188.   —— "Sense and Reference: A Reply", *PR* 65 (1956), pp. 342–61. [See: S80, S82, S101, S187, A45.]

S189.   —— Review of *Translations from the Philosophical Writings of Gottlob Frege*, trans. and ed. P. Geach and M. Black, *PR* 63 (1954), pp. 120–2. [See: F'47.]

S190.   —— Review of R. Wells, "Frege's Ontology", *JSL* 18 (1953), pp. 90–1. [See: S300.]

S191. Martin, G., "Neuzeit und Gegenwart in der Entwicklung des mathematischen Denkens", *Kant Studien*, 45 (1953–4). Reprinted in G. Martin, *Gesammelte Abhandlungen* (Cologne: Kölner Universitäts Verlag, 1961), vol. 1, pp. 138–50.

S192. Martin, R. M., "5.A. Frege on '*Analytisch*' ", in *The Notion of Analytic Truth* (Philadelphia: University of Pennsylvania Press, 1959), pp. 96–9.

S193. —— "On Proper Names and Frege's *Darstellungsweise*", *MO* 51 (1967), pp. 1–8.

S194. —— "On the Frege-Church Theory of Meaning", *Philosophy and Phenomenological Research*, 23 (1963), pp. 605–9. [See: F20, S69, A40.]

S195. Marty, A., [pp. 56–8 of] *Gesammelte Schriften*, Bd. II (Halle: 1918).

S196. Maser, S., *Die ontologischen Grundlagen und ihre Folgen im Werk von Gottlob Frege* (Stuttgart, 1965). Doctoral Dissertation.

S197. Mates, B., Review of Frege's *Begriffsschrift und andere Aufsätze*, ed. I. Angelelli, *JSL* 32 (1967), pp. 240–2. [See: F'49.]

S198. Maxwell, J. J., "Note", *M* 21 (1912), pp. 302–3. [See: S152, A112.]

S199. Mays, W., Review of M. Black, "Frege on Functions", *British Journal for the Philosophy of Science*, 8 (1957–8), p. 167. [See: S49.]

S200. Maziarz, E. A., Review of Frege's *Foundations of Arithmetic*, trans. J. Austin, *The New Scholasticism*, 26 (1952), pp. 91–2. [See: F14.]

S201. McCrea, W. H., Review of Frege's *Foundations of Arithmetic*, trans. J. Austin, *Philosophy*, 26 (1951), pp. 178–80. [See: F14.]

S202. Meckler, L., "Can *Sinn* be a Combination of Properties?", *M* 62 (1953), pp. 248–52. [See: F20, S238, S303, A170.]

S203. Medlin, B., "The Theory of Truth Functions, I and II", *Australasian Journal of Philosophy*, 42 (1964), pp. 1–21; 183–98. [See: F7.]

S204. Menne, A., "Frege und die Entwicklung seines Ansatzes", in *Logik und Existenz* (Meisenheim: Westkulturverlag Anton Hain, 1954), pp. 21–4.

S205. Michaëlis, C. T., Review of Frege's *Begriffsschrift*, *Zeitschrift für Völkerpsychologie und Sprachwissenschaft*, 12 (1880), pp. 232–40. [See: F7, F'53, S59.]

S206. Mortan, G., "Einige Bemerkungen zur Überwindung des Psychologismus durch G. Frege und E. Husserl", *Proceedings of the 12th International Congress of Philosophy*, vol. 12 (Florence, 1961), pp. 327–34.

S207. —— *Gottlob Freges philosophische Bedeutung* (Jena, 1954). Doctoral Dissertation.

S208. Myhill, J., "Two Ways of Ontology in Modern Logic", *RM* 5 (1952), pp. 639–55. [Review: A109.]

S209. Nagel, E., Review of Frege's *Foundations of Arithmetic*, trans. J. Austin, *JP* 48 (1951), p. 342. [See: F14.]

S210. Natucci, A., "*Grundgesetze der Arithmetik* by Gottlob Frege", in *Il concetto di numero e le sue estensioni* (Torino: 1923), pp. 320–33. [See: F23.]

S211. Nidditch, P., "Frege's Logic", in *The Development of Mathematical Logic* (New York: Free Press of Glencoe, 1962), pp. 59–66.

S212. —— "Peano and the Recognition of Frege", *M* 72 (1963), pp. 103–10. [See: S241.]

S213. Osborn, A. D., "Chapter 4, Frege's Attack on Husserl", in *Edmund Husserl and his Logical Investigations* (Cambridge, Massachusetts: 1949), pp. 43–53.

S214. Papst, W., *Gottlob Frege als Philosoph* (Berlin, 1932). Doctoral Dissertation.

S215. Parsons, C., "Frege's Theory of Number", in *Philosophy in America*, ed. M. Black (Ithaca, New York: Cornell University Press, 1965), pp. 180–203. [See F14.]

S216. Passmore, L. [pp. 149–57 of] *A Hundred Years of Philosophy* (London: Duckworth, 1957).

S217. Patzig, G., Vorwort to Frege's *Funktion, Begriff, Bedeutung*, ed. G. Patzig (Göttingen: Vandenhoeck und Ruprecht, 1962). [See: F'48.]

S218. —— Vorwort to Frege's *Logische Untersuchungen*, ed. G. Patzig (Göttingen: Vandenhoeck und Ruprecht, 1966). [See: F'51.]

S219. Peano, G., "Risposta alla lettera del Signor Frege all'Editore", *Rivista di matematica*, 6 (1896–9), 60–1. Reprinted in G. Peano, *Opere scelte* (Rome, 1958), vol. 2, pp. 295–6. [See: F28.]

S220.   Peano, G., Review of Frege's *Grundgesetze der Arithmetik I,* *Rivista di matematica,* 5 (1895), pp. 122–8. Reprinted in G. Peano, *Opere scelte* (Rome, 1958), vol. 2, pp. 187–95. [See: F23.]

S221.   Perelman, C., "Étude sur Gottlob Frege", *Revue de l'Université de Bruxelles* 44 (1938–9), pp. 224–7. Abstract of the author's dissertation.

S222.   —— "Metafizyka Fregego" ["Frege's Metaphysics"], *Kwartalnik filozoficzny,* 14 (1938), pp. 119–42.

S223.   Perna, A., Review of Frege's *Aritmetica e logica,* trans. and ed. L. Geymonat, *Archimede,* 1 (1949), pp. 34–5. [See: F'46.]

S224.   Pietersma, H., "Husserl und Frege", *Archiv für Geschichte der Philosophie,* 49 (1967), pp. 298–323. [See: F24, S139.]

S225.   Piltz, E., "Frege, Friedrich Ludwig *Gottlob*", in *Dozenten Album der Universität Jena, 1858 bis 1908* (Jena: G. Neuenhahn, 1908), p. 19.

S226.   Pivcevic, E., "Husserl versus Frege", *M* 76 (1967), pp. 155–65. [See: F24, S139.]

S227.   Prior, A. N., "Modal Logic in the Style of Frege", in *Time and Modality* (Oxford: Clarendon Press, 1957), pp. 55–62, 71.

S228.   Quick, J. B., Review of Frege's *Foundations of Arithmetic,* trans. J. Austin, *Thought,* 27 (1952), pp. 303–4. [See: F14.]

S229.   Quine, W. V., "On Frege's Way Out", *M* 64 (1955), pp. 145–59. Italian translation: "La via d'uscita di Frege", *Rivista di filosofia* 46 (1955), pp. 371–86. [See: F'47, S75, S102, S234, S252, S270.]

S230.   —— Review of P. Wienpahl, "Frege's 'Sinn und Bedeutung' ", *JSL* 16 (1951), p. 138. [See: S303.]

S231.   Resnik, M. D., "The Context Principle in Frege's Philosophy", *Philosophy and Phenomenological Research,* 27 (1967), pp. 356–65.

S232.   —— "Frege's Methodology: A Critical Study" (Cambridge, Massachusetts, 1964). Doctoral Dissertation, Harvard University.

S233.   —— "Frege's Theory of Incomplete Entities", *Philosophy of Science,* 32 (1965), pp. 329–41.

S234.   —— "Some Observations Related to Frege's Way Out", *Logique et analyse,* N.S. 7 (1964), pp. 139–44. [See: F30, F'47, S102, S229, S270.]

S235.   —— Review of C. Thiel, *Sinn und Bedeutung in der Logik Gottlob Freges*, *Philosophy and Phenomenological Research*, 28 (1967), pp. 303–4.

S236.   Rivetti Barbo, F., "Il senso e il significato di Frege: ricerca teoretica sul senso e designato delle espressioni, e sui valori di verità", in *Studi di filosofia e di storia della filosofia in onore di F. Olgiati* (Milan, 1962), pp. 420–83. [See: F20.]

S237.   —— "Sense, Denotation and the Context of Sentences", in *Contributions to Logic and Methodology in Honor of I. M. Bocheński*, ed. A. Tymieniecka (Amsterdam: North Holland, 1965), pp. 208–42. [See: F20.]

S238.   Rudner, R., "On '*Sinn*' as a Combination of Physical Properties", *M* 61 (1952), pp. 82–4. [See: F20, S202, S303.]

S239.   Runes, D. D., "Frege, Friedrich Ludwig Gottlob", in *Pictorial History of Philosophy* (New York: The Philosophical Library, 1959), p. 324. Includes photograph of Frege.

S240.   Russell, B., "A Letter from Bertrand Russell to Gottlob Frege", trans. B. Woodward in *Source Book in Mathematical Logic*, ed. J. van Heijenoort (Cambridge, Massachusetts: Harvard University Press, 1967), pp. 124–5. [See: S267.]

S241.   —— Appendix A: "The Logical and Arithmetical Doctrines of Frege", in *The Principles of Mathematics* (London: G. Allen, 1903, 2nd edn., 1937), pp. 501–22. Reprinted in 1964 (W. W. Norton Co., New York). [See: S146, S212, S267.]

S242.   Russell, B. and A. N. Whitehead, *Principia Mathematica* (3 vols., Cambridge, England: Cambridge University Press, 1910, 1912, 1913).

S243.   Ryle, G., Introduction to *The Revolution in Philosophy*, ed. A. J. Ayer *et al.* (London: Macmillan; New York: St. Martin's Press, 1956), pp. 1–11.

S244.   —— Review of R. Carnap, *Meaning and Necessity*, *Philosophy*, 24 (1949), pp. 69–76. [See: A36.]

S245.   Schmidt, H. A., "XIV. Normaldeduktiv alternäre → ¬-Aussagenlogik", in *Mathematische Gesetze der Logik* (Berlin, Göttingen, Heidelberg: Springer, 1960), pp. 203–17.

S246.   Scholz, H., "Die Anmerkungen von H. Scholz zur *Begriffsschrift*", in Frege's *Begriffsschrift und andere Aufsätze*, ed. I. Angelelli (Hildesheim: G. Olms, 1964), pp. 115–16. [See: F'49.]

S247.   —— "Gottlob Frege", in *Mathesis Universalis*, ed. H. Hermes *et al.* (Basel and Stuttgart: B. Schwabe, 1961), pp. 268–78. [Review: A97.]

S248.   —— "H. Scholz' Anmerkungen zu *Grundgesetze I*", in Frege's *Kleine Schriften*, ed. I. Angelelli (Darmstadt: Wissenschaftliche Buchgesellschaft, 1967), pp. 420–2. [See: F23, F'52.]

S249.   —— "Was ist ein Kalkül and was hat Frege für eine pünktliche Beantwortung dieser Frage geleistet?", in *Semester-Berichte* (Münster, 1935), 7 sem., pp. 16–47.

S250.   —— Review of the second edition (1934) of Frege's *Grundlagen der Arithmetik*, *DLZ* 56 (1935), pp. 163–70. [See: F14.]

S251.   —— Review of P. F. Linke, "Gottlob Frege als Philosoph", *JSL* 13 (1948), p. 154. [See: S180.]

S252.   —— Review of *Translations from the Philosophical Writings of Gottlob Frege*, trans. and ed. P. Geach and M. Black, *Zentralblatt für Mathematik*, 48 (1954), pp. 1–2. [See: F'47.]

S253.   Scholz, H. and F. Bachmann, "Der wissenschaftliche Nachlaß von G. Frege", in *Actes du congrès international de philosophie scientifique*, [*Paris, 1935*] 8 (1936), pp. 24–30. [See: F45. Review: S175.]

S254.   Scholz, H. and H. Schweitzer, *Die sogenannten Definitionen durch Abstraktion* (Leipzig: F. Meiner, 1935).

S255.   Schotten, H., Review of Frege's *Funktion und Begriff*, *Zeitschrift für Mathematik und Physik*, 38 (1893), Historisch-literarische Abteilung, p. 90. [See: F19.]

S256.   Schröder, E., Review of Frege's *Begriffsschrift*, *Zeitschrift für Mathematik und Physik*, 25 (1880), pp. 81–94. [See: F7, F'53, S59, S149.]

S257.   Schröter, K., *Axiomatierung der fregeschen Aussagenkalküle* (Leipzig: Hirzel, 1943). [See: F7, F23.]

S258.   Searle, J. R., "Russell's Objections to Frege's Theory of Sense and Reference", *A* 18 (1958), pp. 137–43. [See: S146, A140.]

S259.   Sellars, W., "The Paradox of Analysis: A Neo-Fregean Approach", *A* 24 (1963–4), Supplement, pp. 84–98.

S260.   Severi, F., Review of Frege's *Aritmetica e logica*, trans. and ed. L. Geymonat, *Scientia*, 84 (1949), p. 144. [See: F'46.]

S261.   Shearman, A. T., "Definition in Symbolic Logic", *M* 19 (1910), pp. 387–9.

S262.   —— *The Scope of Formal Logic: The New Logical Doctrines Expounded, with Some Criticisms* (London: University of London Press, 1911).

S263.   Shwayder, D. S., "=", *M* 65 (1956), pp. 16–37. [See: F20.]

S264.   Simpson, T. M., "A Note on Sense and Denotation", *Nous*, 1 (1967), pp. 207–9. [See: F20.]

S265.   Sloman, A., "Functions and Rogators", in *Formal Systems and Recursive Functions*, ed. J. N. Crossley and M. Dummett (Amsterdam: North Holland, 1965), pp. 156–75.

S266.   —— Review of Frege's *The Basic Laws of Arithmetic*, trans. and ed. M. Furth, also of J. Walker, *A Study of Frege*, British Journal for the Philosophy of Science, 17 (1966), pp. 249–53. [See: F23; S295.]

S267.   Sluga, H. D., "Frege und die Typentheorie", in *Logik und Logik-Kalkül*, ed. M. Käsbauer and F. von Kutschera (Freiburg i. B. and Munich: K. Alber, 1962), pp. 195–209. [See: F30, S240, S241, S242.]

S268.   Smart, H. R., "Frege's Logic", *PR* 54 (1945), pp. 489–505. [Review: S67.]

S269.   Smith, G. A., "Frege's Theory of Reference" (Detroit: 1967). Doctoral Dissertation, Wayne State University.

S270.   Sobociński, B., "L'analyse de l'antinomie russellienne par Leśniewski: IV. La correction de Frege", *Methodos*, 1 (1949), pp. 220–8. [See: S102, S229, S234.]

S271.   Somenzi, V., Review of Frege's *Aritmetica e logica*, trans. and ed. L. Geymonat, *Sigma*, 1 (1948), pp. 436–47.

S272.   Sommers, F., "On a Fregean Dogma", in I. Lakatos (ed.), *Problems in the Philosophy of Mathematics* (Amsterdam: North Holland, 1967).

S273. Stammler, G. [§§58–65 of] *Begriff, Urteil, Schluß* (Halle a.d. S.: M. Niemeyer, 1928), pp. 171–89.

S274. Steck, M., [Remarks with] "Ein unbekannter Brief von Gottlob Frege über Hilberts erste Vorlesung über die Grundlagen der Geometrie", in *Sitzungsberichte der Heidelberger Akademie der Wissenschaften: Mathematisch-naturwissenschaftliche Klasse 1940* (1940), nr. 6. [See: F42, F43, S132.]

S275. Steele, D. A., Review of Frege's *Foundations of Arithmetic*, trans. J. Austin, *Scripta Mathematica*, 17 (1951), pp. 260–2. [See: F14.]

S276. Sternfeld, R., *Frege's Logical Theory* (Carbondale, Illinois: Southern Illinois University Press, 1966).

S277. —— "A Restriction in Frege's Use of the Term 'True' ", *Philosophical Studies*, 6 (1955), pp. 58–64.

S278. Stier, F., ["Remarks on E. Abbe's *Gutachten* (1879) Concerning Frege's Promotion to *Ausserordentlicher Professor*"], in *Ernst Abbes akademische Tätigkeit an der Universität Jena. — Jenaer Reden und Schriften* (Jena, 1955), Heft 3, Bestand C, nr. 612, pp. 26 and 28. [See: S1.]

S279. Stoothoff, R. H., "Note on a Doctrine of Frege", *M* 72 (1963), pp. 406–8. [See: S21.]

S280. —— Review of B. V. Birjukov, *Two Soviet Studies on Frege*, trans. and ed. I. Angelelli, *PQ* 16 (1966), p. 396. [See: S45, S46, S47.]

S281. —— Review of Frege's *The Basic Laws of Arithmetic*, trans. and ed. M. Furth, *PQ* 16 (1966), p. 395. [See: F'50.]

S282. Sykes, R. D., Review of G. E. M. Anscombe and P. Geach, *Three Philosophers*, *Australasian Journal of Philosophy*, 40 (1962), pp. 378–83. [See: S22.]

S283. Tannery, P., Review of Frege's *Begriffsschrift*, *Revue philosophique*, 8 (1879), pp. 108–9. [See: F7, F'53, S59.]

S284. Thiel, C., *Sinn und Bedeutung in der Logik Gottlob Freges* (Meisenheim am Glan: A. Hain, 1965). Doctoral Dissertation, Erlangen. [See: F20, F23.] English translation by T. J. Blakeley, *Sense and Reference in Frege's Logic* (Dordrecht, Holland: D. Reidel, 1968).

S285. Thomae, J., "Bermerkungen zum Aufsätze des Herrn Frege", *JDMV* 15 (1906), p. 56. [See: F35, F36, F37, S285, S287.]

S286. —— "Gedankenloser Denker, eine Ferienplauderei", *JDMV* 15 (1906), pp. 434–8. [See: F35, F36, F37, S285 S287.]

S287. —— "Erklärung", *JDMV* 15 (1906), pp. 590–1. [See: F35, F36, F37, S285, S286.]

S288. Trinchero, M., "La fortuna di Frege nell'Ottocento", *Rivista di filosofia*, 55 (1964), pp. 154–86.

S289. Valpola, V., "On the Concept of Observational Truth", *Proceedings of the 12th International Congress of Philosophy*, 5 (1960), pp. 531–5.

S290. Veatch, H., Review of *Translations from the Philosophical Writings of Gottlob Frege*, trans. and ed. P. Geach and M. Black, *The Thomist*, 17 (1954), pp. 104–11. [See: F'47.]

S291. Venn, J., "Chapter XX, Historical Notes: 15. Frege's Scheme", in *Symbolic Logic* (London: Macmillan, 1881), p. 415. [See: F7.]

S292. —— Review of Frege's *Begriffsschrift*, *M* 5 (1880), p. 297. [See: F7, F'53, S59.]

S293. Vuillemin, J., "L'élimination des définitions par abstraction chez Frege", *Revue philosophique*, 156 (1966), pp. 19–40.

S294. —— "Sur le jugement de récognition (*Wiedererkennungsurteil*) chez Frege", *Archiv für Geschichte der Philosophie*, 46 (1964), pp. 310–25.

S295. Walker, J., *A Study of Frege* (Oxford: Blackwell, 1965). [Review: S62.]

S296. —— Review of B. Birjukov, *Two Soviet Studies on Frege*, *Philosophical Books* 7 (1966), pp. 4–7. [See: S45, S46, S47.]

S297. Wang, H., "IV. The Axiomatization of Arithmetic: §6. Dedekind and Frege" and "XVI. Different Axiom Systems: §6. The Systems of Ackermann and Frege", in *A Survey of Mathematical Logic* (Peking: Science Press; Amsterdam: North Holland, 1963), pp. 79–81, 423–31. [See: F23, A51.]

S298. Warner, D. H. J., "Form and Concept", *Journal of the History of Philosophy*, 3 (1965), pp. 159–66. [See: A155.]

S299. Wedberg, A., "Chapter III, Logik och aritmetik: Gottlob Frege", in *Filosofiens historia* (Stockholm: Bonniers, 1966).

S300. Wells, R., "Frege's Ontology", *RM* 4 (1951), pp. 537–73. [See: S36, S116. Review: S190.]

S301. Wells, R., "Is Frege's Concept of Function Valid?", *JP* 60 (1963), pp. 719–30. [See: S28.]

S302. White, M., "On the Church-Frege Solution of the Paradox of Analysis", *Philosophy and Phenomenological Research*, 9 (1948–9), pp. 305–8. [See: S71, A42.]

S303. Wienpahl, P. D., "Frege's *Sinn* and *Bedeutung*", *M* 59 (1950), pp. 483–94. [See: F20, S202, S238. Review: S230.]

S304. Wilder, R. L., "VIII.4.1. Frege's Arithmetic" and "IX. The Frege-Russell Thesis: Mathematics an Extension of Logic", in *Introduction to the Foundations of Mathematics* (London, New York, Sydney: Wiley, 1952, reprinted 1965), pp. 208, 219–45.

S305. Williams, C., Review of G. E. M. Anscombe and P. Geach, *Three Philosophers*, *PQ* 13 (1963), pp. 270–1. [See: S22.]

S306. Zermelo, E., "Anmerkung", in G. Cantor, *Gesammelte Abhandlungen* (Berlin: 1932). Remarks on Cantor's review of Frege's *Grundlagen der Arithmetik*. [See: F14, S60.]

ADDITIONAL SOURCES

A1. Arms, R., "The Relation of Logic to Mathematics", *MO* 29 (1919), pp. 146–52. Frege topics: Frege's arguments against psychologism in mathematics and logic.

A2. Bachelard, S., Avant-Propos to *La Logique de Husserl* (Paris: Presses Universitaires de France, 1957). Frege topics: Frege's critique of Husserl's *Philosophie der Arithmetik*, Husserl's critique of Frege's *Grundlagen der Arithmetik*.

A3. Bar-Hillel, Y., "Bolzano's Definition of Analytic Propositions", *T* 16 (1950), pp. 91–117. Also appears in *Methodos*, 2 (1950), pp. 32–55. Frege topics: Bolzano's versus Frege's definition of analytic proposition.

A4. —— Review of A. Church, "The Need for Abstract Entities in Semantic Analysis", *JSL* 17 (1952), pp. 137–9. [See: S69.] Frege topics: categorematic and syncategorematic expressions, Frege's semantics.

A5. —— Review of W. V. Quine, "Semantics and Abstract Objects" (and comments on this paper by M. Black), *JSL* 17 (1952), pp. 136–7. Frege topics: naming, ontology, sense and denotation, truth values.

A6.   Bar-Hillel, Y., and A. A. Fränkel, *Foundations of Set Theory* (Amsterdam: North Holland, 1958). Frege topics: logicism, Russell's Paradox.

A7.   Barker, S., *Philosophy of Mathematics* (Englewood Cliffs, New Jersey: Prentice-Hall, 1964). Frege topics: definition of number, logicism, realism and the nature of numbers, truths of geometry.

A8.   Bauch, B., *Die Idee* (Leipzig: E. Reinicke, 1926). Frege topics: concepts, definition of number, functions.

A9.   ——— *Das Naturgesetz* (Berlin and Leipzig: Teubner, 1924). Frege topics: concepts, functions, generality, levels of functions, "saturation" of functions.

A10.   ——— "Über den Begriff des Naturgesetzes", *Kant Studien*, 19 (1914), pp. 303–37. Frege topics: concepts, functions, judgements, levels of functions, psychologism.

A11.   ——— *Wahrheit, Wert und Wirklichkeit* (Leipzig: F. Meiner, 1923). Frege topics: functions, judgements, propositions, truth values.

A12.   Benacerraf, P., "Logicism, Some Considerations" (Princeton: 1960). Doctoral Dissertation. Frege topic: logicism.

A13.   ——— "What Numbers Could Not Be", *PR* 74 (1965), pp. 47–73. Frege topic: definition of number.

A14.   Benacerraf, P., and H. Putnam, Introduction to *Philosophy of Mathematics, Selected Readings*, ed. P. Benacerraf and H. Putnam (Englewood Cliffs, New Jersey: Prentice-Hall, 1964), pp. 1–27. Frege topics: concept of number, existence of mathematical entities, logicism, mathematical induction.

A15.   Berg, J., *Bolzano's Logic* (Stockholm, Göteborg, Uppsala: Almqvist and Wiksells, 1963). Frege topics: analyticity, comparison of Frege's and Bolzano's logic, definition of number, empty propositions, judgements, logistic systems, propositions, truth values.

A16.   Beth, E. W., "Carnap's Views on the Advantages of Constructed Systems Over Natural Languages in the Philsophy of Science", in *The Philosophy of Rudolf Carnap*, ed. P. A. Schilpp (La Salle, Illinois: Open Court, 1963), pp. 469–502. Frege topics: Frege's influence on Carnap, Frege's influence on Husserl, intension and extension, logicism, psychologism, sense and denotation, set theory, synthetic *a priori* character of geometric principles.

A17. Beth, E. W., "Hundred Years of Symbolic Logic", *Dialectica*, 1 (1947), pp. 331–46. Frege topic: logicism.

A18. —— "La sémantique et sa portée philosophique", *Semantica* (Archivio di filosofia, 1955), pp. 41–62. Frege topics: Frege's contributions to logic and semantics (general comments).

A19. —— "Wiskunde, logica en natuurphilosophie op het Congrès— Descartes", *Algemeen Nederlands tijdschrift voor wijsbegeerte en psychologie*, 31 (1937-8), pp. 130–42. Frege topic: Frege's contributions to the foundations of mathematics.

A20. —— Review of A. Heyting, "Formal Logic and Mathematics", *JSL* 14 (1949), p. 195. Frege topics: Frege's contributions to logic and mathematics, Frege's influence on Hilbert. [See: S131.]

A21. Betsch, C., *Fiktionen in der Mathematik* (Stuttgart: Frommanns, 1926). Frege topics: definition, definition of number, psychologism.

A22. Bird, O., "The History of Logic" (a review of W. Kneale and M. Kneale, *The Development of Logic* and I. Bocheński, *A History of Formal Logic*), *RM* 16 (1963), pp. 491–502. Frege topics: judgement and content, propositional functions, sense and denotation, truth functions. [See: S54, S167.]

A23. Black, M., "Comments on Quine's 'Semantics and Abstract Objects' ", *Proceedings of the American Academy of Arts and Sciences*, 80 (1951), pp. 97–9. Frege topics: extensions, names of general terms. [See: A5.]

A24. —— *The Nature of Mathematics* (London: Kegan Paul, 1933; New York: Harcourt, 1935). Frege topic: logicism.

A25. —— "Reasoning with Loose Concepts", *Dialogue*, 2 (1963), pp. 1–12. Frege topics: definition of 'concept', law of excluded middle.

A26. —— Review of A. Church, *Introduction to Mathematical Logic*, vol. 1, *JSL* 22 (1957), pp. 286–9. Frege topic: Church's modification of Frege's semantics.

A27. Bocheński, I., *A Précis of Mathematical Logic* (Dordrecht, Holland: D. Reidel, 1959). German edition: *Grundriß der Logistik* (Paderborn: F. Schöningch, 1954). French edition: *Précis de logique mathématique* (Bussum, Holland: F. G. Kroonder, 1949). Frege topic: Frege's contributions to logic.

A28.   Bohnert, H., "Carnap on Definition and Analyticity", in *The Philosophy of Rudolf Carnap*, ed. P. A. Schilpp (La Salle, Illinois: Open Court, 1963), pp. 407–30. Frege topic: psychologism.

A29.   Britzelmayr, W., "Interpretation von Kalkülen", *S* 7 (1948–9), pp. 50–7. Frege topics: 'beurteilbarer Inhalt', proposition, thought, truth value.

A30.   Brunschvicg, L., *Les étapes de la philosophie mathématique* (Paris: F. Alcan, 1922). Frege topics: functions, variables.

A31.   Burkamp, W., *Logik* (Berlin: E. S. Mittler and Son, 1932). Frege topics: concept, Frege's contributions to logic, functions, logical symbols, propositional functions.

A32.   —— *Wirklichkeit und Sinn* (Berlin: Junker and Dünnhaupt, 1938). Frege topic: criticism of Frege–Russell concept of number.

A33.   Carnap, R., *The Logical Syntax of Language*, trans. A. Smeaton [Countess von Zeppelin] (London: Routledge and Kegan Paul, 1937, 1949, 1951, 1954. Also published by Humanities Press, N. Y., 1956, and Littlefield Adams, Paterson, N. J., 1959). German edition: *Logische Syntax der Sprache* (Vienna, 1934). Frege topics: analyticity, classes, class-expressions, concepts, courses-of-values, definition of number, descriptions, extensions, functions, intensions, logicism, negation, Russell's Paradox, type theory, universal operators, use-mention distinction.

A34.   —— "The Development of My Thinking", in *The Philosophy of Rudolf Carnap*, ed. P. A. Schilpp (La Salle, Illinois: Open Court, 1963), pp. 3–43. Frege topics: Carnap's experience as a student of Frege, Frege's influence on Carnap, Frege's influence on the Polish school, Frege's influence on Wittgenstein.

A35.   —— "Die logizistische Grundlegung der Mathematik", *E* 2 (1931), pp. 91–105. Frege topic: logicism.

A36.   —— *Meaning and Necessity* (Chicago: University of Chicago Press, 1947, 1956, 1960). Frege topics: definition of number, descriptions, general semantical method, interchangeability, name-relation, oblique contexts, propositions, sense and denotation. [See: S180. Reviews: S179, 244.]

A37.   Carruccio, E., *Mathematics and Logic in History and in Contemporary Thought* (Chicago: Quigly Aldine, 1964). Frege topic: sketch of Frege's logistic programme. [Review: A99.]

A38.   Cassirer, Eva, Review of G. E. M. Anscombe, *An Introduction to Wittgenstein's Tractatus*, British Journal for the Philosophy of *Science*, 14 (1963–4), pp. 359–66. Frege topic: assumption versus assertion.

A39.   Church, A., "Connotation", in *Encyclopaedia Britannica* (Chicago, London, Toronto: Benton, 1960), vol. 6, p. 275. Frege topic: sense and denotation. [See S194.]

A40.   —— *Introduction to Mathematical Logic*, vol. I (Princeton: Princeton University Press, 1956, 1958, 1962). Frege topics: assertion sign, concepts, constants, equality of senses, Frege's contributions to logic, identity, oblique contexts, proper names, rule of substitution, sense and denotation, truth functions, truth values, variables.

A41.   —— "Propositions and Sentences", in I. Bocheński *et al.*, *The Problem of Universals* (South Bend, Indiana: University of Notre Dame Press, 1956), pp. 3–11. Frege topic: propositions.

A42.   —— Review of M. Black, "The 'Paradox of Analysis' Again: A Reply", *JSL* 11 (1946), p. 133. Frege topics: identity, paradox of analysis, sense and denotation. [See: S302.]

A43.   —— Review of M. Farber, *The Foundations of Phenomenology*, *JSL* 9 (1944), pp. 63–5. Frege topics: Frege's concept of number, Frege's influence on and critique of Husserl, psychologism.

A44.   —— Review of C. J. Keyser, "Charles Sanders Peirce as a Pioneer", *JSL* 6 (1941), pp. 161–2. Frege topic: invention of the propositional function.

A45.   —— Review of W. V. Quine, "Note on Existence and Necessity", *JSL* 8 (1943), pp. 45–7. Frege topics: meanings, ordinary and oblique contexts, propositions, sense and denotation.

A46.   Copi, J. M., "Symbolic Logic", in *Encyclopedia International*, 1st edn. (New York, Montreal, Mexico City, Sydney: Grolier, 1964), vol. 17, pp. 449–50. Frege topic: logistic systems.

A47.   Costello, H. T., "Notes on Logic: Introduction", *JP* 54 (1957), pp. 230–1. Frege topic: Frege's recommendation to Wittgenstein that he should study with Bertrand Russell.

A48.   Danto, A., Review of P. Geach, *Reference and Generality*, *PR* 61 (1964), pp. 122–3. Frege topics: predicates, proper names. [See A66.]

A49.   Davidson, D., "The Method of Extension and Intension", in
       The Philosophy of Rudolf Carnap, ed. P. A. Schilpp (La Salle,
       Illinois: Open Court, 1963), pp. 311–49. Frege topics: antimony
       of the name relation, identity, oblique contexts, paradox of
       analysis, sense and denotation.

A50.   —— "Theories of Meaning and Learnable Languages", *Proceed-
       ings of 1964 International Congress for Logic, Methodology and
       Philosophy of Science* (Amsterdam: North Holland, 1965), pp. 383–
       94. Frege topic: sense and denotation.

A51.   Dedekind, R., [A Letter from R. Dedekind], in H. Wang, "The
       Axiomatization of Arithmetic", *JSL* 22 (1957), pp. 150–1. Frege
       topic: Dedekind's reaction to Frege's *Begriffsschrift* and *Grund-
       lagen*. [See: F7, F14, S297, A52.]

A52.   —— Preface to the Second Edition of *Was sind und was sollen die
       Zahlen?* (Braunschweig: F. Vieweg, 1893). English translation by
       W. W. Beman, in R. Dedekind, *Essays on the Theory of Numbers*
       (Chicago: Open Court, 1901). Frege topic: the relation of this
       work to Frege's *Grundlagen*. [See: F14, A51.]

A53.   Dummett, M., "Truth", *PAS* 59 (1958–9), pp. 141–62. Reprinted
       in *Truth*, ed. G. Pitcher (Englewood Cliffs, New Jersey: Prentice-
       Hall, 1964). Frege topics: concepts, functions, meanings of pro-
       positions, relations, sense and denotation, truth values.

A54.   —— Review of M. Black, "Presupposition and Implication",
       JSL 25 (1960), pp. 338–9. Frege topic: Frege's use of assertion
       and presupposition. [See: S51.]

A55.   —— Review of G. Boole, *Studies in Logic and Probability*, ed.
       R. Rhees, *JSL* 24 (1959), pp. 203–9. Frege topic: Frege, not
       Boole, is the "father of modern logic".

A56.   Egidi, R., "Il problema della sinonimia nella semantica", *Ras-
       segna di filosofia*, 7 (1958), pp. 255–69. Frege topic: synonymy.

A57.   Enriques, F., *The Historic Development of Logic*, trans. J. Rosen-
       thal (New York: Henry Holt, 1929). Frege topic: Frege's logic.

A58.   Eves, H. and C. V. Newsom, *An Introduction to the Foundations
       and Fundamental Concepts of Mathematics* (New York: Holt,
       Rinehart, and Winston, 1958). Frege topics: definition of number,
       logicism, Russell's Paradox, symbolic logic.

A59.   Farber, M., *The Foundation of Phenomenology: Edmund Husserl and the Quest for a Rigorous Science of Philosophy* (Cambridge, Massachusetts: Harvard University Press, 1943). Frege topics: Frege's criticism of Husserl, Frege's concept of number.

A60.   Feys, R., Review of L. Kattsoff, *A Philosophy of Mathematics, JSL* 13 (1948), pp. 208–12. Frege topics: definition of number, Frege's symbolism, hereditary property, many-one relations, one-to-one relations, ranges of values.

A61.   Fischer, L., *Die Grundlagen der Philosophie und der Mathematik* (Leipzig: F. Meiner, 1933). Frege topic: Frege's logistic programme.

A62.   Freudenthal, H., "The Main Trends in the Foundations of Geometry in the 19th Century", in *Logic, Methodology and Philosophy of Science*, ed. E. Nagel *et al.* (Stanford: Stanford University Press, 1962), pp. 613–21. Frege topic: Frege's criticism of Hilbert.

A63.   Geach, P., "Entailment", *PAS SV* 32 (1958), pp. 157–72. Frege topics: numerical identity, proper names, propositions.

A64.   —— "Identity", *RM* 21 (1967), pp. 3–12. Frege topic: Frege's theory of identity.

A65.   —— "Form and Existence", *PAS* 59 (1954–5), pp. 251–72. Frege topics: concept and object, functions, marks of a concept, properties of a concept.

A66.   —— *Reference and Generality* (Ithaca: Cornell University Press, 1962). Frege topics: concepts, referring expressions, two kinds of copula. [Review: A48.]

A67.   —— "Subject and Predicate", *M* 59 (1950), pp. 461–82. Reprinted in *Readings in Logic*, ed. R. Houde (Dubuque, Iowa: W. C. Brown, 1958), pp. 62–83. Frege topics: concept and object, definite descriptions, identity, naming.

A68.   *Geschichte der Universität Jena, 1548/58–1958: Festgabe zum vierhundertjährigen Universitätsjubiläum* (Jena: G. Fischer, 1958), vol. I, p. 478; vol. II, pp. 118 and 584. Frege topics: Frege's habilitation, Frege's pension, Frege's predecessors, some important dates in Frege's career.

A69.   Geymonat, L., "I problemi del nulla e delle tenebre in Fredegiso di Tours", *Rivista di filosofia*, 43 (1952), pp. 280–8. Frege topics: identity, platonism, sense and denotation.

A70. Gödel, K., "Russell's Mathematical Logic", in *The Philosophy of Bertrand Russell*, ed. P. A. Schilpp (La Salle, Illinois: Open Court, 1944, 1951, 1963), pp. 125–53. Reprinted (New York: Harper & Row, 1963). Frege topics: *characteristica universalis*, precision and rigour in logic, 'the', theory of truth.

A71. Goodstein, R., "On the Nature of Mathematical Systems", in *Logica, Studia Dedicata P. Bernays* (Neuchâtel, Switzerland: Éditions du Griffon, 1959), pp. 92–112. Reprinted as "The Nature of Mathematics" in R. Goodstein, *Essays in the Philosophy of Mathematics* (Leicester, England: Leicester University Press, 1965), pp. 97–115. Frege topics: definition of number, psychologism, sense, and denotation.

A72. —— "Pure and Applied Mathematics", *Ratio*, 6 (1964). Reprinted in R. Goodstein, *Essays in the Philosophy of Mathematics* (Leicester, England: Leicester University Press, 1965), pp. 126–38. Frege topics: formalization, proof theory.

A73. Grünbaum, A., Review of H. Reichenbach, *The Rise of Scientific Philosophy*, *Scripta Mathematica*, 19 (1953), pp. 48–54. Frege topic: existence of mathematical entities.

A74. Hermes, H., and H. Scholz, "Mathematische Logik", in *Enzyklopädie der mathematischen Wissenschaften*, Band I (Leipzig: Teubner, 1952). Frege topic: Frege's contributions to mathematical logic.

A75. Hilbert, D., "On the Foundations of Logic and Arithmetic", *MO* 15 (1905), pp. 338–52. Frege topics: concept of whole number, inference by complete induction, logical paradoxes, logicism.

A76. Hiż, H., "Logika" in "Filozofia w Stanach Zjednoczonych 1939–1947" ["Philosophy in the United States, 1939–1947"]. *Przegląd filozoficzny*, 44 (1948), pp. 241–9. Frege topic: Frege's influence on American logic.

A77. —— Review of W. Tatarkiewicz, *Historia filozofii*, *JSL* 16 (1951) p. 287. Frege topics: antipsychologism, denotations of sentences, Frege's philosophical importance, truth values.

A78. Husserl, E., *Logische Untersuchungen* (Halle: N. Niemeyer, 1900–1). Frege topic: sense and denotation.

A79. Ingalls, D., "The Comparison of Indian and Western Philosophy", *Journal of Oriental Research*, 22 (1952–3), pp. 1–11. Frege topic: the definition of number. [Review: A100.]

A80.   Isimoto, A., "Kindai ronrigaku no tenbô" ["A Survey of Modern Logic"] *Sisô*, 347 (1953), pp. 97–106. Frege topic: Frege's contributions to modern logic.

A81.   Johansen, H., "Die Russellsche Theorie der definiten Deskriptionen vom Standpunkt der Sprachwissenschaft aus betrachtet", *T* 18 (1952), pp. 32–58. Frege subjects: definite descriptions, sense and denotation, thoughts.

A82.   Jørgensen, J., "Einige Hauptpunkte der Entwicklung der formalen Logik seit Boole", *E* 5 (1935–6), pp. 131–42. Frege topic: Frege's contributions to formal logic.

A83.   Jourdain, P. E. B., "Logic and Psychology", *MO* 27 (1917), pp. 460–7. Frege topic: Frege's logic and its purposes.

A84.   —— "The Philosophy of Mr. B*rtr*nd R*ss*ll", *MO* 21 (1911), pp. 481–508. Frege topic: Frege's contributions to logic.

A85.   —— "Some Modern Advances in Logic", *MO* 21 (1911), pp. 564–6. Frege topic: Frege's contributions to the advancement of logic.

A86.   —— "Transfinite Numbers and the Principles of Mathematics", *MO* 20 (1910), pp. 93–118. Frege topic: Frege's logic and its application to mathematics.

A87.   —— Review of H. Berkeley, *Mysticism in Modern Mathematics*, *M* 20 (1911), pp. 88–97. Frege topics: definition of numbers, psychologism.

A88.   —— Review of P. Natorp, *Die logischen Grundlagen der exakten Wissenschaften*, *M* 20 (1911), pp. 552–60. Frege topics: concepts, numbers. [See: A112.]

A89.   Kalish, D., "Logical Form", *M* 61 (1952), pp. 57–71. Frege topic: a comparison of Frege and Russell on definite descriptions.

A90.   Kambartel, F., "Einleitung des Herausgebers", in B. Bolzano, *Grundlegung der Logik*, ed. F. Kambartel (Hamburg: F. Meiner, 1963), pp. vii–lxxi. Frege topic: comparison of Bolzano's and Frege's logic.

A91.   Kaplan, D., "Foundations of Intensional Logic" (Los Angeles: 1964). Doctoral Dissertation, UCLA. Frege topic: Frege's semantics.

A92.   Kattsoff, L., *Logic and the Nature of Reality* (The Hague: M. Nijhoff, 1956). Frege topics: functions and variables, negation.

A93.   Kemeny, J., "Semantics as a Branch of Logic", in *Encyclopaedia Britannica* (Chicago, London, Toronto: Benton, 1960), vol. 20, pp. 113c–113d. Frege topic: sense and denotation.

A94.   Kneale, W., "The Province of Logic", in *Contemporary British Philosophy*, ed. H. D. Lewis (London: G. Allen and Unwin; New York: Macmillan, 1956), pp. 237–61. Frege topic: Frege's influence on logic.

A95.   Körner, S., *The Philosophy of Mathematics* (London: Hutchinson University Library, 1960). Frege topics: classes, definition, definition of number, logicism, principle of abstraction, quantification, sense and denotation.

A96.   Kraszewski, Z., "Zagadnienie intensjonalności" ["On the Problem of Intensionality"], *Studia filozoficzne*, 3 (1959), pp. 147–53. Frege topics: Frege's treatment of intensional contexts, sense and denotation.

A97.   Kreisel, G., Review of H. Scholz, "Gottlob Frege" (in *Mathesis Universalis*), *JSL* 28 (1963), p. 286. Frege topic: Russell's Paradox in Frege's system. [See: S247.]

A98.   Küng, G., *Ontologie und logistische Analyse der Sprache* (Vienna: Springer, 1963). Frege topics: antipsychologism, Frege's contributions to logic, Frege's relations with Wittgenstein, functions, logicism, meaning of a proposition, quantification, sense and denotation, truth values, whole-part relation.

A99.   Lemmon, E. J., Review of E. Carruccio, *Mathematics and Logic in History and Contemporary Thought*, trans. J. Quigly, *Journal of the History of Philosophy*, 5 (1967), pp. 98–9. Frege topics: propositional calculus, quantifiers. [See: A37.]

A100. —— Review of D. Ingalls, "The Comparison of Indian and Western Philosophy", *JSL* 21 (1956), pp. 387–8. Frege topic: definition of number. [See: A79.]

A101. Lewis, C. I., *A Survey of Symbolic Logic* (Los Angeles: University of California Press, 1918). Reprinted, minus Chapters V and VI (New York: Dover; and London: Constable, 1960). Frege topics: Frege's logistic programme and its relation to Peano and Russell, Frege's symbolism.

A102. Lewy, C., "Entailment and Necessary Propositions", in *Philosophical Analysis*, ed. M. Black (Englewood Cliffs, New Jersey: Prentice-Hall, 1950, 1963), pp. 183–97. Frege topic: necessity of self-identity propositions.

A103.   Linke, P., "Die Implikation als echte Wenn-so-Beziehung", *Wissenschaftliche Zeitschrift der Friedrich-Schiller-Universität Jena*, 3 (1953-4), pp. 107-8. Frege topic: the meaning of 'if-then' statements.

A104.   —— "Logic and Epistemology", in *Philosophy Today*, ed. E. Schaub (Chicago and London: Open Court, 1928), pp. 359-92. This is a reprint of "The Present Status of Logic and Epistemology in Germany", *MO* 36 (1926), pp. 222-55. Frege topics: antipsychologism, concepts and functions, formal logic, Frege's influence on Husserl, logical laws, logicism, meanings of the term 'law'.

A105.   —— "Warum philosophische Wissenschaft?", *Wissenschaftliche Zeitschrift der Friedrich-Schiller-Universität Jena*, 2 (1952-3), pp. 25-38. Frege topics: assertion, judgements.

A106.   —— "Was ist Logik?", *Zeitschrift für philosophische Forschung*, 6 (1951-2), pp. 372-89. Reprinted in *Wissenschaftliche Zeitschrift der Friedrich-Schiller-Universität Jena*, 3 (1953-4), pp. 179-90. Frege topics: antipsychologism, the place of judgements in logic, laws of thought and laws of logic.

A107.   Lorenzen, P., "Grundlagen der Mathematik", in *FIAT Review of German Science, 1939-1946: Pure Mathematics*, Part I (Wiesbaden: Dieterich'sche Verlagsbuchhandlung, 1948), pp. 11-22. Frege topic: the connection between the notion of a mathematical theory due to Schröter and the notions and ideas of Frege.

A108.   —— *Formale Logik* (Berlin: W. de Gruyter, 1958). English translation by F. J. Crosson (Dordrecht, Holland: D. Reidel, 1965). Frege topics: conditionality, descriptions, extensions, intensions, propositions, truth values.

A109.   Marshall, W., Review of J. Myhill, "Two Ways of Ontology in Modern Logic", *JSL* 18 (1953), pp. 91-2. Frege topics: incompleteness of functions, logically complex objects. [See: S208.]

A110.   Martin, G., "Methodische Probleme der Metaphysik der Zahl", *Studium Generale*, 6 (1953). Reprinted in G. Martin, *Gesammelte Abhandlungen* (Cologne: Kölner Universitäts Verlag, 1961), pp. 125-36. Frege topic: logicism.

A111.   Mates, B., *Stoic Logic* (Los Angeles: University of California Press, 1953, 1961). Frege topics: conditionals, predicates, sense and denotation.

A112. Natorp, P., *Die logischen Grundlagen der exakten Wissenschaften* (Leipzig and Berlin: Teubner, 1910). Frege topic: logicism. [See: S152, S198. Review: A88.]

A113. Ogden, C. K. and I. A. Richards, *The Meaning of Meaning* (New York: Harcourt, Brace, 1923, 1926, 1930, 1936, 1946, 1960; London: Routledge and Kegan Paul, 1949). Frege topic: sense and denotation.

A114. Paci, E., "Fondazione e construzione logica del mondo in Carnap", in *Logica e analisi* (Archivio di Filosofia, 1966), pp. 95–107. Frege topics: Frege's influence on Carnap, Husserl's critique of Frege, sense and denotation.

A115. Pap, A., *Semantics and Necessary Truth* (New Haven: Yale University Press, 1958), pp. 44–6, 274–7. Frege topics: analyticity, definition, paradox of analysis.

A116. Peano, G., "Studii di logica matematica", *Atti della Reale Accademia delle Scienze di Torino*, 32 (1896–7), pp. 565–83. Reprinted in G. Peano, *Opere scelte* (Rome: Edizioni Cremonese, 1958), vol. II, pp. 201–17. German translation by G. Bohlmann and A. Schlepp, in G. Peano, *Angelo Genocchi Differentialrechnung und Grundzüge der Integralrechnung* (Leipzig: 1899), pp. 336–52. Frege topics: Frege's logic, Frege's versus Peano's use of material implication.

A117. Peters, F., "Russell on Class Theory", *S* 15 (1963), pp. 327–35. Frege topic: relation-concepts.

A118. Popovich, M. V., "Philosophic Aspects of the Problem of Meaning and Sense", *Soviet Studies in Philosophy*, 1 (1963), pp. 23–31. Frege topics: extensional logic, identity, names, objects, sense and denotation, truth values.

A119. Prior, A. N., *Formal Logic* (Oxford: Clarendon Press, 1955, 1962). Frege topics: axioms of propositional calculus, class inclusion, conjunction, levels of concepts, postulate sets for logical calculi, proof of Frege's third axiom, proper names, propositional functions, truth functions.

A120. Quine, W. V., "Carnap and Logical Truth", in *The Philosophy of Rudolf Carnap*, ed. P. A. Schilpp (La Salle, Illinois: Open Court, 1963), pp. 385–406. Italian translation in *Rivista di filosofia*, 48 (1957), pp. 3–29. Frege topic: logicism.

A121. Quine, W. V., *From a Logical Point of View* (Cambridge, Massachusetts: Harvard University Press, 1953, 1961). Frege topics: ancestral of a relation, definition of number, identity contexts, individual concepts, logicism, naming, oblique contexts, ontology, propositions, reference to truth values, theory of classes. [See: S180.]

A122. —— "Identity, Ostension and Hypostasis", *JP* 47 (1950), pp. 621–33. Frege topic: identity. [See: S36, S81.]

A123. —— "Logic, Symbolic", in *Encyclopedia Americana*, International Edition (1965), vol. 17, pp. 690–6. Frege topic: Frege's contributions to symbolic logic.

A124. —— *Mathematical Logic* (Cambridge, Massachusetts: Harvard University Press, 1940, 1951, 1961). Frege topics: abstraction, axioms and rules of inference, definition of number, descriptions, inclusion and membership in classes, logicism, material implication, mathematical induction, ordinary ancestral, proper ancestral, quantification, relative product and image, successor function, use and mention. [See: S103.]

A125. —— *Methods of Logic* (New York: Holt, Rinehart and Winston, 1950, 1959, 1961). Frege topics: definition of number, logicism, material implication, meanings, quantification, truth functions.

A126. —— "Ontological Reduction and the World of Numbers", *JP* 61 (1964), pp. 209–16. Frege topics: definition of number, ontology.

A127. —— Preface to J. T. Clark, *Conventional Logic and Modern Logic* (Woodstock, Maryland: Woodstock College Press, 1952), pp. v–vii. Frege topic: Frege's contribution to logic.

A128. —— "Semantics and Abstract Objects", *Proceedings of the American Academy of Arts and Sciences*, 80 (1951), pp. 90–6. Frege topics: naming, ontology, sense and denotation, truth values.

A129. —— *Set Theory and Its Logic* (Cambridge, Massachusetts: Harvard University Press, 1963). Frege topics: ancestral of a relation, axiom of infinity, class abstraction, definition of number, function abstraction, law of concretion.

A130. —— "Unification of Universes in Set Theory", *JSL* 21 (1956), pp. 267–79. Frege topics: classes, functional abstraction, sentences as singular terms.

A131.   —— "Whitehead and the Rise of Modern Logic", in *The Philosophy of Alfred North Whitehead*, ed. P. A. Schilpp (New York: Tudor, 1944), pp. 125–63. Frege topic: Frege's versus Whitehead's logic.

A132.   —— Review of A. Church, "A Formulation of the Simple Theory of Types", *JSL* 5 (1940), pp. 114–15. Frege topics: class abstraction, Fregean approach to a theory of types, functional abstraction, relational abstraction, relations, truth values.

A133.   Quinton, A., "The *A Priori* and the Analytic", *PAS* 64 (1963–4), pp. 31–54. Frege topic: analyticity.

A134.   Rabus, L., *Die neuesten Bestrebungen auf dem Gebiete der Logik bei den Deutschen und die logische Frage* (Erlangen: 1880). Frege topics: assertible contents, asserting, judging.

A135.   Rescher, N. and J. Thomson, Review of V. Valpola, "Über Namen", *JSL* 16 (1951), pp. 212–13. Frege topics: logical truth, proper names, sense and denotation.

A136.   Rovighi, S. V., "Capitolo secondo", of *La filosofia di Edmund Husserl* (Milan: Società Editrice, 1939). Frege topic: Frege's critique of Husserl's *Philosophie der Arithmetik*. [See: F24.]

A137.   Russell, B., *Introduction to Mathematical Philosophy* (London: G. Allen, 1919). Frege topic: logicism.

A138.   —— "Logic as the Essence of Philosophy", in *Our Knowledge of the External World* (London: G. Allen, 1914). Reprinted in *Essays in Logic from Aristotle to Russell*, ed. R. Jager (Englewood Cliffs, New Jersey: Prentice-Hall, 1963), pp. 120–39. Frege topic: propositions.

A139.   —— "My Mental Development", in *The Philosophy of Bertrand Russell*, ed. P. A. Schilpp (London: Tudor, 1944, 1951), pp. 3–20. Reprinted (New York: Harper and Row, 1963). Frege topic: Russell's relation to Frege.

A140.   —— "On Denoting", *M* 14 (1905), pp. 479–93. Reprinted in *Readings in Philosophical Analysis*, ed. H. Feigl and W. Sellars (New York: Appleton-Century-Crofts, 1949), pp. 103–15, and also in *Meaning and Knowledge, Systematic Readings in Epistemology*, ed. E. Nagel and R. Brandt (New York: Harcourt, Brace and World, 1965), pp. 78–87. Frege topics: definite descriptions, denoting expressions, sense and denotation. [See: S44, S146, S147, S258.]

A141. Schnelle, H., *Zeichensysteme zur wissenschaftlichen Darstellung* (Stuttgart and Bad Connstatt: F. Frommann, 1962). Frege topic: Frege's symbolism.

A142. Scholz, H., *Geschichte der Logik* (Berlin: Junker and Dünnhaupt, 1931). Frege topic: Frege's contributions to logic.

A143. —— "Die klassische deutsche Philosophie und die neue Logik", in *Actes du congrès international de philosophie scientifique (Paris: 1936)*, vol. 8, pp. 1–8. Frege topic: Frege's contributions to logic. [Review: S174.]

A144. —— "Die Wissenschaftslehre Bolzanos", *Mathesis Universalis* (Basel, Stuttgart: Benno Schwabe, 1961), pp. 219–67. Frege topic: Frege's critique of Hilbert.

A145. —— "Zur Erhellung des Verstehens", in *Geistige Gestalten und Probleme, Eduard Spranger zum 60. Geburtstag*, ed. H. Wenke (Leipzig: Quelle and Meyer, 1942), pp. 291–310. Frege topics: mathematics, propositions, symbolic logic, truth values.

A146. Schomerus, F., *Werden und Wesen der Carl-Zeiss-Stiftung* (Stuttgart: G. Fischer, 1955), p. 246. Frege topic: Frege's pension from the Carl-Zeiss-Stiftung.

A147. Shearman, A. T., *The Development of Symbolic Logic* (London: Williams and Norgate, 1906). Frege topics: cardinal numbers, class membership, Frege's extension of symbolic logic, implication, propositional calculus, universal propositions, Venn's critique of Frege.

A148. Shwayder, D. S., "*Gegenstände* and Other Matters", *Inquiry*, 7 (1964), pp. 387–413. Frege topics: definition, Frege's influence on Wittgenstein, function names, propositions, sense and denotation.

A149. Smiley, T. J., "Propositional Functions", *PAS, SV* 34 (1960), pp. 33–46. Frege topic: propositional functions.

A150. Sobociński, B., "In Memoriam Jan Łukasiewicz", *Philosophical Studies (Maynooth)*, 6 (1956), pp. 3–49. Frege topics: Łukasiewicz' relation to Frege, propositional calculus.

A151. Sosa, E., "The Semantics of Imperatives", *American Philosophical Quarterly*, 4 (1967), pp. 57–64. Frege topic: sense of questions and imperatives.

A152. Stanosz, B., "Znaczenie i oznaczanie a paradoks intensjonalności" ["Meaning and Designation and the Paradox of Intensionality"], *Studia filozoficzne*, 2 (1965), pp. 19–48. Frege topics: Frege's logic and semantics, intensionality, sense and denotation.

A153. Stegmüller, W., *Das Wahrheitsproblem und die Idee der Semantik* (Vienna: Springer, 1957). Frege topic: sense and denotation.

A154. Sternfeld, R., "Philosophical Principles and Technical Problems in Mathematical Logic", *Methodos*, 8 (1956), pp. 269–88. Frege topic: Frege versus Russell and Gödel on classes.

A155. Strawson, P. F., *Individuals* (London: Methuen, 1959; reprinted, New York: Doubleday Anchor, 1963. Frege topics: concepts and objects, proper names, subject-predicate, saturated and unsaturated entities. [See: S298.]

A156. Tarski, A., *Introduction to Logic and to the Methodology of Deductive Sciences*, trans. O. Helmer (Oxford: Oxford University Press, 1941). Frege topic: Frege's contributions to logic.

A157. Thomson, J. F., Review of R. Rudner, "On *Sinn* as a Combination of Physical Properties", *JSL* 18 (1953), p. 89. Frege topic: sense and denotation. [See: S238.]

A158. —— Review of D. S. Shwayder, "=", *JSL* 21 (1956), p. 383. Frege topics: proper names, sense and denotation. [See: S263.]

A159. Thomson, J. and N. Rescher, Review of V. Valpola, "Über Namen", *JSL* 16 (1951), pp. 212–13. Frege topics: logical truth, proper names, sense and denotation. [See: A161.]

A160. Thompson, M. H. Jr., "The Logical Paradoxes and Peirce's Semiotic", *JP* 46 (1949), p. 520. Frege topic: Frege versus Peirce on functions.

A161. Valpola, V., "Über Namen: Eine logische Untersuchung", *Annales Academiae Scientiarum Fennicae*, ser. B, 68 (1950). Frege topics: logical truth, proper names, sense and denotation. [Review: A159.]

A162. [Venn, J.], *Books on Logic Presented to the Library by John Venn* (Cambridge, England: Cambridge University Press, 1889). Frege topic: Frege works owned by Venn.

A163. Waismann, F., "How I See Philosophy", in *Contemporary British Philosophy*, ed. H. D. Lewis (London: G. Allen and Unwin, 1956), pp. 447–90. Reprinted in *Logical Positivism*, ed. A. J. Ayer (New York: Free Press, 1959). Frege topic: Frege and philosophic method.

A164. Waismann, F., *Introduction to Mathematical Thinking*, trans. T. J. Benac (New York: Harper, 1959). English translation of *Einführung in das mathematische Denken* (Vienna: F. Ungar, 1936). Italian translation of this work: *Introduzione al pensiero matematico* (Turin, 1939). Frege topics: critique of formalism, definition of number, logicism. [Review: S85.]

A165. —— *The Principles of Linguistic Philosophy* (London: Macmillan; New York: St. Martin's, 1965). Frege topics: concept and object, definition of number, delimitation of concepts, formalism, fundamental propositions of logic, meaning, names, the task of philosophy.

A166. Wang, H., "The Axiomatization of Arithmetic", *JSL* 22 (1957), pp. 145–58. Frege topics: analytic-synthetic, ancestral of a relation, classes, concept, deduction, definition of number, Frege's relation to Dedekind, logicism, relation.

A167. —— "Eighty Years of Fundamental Studies", in *Logica, studia dedicata P. Bernays* (Neuchâtel, Switzerland: Griffon, 1959), pp. 262–93. Frege topics: classes, concepts, definition of number, Frege's propositional calculus and predicate calculus, logicism, relations, type theory of predicates.

A168. Wells, R., Review of A. Church, "A Formulation of the Logic of Sense and Denotation", *JSL* 17 (1952), pp. 133–4. Frege topic: developing the Fregean approach. [See: S67.]

A169. White, M., *Toward Reunion in Philosophy* (Cambridge, Massachusetts: Harvard University Press, 1956). Frege topics: analyticity, Frege's argument for the existence of meanings, identity and synonymy, logicism, sense and denotation, truth values.

A170. Wienpahl, P., "More About the Denial of Sameness of Meaning", *A* 12 (1951), pp. 19–23. Frege topic: sense and denotation. [See: S202.]

A171. —— "Wittgenstein and the Naming Relation", *Inquiry*, 7 (1964), pp. 329–47. Frege topics: Frege's influence on Wittgenstein, propositions.

A172. Wittgenstein, L., *Remarks on the Foundations of Mathematics*, ed. G. E. M. Anscombe *et al.*, trans. G. E. M. Anscombe (New York: Macmillan, 1956). Frege topics: immediate realization of truth, laws of thought, logical calculus, new kind of insanity, number, straight lines. [See: S178.]

A173. —— *Tractatus Logico-Philosophicus* (Annalen der Naturphilo-sophie, 1921). English trans. by C. K. Ogden (London, 1922, 1933). English translation by D. Pears and B. McGuinness (London: Routledge and Kegan Paul, 1961, 1963). Frege topics: definitions and the introduction of signs, Frege's logic, functions, generality, judgement stroke, rules of inference, logical constants, logical objects, names, propositions, sense and denotation, truth values.

A174. von Wright, G. H., *Den logiska empirismen: En huvudriktning i modern filosofi* [*Logical Empiricism: A Leading Movement in Modern Philosophy*] (Helsinki, 1943). Frege topic: logicism.

A175. —— "Ludwig Wittgenstein, a Biographical Sketch", *PR* 64 (1955), pp. 527–45. Frege topic: Frege's advice to Wittgenstein.

A176. Zilli, M., "Le attitudini proposizionali", *Rassegna di filosofia*, 6 (1957), pp. 338–54. Frege topics: definite descriptions, sense and denotation.

INDEX